PAINTING WITH ANNIGONI

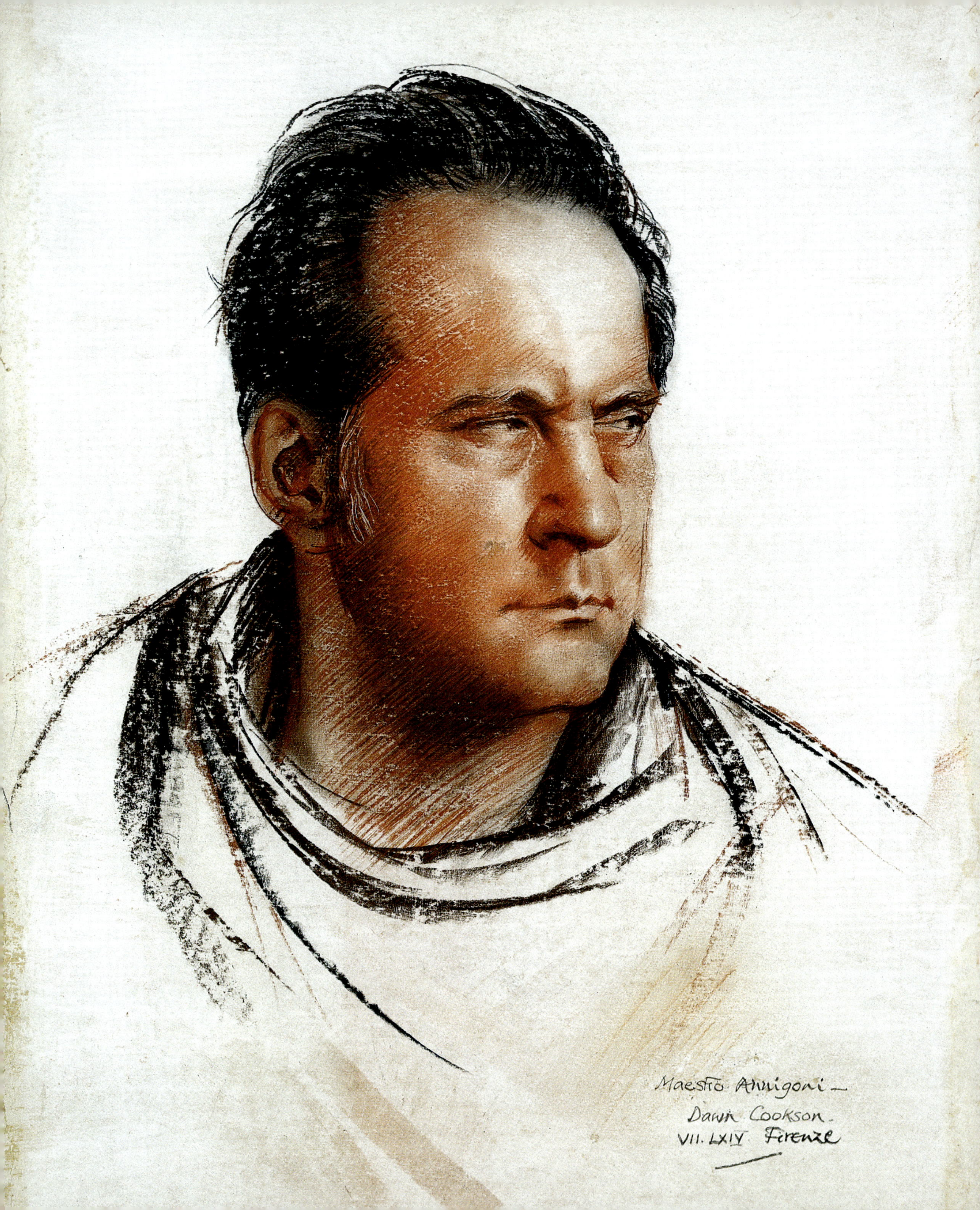
Maestro Annigoni –
Dawn Cookson.
VII. LXIV Firenze

PAINTING WITH ANNIGONI

A Halcyon Decade as a Student in Florence 1958-68

Dawn Cookson

UNICORN PRESS
LONDON

A tribute to the late and great painter
Pietro Annigoni

Unicorn Press
21 Afghan Road
London SW11 2QD

email unicorn@tradford.demon.co.uk
website www.boydell.co.uk

Published by Unicorn Press 2000

ISBN 0 906290 37 6

Designed by Jonathan Raimes, Foundation Publishing Limited

Printed in Belgium by Snoeck-Ducaju & Zoon

CONTENTS

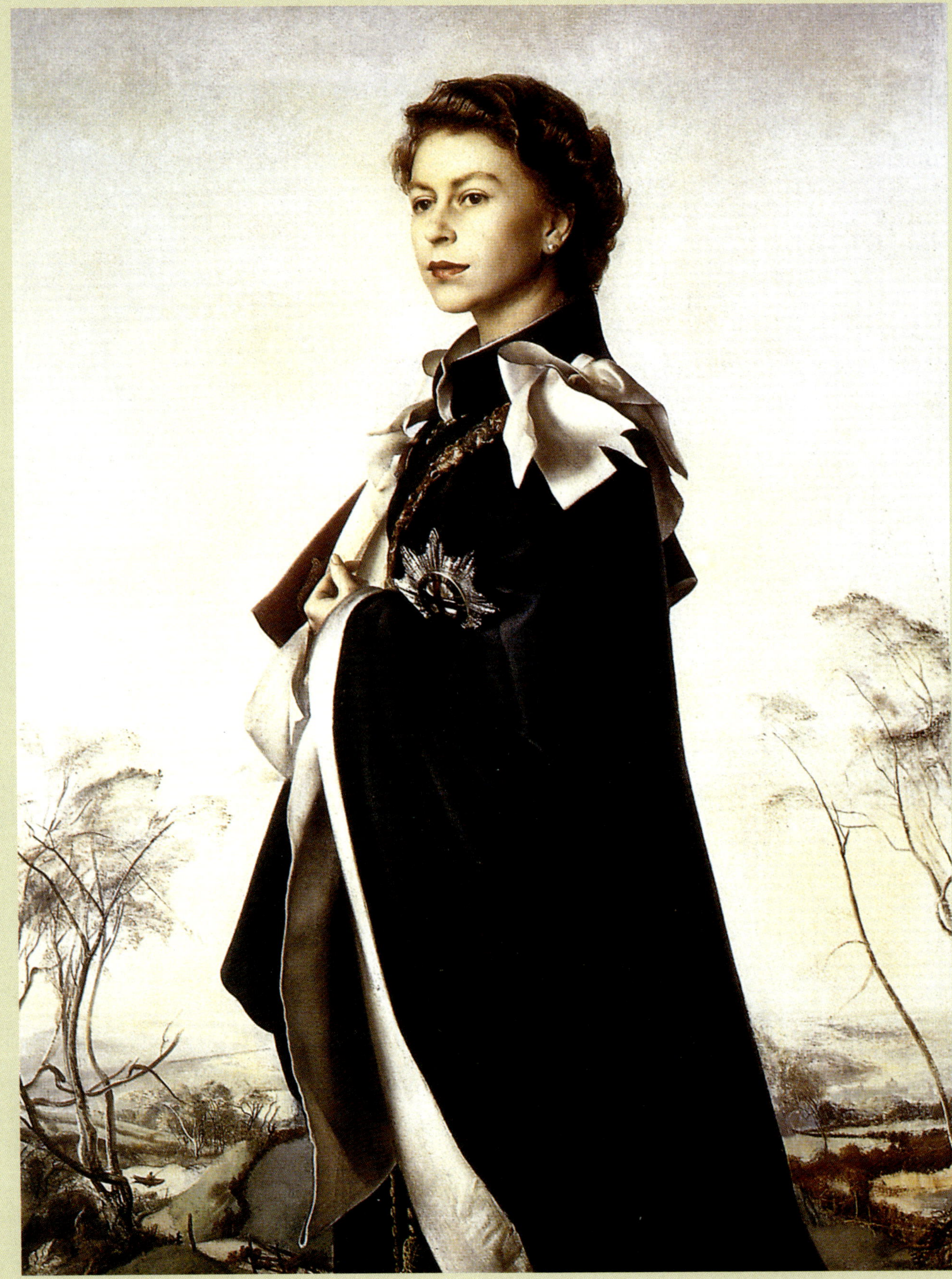

FOREWORD

I must confess that I almost always feel a certain embarrassment when asked to speak publicly or write about Pietro Annigoni; not only through a natural reticence but also because it seems I am expected to make a critical judgement of his work, as if being his son is enough to compensate for my limited knowledge of art history and confers on me a special insight I do not possess.

As one among the many admirers of his work, what most attracts me to him is his extraordinary humanity. The privilege of closeness has enabled me to appreciate every aspect of his personality and I am convinced that if he had not been a great painter he would still have been a great man. So it is with joy that I agreed to write these few lines of introduction to Dawn Cookson's *Painting with Annigoni*, a book which has really moved me since it is completely different from any other so far published about my father. Considering that the author was among the most diligent and loyal pupils of the Maestro and is herself a respected painter, one might expect her book to be a sort of manual for experts, aimed at a group of specialists and followers of contemporary figurative art. But it is nothing of the sort; the book, much more than a homage to Annigoni, is a rare and valuable evocation of a past era perhaps still too recent for anybody to have felt the need to study in depth, yet which is rich in ideas and is in many respects unrepeatable – as past events mostly are.

This was the period between 1950 and 1960, in which Europe, emerging from the tragedy of the Second World War, was bursting with new vitality. Like a tree just pruned, it was uncertain in which direction to grow its new branches and was wavering between reverting to its old traditions, following the brutal scar of fascism, and the temptation to be seduced by the trappings of the more imminent globalisation.

It was a brief and intense period in which the culture and pride of the old defeated continent made a huge effort to present itself as an alternative to the model imported by the victors across the Atlantic. Before the powerful forces of finance and supremacy submerged all individuality in the huge melting pot of a new and indefinable western civilisation. *Painting with Annigoni* takes us back through the innocence, the freshness, the acute observations and enthusiasm of a young English woman, still a novice, right in the centre of this scenario, in a Florence that was its very hub thanks to the interweaving of everyday happenings, personalities, discussions, ideals, tastes and smells around and about the privileged observatory of Annigoni's studio. The studio was a kind of microcosm, mirror and synthesis such as the Italian playwright Goldoni captured in his tragi-comedies with real characters and witty dialogue surrounding him for inspiration. On this stage, Annigoni, still young, already renowned but unaffected by fame and oblivious to his own charisma, performed the dual role of principal player and choreographer of a spectacle in which each character was simultaneously actor and observer.

Dawn Cookson, herself both actress and spectator, has managed to recollect and describe these events in a most original language and with typical British reserve mellowed by fond memory; her feelings without being stifled. The result has a poetic dimension which though perhaps unintentional is for this very reason all the more genuine.

There is no doubt that the main character in this book is Annigoni, but I would venture to suggest that he is not the true protagonist; neither is Dawn, since, despite assuming the crucial role of narrator in the first person, she chooses to stay in the background. Perhaps the true protagonist of *Painting with Annigoni* is an entire generation of which I was also a member and which, in those years, close and distant to us at the same time, lived out its great dream before having to face the banality of a world where it seems only numbers count.

Benedetto Annigoni, 1999

Opposite: Annigoni's 1955 portrait of HM The Queen, commissioned by the Worshipful Company of Fishmongers

INTRODUCTION

Much has been written about the famous Italian painter, Pietro Annigoni, who died at the age of 78 on 28 October 1988, having dedicated his entire life to art.

For his many admirers, friends, followers and pupils, his death was the end of an era. I was one of those fortunate few, privileged to have been accepted in 1958 – despite being a foreigner and female – into the 'inner sanctum' of his Florentine studio, where I worked for many months of every year until 1968. This was an unforgettable experience and proved to be the most important and influential period of my life, changing its whole course.

I wanted to recapture and record my personal memories of the events influencing the lives of the pupils who emanated from this studio, and those who were drawn from far and wide towards it. We were all affected by Annigoni's charismatic personality, vision, strength of character and positive determination.

It is said that everything viewed in retrospect appears better than it was in reality. Memories may often be veiled in nostalgia and some facts forgotten. This book covers the most exciting years of my life when every day was filled with anticipation and unexpected encounters both in and out of that unique studio. Most of all, there was total commitment to painting and a constant struggle to improve.

Annigoni was relatively unknown in England until in 1955 he became famous, almost overnight, with his first striking portrait of Queen Elizabeth II, exhibited at the Royal Academy. This painting, now known worldwide, stood out among the hundreds of other exhibits and drew unprecedented crowds of admirers. Here was a beautiful and imaginative portrait of great stature, combining regality with simplicity. Unadorned by crown or jewels, the young bareheaded Queen stands almost life-size against the background of a clear blue sky, wearing the flattering blue cape and Order of the Garter – the only emblem of pageantry depicting an isolated figure of a young woman gazing into the future, and more importantly, a young queen on the threshold of a new Elizabethan age. This was a startlingly fresh portrayal contrasting with many other formal and often stiff Royal Portraits. The only artistic licence the artist has permitted himself is in the background: the far distant, low-lying Italianate landscape, with a small boat on a lake and a solitary fisherman, reminders of his own private love for his boat and fishing, and also a subtle allusion to the Worshipful Company of Fishmongers who commissioned the painting. When the letter of commission arrived, he thought someone was playing a joke on him and remarked to one of his English pupils (Tim Whidbourne) 'You English have an extraordinary sense of humour; some fishmongers have asked me to paint your queen.' He then threw the letter into a waste-paper-basket. Fortunately, Tim retrieved it and assured Annigoni that this was not a joke but a serious enquiry from a prestigious and ancient guild which was honouring him with a very important commission.

When exhibited, the painting caused a furore with the public and there was widespread publicity – as well as much controversy and adverse comment from the art critics. A notable media personality, the late Malcolm Muggeridge, interviewing Annigoni on television with a panel of journalists, asked him, 'What is the difference between your style of painting and a good photograph?'

Annigoni's controlled reply was blunt: 'If you are unable to tell the difference, I really see no reason to waste my time answering'.

There were many harsh criticisms from art intellectuals, but for the thousands who flocked to the Royal Academy's Summer Exhibition in 1955 the painting was an outstanding success.

I was one of those admirers of this so-called new Renaissance painter. This artist made such an impact upon me, that I was determined somehow or other to meet him. But how, when and where were at that time not so easy. Where there is a will, however, there is also a way. Fate intervenes many times in our life for good or bad. Some believe that what will be, will be. I prefer 'it will be if you make it'.

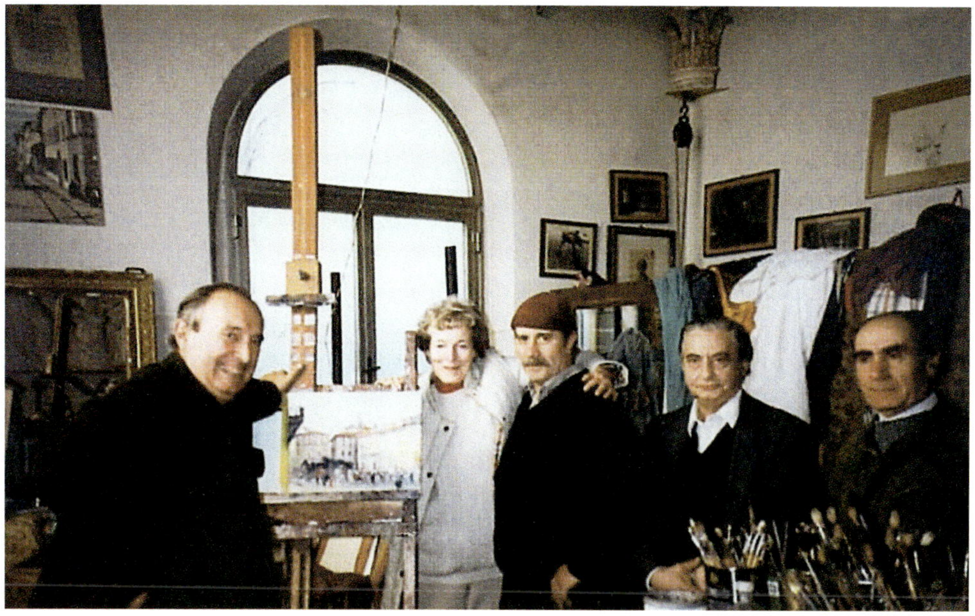

The reunion with old colleagues in May 1997 in the studio of Romano Stefanelli, Florence

I hope that this account will not be judged as either superficial or presumptuous by my contemporaries. There were many amusing occasions that formed part of our life in Florence in those happy years and cemented the bond between the Maestro and his pupils and friends. The studio was like a workshop of medieval times, with the apprentices working alongside the master, whose influence was very strong. Annigoni did not suffer fools, pretensions or excuses. He was the most single-minded and generous man I have ever met. A harsh critic, demanding and strong-willed; of erratic mood swings; with a boyish sense of humour and sharp wit, easily angered, inwardly sensitive, outwardly magnanimous, he was truly a man for all seasons and all conditions of people.

Now, after 40 years of painting and in the winter of whatever remains of my life, I am prompted by an urgent desire to record some of those most influential years. When time permitted, I kept brief diaries for reference, and I wrote many hundreds of letters to my parents recounting daily events in detail. Fortunately, my memory of that time is still vivid in substance, if not in detail.

Annigoni's passing left a vacuum of great sadness and sense of loss, most of all for his wife Rossella, his son Benedetto and his daughter Maria Ricciarda. It was deeply felt by all the friends, colleagues and pupils who loved and respected him, and the many all over the world who admired him. Since his death, many old friends who formed a great part of his 'entourage' have gone. Only my contemporaries from the studio and others who followed in subsequent years remain. Now too that wonderful studio has been sold. Only memories echo round the walls that could have told a thousand tales. But the prolific output of paintings, drawings, etchings, lithographs and sculpture created there will live on in many parts of the world.

In April 1997 I visited the studio once more before the sale and talked at length with Palmiro Meacci who had been Annigoni's secretary, agent and companion since the death of his closest friend, Riccardo Noferi. The place was so sad without Annigoni's magnetic presence. His old rocking chair behind the easel at which he worked was a poignant reminder. There was an all-pervading silence and emptiness with only a few of his paintings left there. Opposite his studio a few more steps led into his private book-lined study. Opening the door, I could visualize the burly figure sitting at his perpetually cluttered desk with a torn-in-half Gauloise cigarette smouldering between his fingers (a vain attempt to reduce his heavy smoking) while sorting out the accumulating piles of papers and appointments between intrusive phone calls. Now all was silent. The desk was bare and everything tidy, cold and lifeless. I retreated hastily and climbed up the rickety staircase to the attic where I had spent so many hours toiling over 'gessos', and onto the outside terrace from which the familiar view was much the same except for the intrusion of satellite dishes and too many coats of paint covering the patina of those weathered walls. Only Brunelleschi's Duomo, timeless and unchanged, dominated the heavenly sky-scape creating a feeling of hope in the eternal life into which Annigoni had entered.

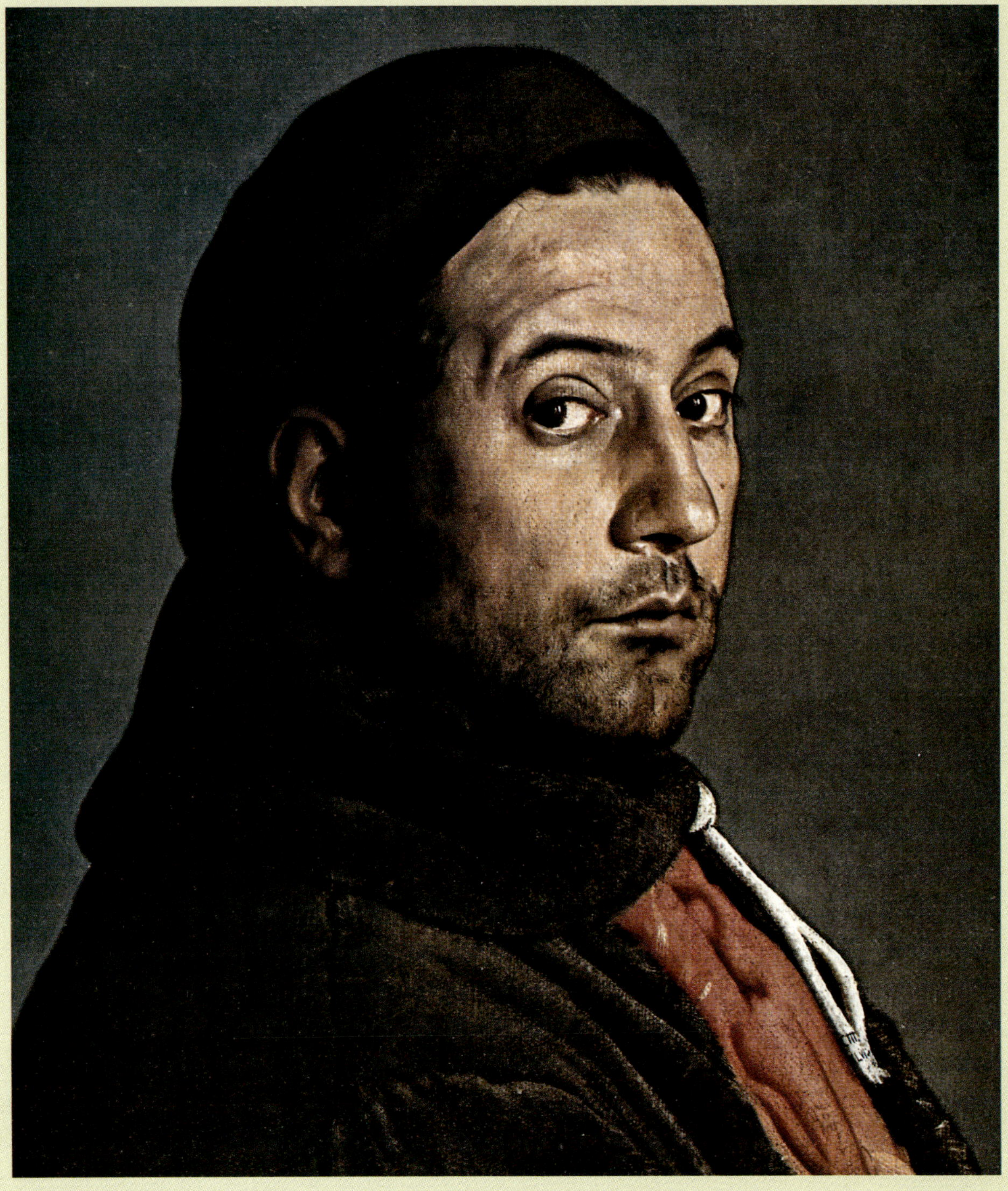

MEETING THE MAESTRO

My original art training was a five-year course of drawing and painting from life at the Birmingham College of Art. We were taught to draw in those days from the skeleton to the life model. However, I soon learnt that it took more than that to become an artist – and especially a painter. Most students turned to teaching as the next stage but, barely out of art school, with what practical experience, let alone knowledge?

It is never easy to earn a living as a painter and a living is hard-earned as a teacher. I tried teaching for a while, as well as commercial art, and was becoming in a sense a Jack of all trades and master of none. I saw the danger of drifting horizontally instead of moving forward and knew that I needed to focus my vision on learning more about art and its history.

Fortunately, an Italian friend of mine suggested that I should go to Italy and join a fine arts course at the famous Università per Stranieri (University for Foreigners) in the ancient Etruscan city of Perugia in Umbria. Possessing already a great love of Italy and having some knowledge of the language, I decided to take a sabbatical, with nothing to lose except money but every prospect of gaining my goal. That was the first step in the right direction and one that I was never to regret.

In the summer of 1955 I set off on the long train journey and started to realize the dream of a totally different way of life. Living under the hot sun in that historic hill town of ancient culture, I had my eyes opened to architecture, antiquity and some of the greatest paintings in the world. I walked for miles, discovering numerous churches in almost every street and piazza, from vast cathedrals to the smallest chapels, many of which contained great works of art.

Opposite: Annigoni's self-portrait

I recognized paintings I had hitherto only seen on slides at lectures. To come face to face with the originals from the thirteenth to sixteenth centuries was an overwhelming experience. Added to all this was the sheer joy of participating in the Italian way of life, lodging with local families of great warmth alongside other students of many nationalities.

My avid desire to improve my painting was not satisfied by my short spell of studies at the Accademia delle Belle Arti in Perugia. The *maestri* and *professori* rarely appeared in the life room, and when they did they seldom gave any valuable constructive criticism other than *Non c'è male; va avanti, coraggio* ('Not bad; keep going, have courage') or similar platitudes. The fine art lectures at the university were given by very erudite and eloquent professors of art history, who communicated their knowledge in voluble Italian which was hard to keep pace with. My Italian improved rapidly. Each Sunday we were expected to attend highly concentrated tours of art in Umbria, covering cathedrals, convents, museums and galleries. These started at 6 a.m., when the coach departed, and continued throughout the heat of the day with intensive lectures until we returned to base at sunset, completely exhausted. Impressions from them were recorded forever in my mind.

Through seeing the quality of the paintings at close hand and analysing them in great detail, my appetite to learn was increased, particularly about the craft and technique of the medium of tempera, which was the earliest known and was used with great skill by the masters of the Sienese school of the thirteenth through to the early fifteenth century, when oil painting developed. So Perugia was to provide a natural stepping stone on the road to Florence.

Among my fellow students I had befriended a Swiss girl, Edith Wittwer, a kindred spirit, and together we decided to spend a weekend in Florence to explore as much of the city as we could in two brief days. What a hope!

While walking down one of the narrow old streets leading off from the centre, we managed to find a lodging for two nights in Via Pandolfini 26, with an old couple called Giunti. It was very clean, basic, cheap and central. I made a note of this *punto d'appoggio*, little knowing then that I would be making it my home the following year. We wandered down the many back streets of the artisans' quarter, where the pavements are barely wide enough for one person to walk, and eventually found ourselves in Borgo degli Albizzi, a busy street bustling with traffic and lined with old buildings of monumental proportions, each with its own huge *portone* (a large double door) and brass letter plate indicating the names of the occupants.

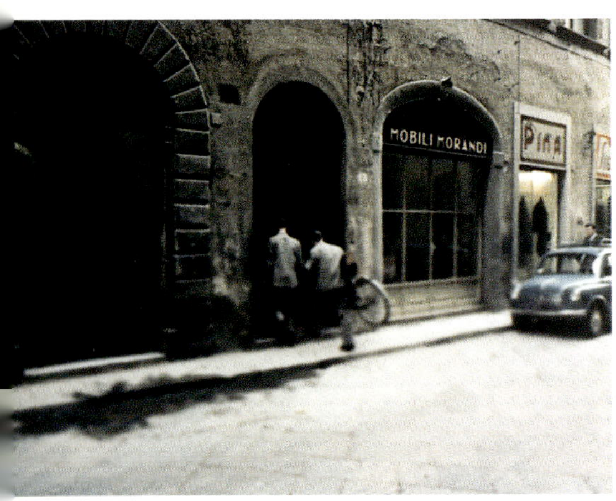

At No. 8, the door was open to the entrance hall, and by the bell were the words 'Annigoni – Studio'. I could hardly believe my luck. In the hall were various letter boxes indicating that the *studio di pittura* (painters' studio) was on the fourth floor. We climbed in semi-darkness up four flights and 99 hard stone steps to reach the top landing, from which a dark passage led to two final doors. Here the only indication as to which was the studio was a small indecipherable emblem and above it, written in pencil, simply 'P. Annigoni'.

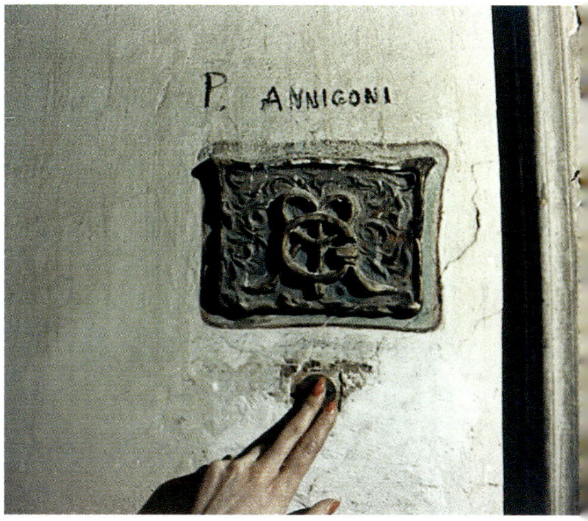

I pressed the bell. A shutter above the landing opened and a voice called out, *'Chi è?'* ('Who is it?'). We looked up in the direction of the voice and saw an old man leaning out of an internal window above. *'Cosa vuole'* ('What do you want?'). I asked for Annigoni. *'Il Maestro non c'è'* – 'He's not here; he is in England.' And with that he banged the shutter closed and my hopes were dashed. At least I knew now where he lived and would meet him somehow, sooner or later. Meanwhile Edith and I spent two days walking all over the centre of Florence, on relentless hard stones, briefly visiting a few churches, crossing the Ponte Santa Trinità, pausing to admire the beautiful piazzas and limiting our cultural tour to only one of the famous galleries for sheer lack of time and physical and mental exhaustion.

I had visited Florence only once before, in the early fifties, when rebuilding was still in progress following the end of the war. It was a very different city then, and now, thanks to the resilience of the Florentine people, it had emerged from the harrowing years of bombardment and suffering and had been restored with such adherence to historical records in every detail that the wounds of the battle could hardly be seen.

We had seen little of it that weekend, but enough to get our bearings and the feel of Florence in the best possible way – on foot – avoiding the typical tourist trap of seeing everything at great speed and assimilating nothing. We slept all the way back on the train to Perugia, exhausted yet inspired, to resume our studies on Monday morning.

I could write much more about my experiences in Umbria, my lodgings and everyday life, and most of all my discovery of the hill towns from the borders of Tuscany through the Piero della Francesca country, which instilled in me a deep and abiding admiration for that brilliant and unique painter, amongst so many other great masters of his time. I felt that my re-awakening to the endless horizon of artistic studies could not now be abandoned because my brief sabbatical had come to an end, and I had to return to England.

I had previously been approached for a design job in industry with a well-known British company in the north, manufacturing man-made materials – scope for development, a chance to travel, good pay and full time employment. I had gone for an interview and been short-listed, with every prospect of being given the job.

But Italy had meanwhile got into my system, with Annigoni as my goal, though I had not even met him yet. This was the big decision and a turning point. Which road should I take? A lucrative and secure job as a designer, with prospects? Or a return to Italy to study as a painter, with no secure future.

As I agonized over my decision, fate intervened. I read in the newspapers that Annigoni was in England painting a portrait of HRH The Duchess of Kent. I managed to obtain his temporary address at a studio he used in Kensington and wrote immediately requesting an appointment. I received a surprisingly prompt reply from his English secretary, Cedra Osborne. I was invited to bring some of my work to London on 20 July 1956.

I shall never forget that meeting. I was full of nervous tension. He received me, glanced over some of my work and asked what I wanted from him. 'Criticism and advice,' I replied, explaining briefly my position, my basic training and most of all my desire to be able to study under him.

He looked at me sternly and produced a small photograph of an exquisitely drawn portrait of a woman. It was strong and impressive. 'This is done by one of my Italian pupils, and when you can produce something like it, I will consider you. Meanwhile, the best advice I can give you is to go to the studio of Nerina Simi in Florence, where that pupil learnt to draw. She is a very gifted and unique teacher. You have the possibility of doing better, provided you work hard and dedicate yourself to one road only – and it is long and difficult.' He wrote Signorina Simi's address on his card and handed it to me. I thanked him. In parting he said, 'You will thank me by what you do and show for it,' adding, '*Forza, coraggio e arrivederci!*' – a phrase that was to become familiar.

He had given me a challenge, not discouragement. That made me decide to abandon the offer of a safe yet uninspiring job which would imprison me and take the plunge into the unknown: head for Florence again and this time the Simi studio with his recommendation. The turning point had come and it was to change my whole future. So, in the autumn of 1957, began my halcyon decade in Italy.

The first thing was to establish a lodging, and I decided to write in advance to the old couple Giunti with whom I had stayed previously with Edith. Their home was ideally placed and familiar. So, following a summer holiday at Riccione in September, I went to Florence, where I had to wait until 14 October for the Simi studio to open. Meanwhile, I was settling in to the top floor room. For 500 lire per day I had the use of the kitchen and bathroom, both of which where very antiquated and the latter hardly used. The wood-burning stove was apparently never lit; hot water had to be boiled in a large pan on the only gas stove in the kitchen. It required considerable dexterity to get it to the bathroom and use it to the best advantage while standing in the vast empty bath in a freezing cold atmosphere with draughts penetrating through every crack in the roof. It was not the most comfortable place for ablutions, nor the most private. It led directly from the kitchen-cum-sitting-room where the old couple spent most of their time, he reading newspapers and she knitting by an inadequate stove. There was only cold running water, which did not always run during the summer. Ever since then I have never wasted water.

In those beautifully mild early autumn days, this deprivation was not so acutely felt. I had a little electric heater in my room and got on well with the old couple. I usually ate out at a nearby trattoria in the evenings and enjoyed lunch in my room: delicious Italian bread, cheese, salad and wine, sitting by the huge tall window which, being on the top floor, looked over the roof tops and caught the morning sunshine. I was immensely happy and relatively carefree – eating well and comfortably accommodated for 1500 lire a day – a price which would hardly buy a cappuccino today.

Via Pandolfini was central and so rather noisy during the day, as most of the very old, large buildings housed business premises, lawyers' offices and shops. But way up on the upper floors, were private apartments and *pensioni* which later on would be converted to luxury penthouses with fabulous views over Florence. As in many buildings, there was no lift at No. 26, with six floors and half landings – and in my case, 96 steps – to be climbed to the top. It was good exercise having to negotiate them at least four to six times daily, the effect of which was to counteract my daily consumption of irresistible pasta and bread, which I adored. Luckily, I never gained a kilo while living there.

Studio Simi

I was looking forward to the opening, on 14 October, of the autumn term at the studio of Nerina Simi in Via Tripoli. This was only a fifteen-minute walk from my lodgings, across the Piazza Santa Croce, which was dominated by the magnificent fourteenth-century church of that name, containing some of Giotto's finest frescos in the Capella dei Pazzi. In the centre of that typical Tuscan stone square stood the statue of one of his famous sons, the poet Dante. From there it was a short distance to the National Library, which less than a decade later was to suffer devastating flood damage to countless and priceless volumes documenting the history and culture of Florence and elsewhere. The long narrow Via Tripoli joined another large and not so beautiful square, Piazza Piave, a crossing place for continuous traffic from both sides of the River Arno. This was a noisy walk, but once inside the old building of No. 1, which formed the corner of the square, and up a mere three flights of stairs, one entered a small world of another era.

Studio Simi with pupils and some of her father's paintings

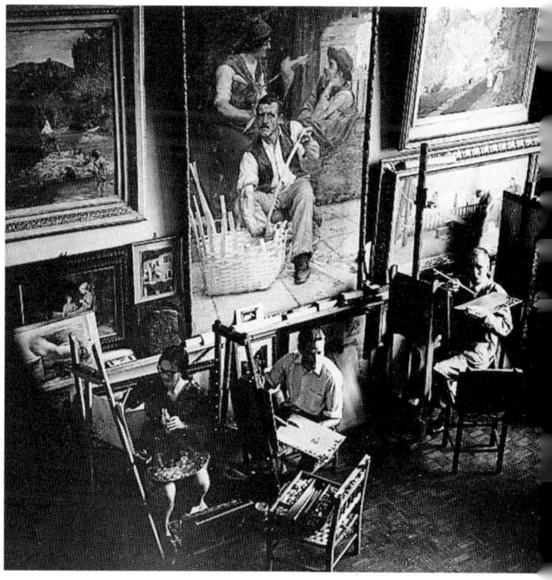

The large studio had a tall, wide north-facing window looking onto the square below. It was crammed with chairs and easels on three sides, with a raised dais at the back, on which the models posed. It was heated by an antiquated coke-burning iron stove which did its best against constant draughts from the roof and window.

The studio was always full. Positions were jockeyed for and tenaciously 'bagged' by pupils of various nationalities. The walls were covered with oil paintings, mostly by Nerina's father, Filadelfo Simi, who was an acknowledged painter of the nineteenth century and a former pupil of Gérôme in Paris. Filadelfo was a contemporary of the Italian Macchiaioli of 1850–60, so called because they used dappled patches of colour or smudges, in a similar way to the

French Impressionists and were influenced by the Barbizon school of Corot and Corbet. This Italian school was led by the great painters Fattori, Signorini, Lega and Boldini. Nerina had worked under and assisted her father as part of her early training. Few women then had the freedom to pursue their own careers publicly, and female artists mostly turned to teaching. With her singular background of two generations of painters and a long working life dedicated almost entirely to teaching and painting, she was a truly vocational teacher, unique in her time and a rarity nowadays. She lived into her nineties, a diminutive little lady with piercing brown eyes, her greying hair drawn back into a neat bun, dressed perpetually in a black overall with only a white blouse and a single string of pearls to relieve the sombre attire.

She must have been in her sixties when I joined her class but no one ever knew her exact age, and during the twenty years I knew her, she never seemed to change. Increasing and crippling arthritis, failing eyesight and frail health in the latter years obliged her to remain seated in her small adjoining living room, from where she continued to give criticisms of her pupils' work. These were still as perceptive and constructive as in her active days when she passed continually from pupil to pupil, giving individual tutoring with a never-failing and accurate eye for detail, proportion, form and *chiaroscuro* (shading). Nothing and no one escaped her attention, and she seemed indefatigable, teaching a three-hour session every morning and afternoon. The mornings were devoted to the study of the nude and the afternoons to portrait and still-life in order to learn composition and proportion. She insisted on drawing as the basic essential. She believed that most of the problems of painting could be solved by the study of the human form, which was surely the most difficult and challenging. How right she was! She trained the eye to see, to measure proportions and space and to observe the effect of light on surfaces. The time taken was unimportant compared with the experience gained by deep observation and continual study. She would often repeat 'You will arrive to see and understand' in her measured English interspersed with her native language. As she had never been to England, her English was remarkable. Personally, I learnt more in three months in her studio than during the five years of my earlier study at art college. I owe much to her teaching and criticism, which was always consistent with that of Annigoni.

She possessed the quiet charm of a well-bred and educated woman of her generation, and never gave way to modern trends or short cuts. She was a disciplinarian in her studio, where lapses into conversation were frowned upon. 'You cannot concentrate and chatter,' she would say. She was also very human and warm-hearted and, despite her relatively sheltered life, very broad-minded and understanding to anyone with problems or needing advice or comfort. Surrounded as she was in the main by young students, she listened to their opinions and attitudes, never condemning, even if sometimes disapproving, summing up their potential as would-be painters and tirelessly

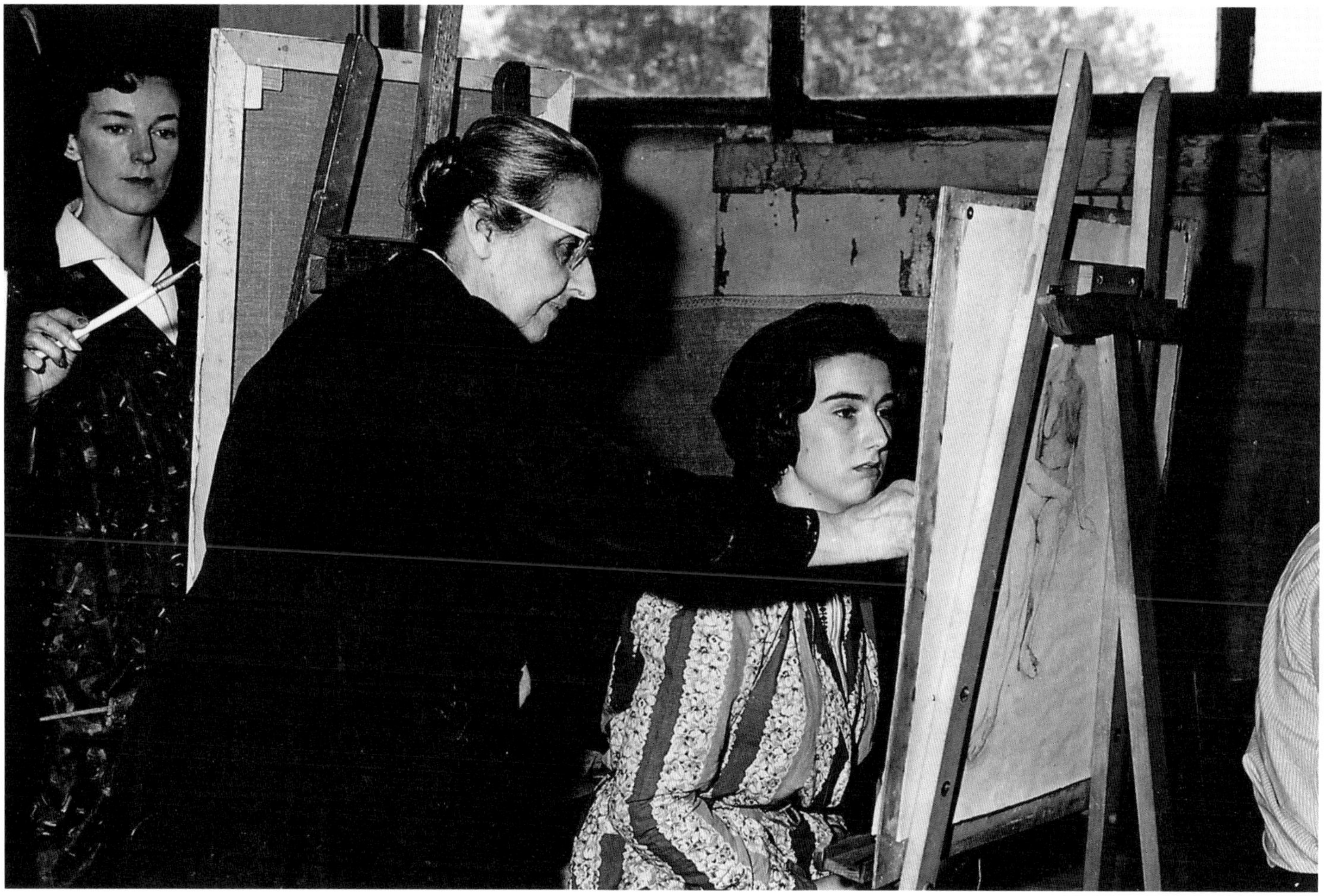

Signorina Simi correcting work

giving her all to each individual whatever sex, age or nationality.

From the main studio a very narrow door opened onto a small room full of props and plaster casts for still-life study, more paintings of the Simi school and many books. Here, there was only room for one or two students to set up a composition in the rather dim light from a small window overlooking Via Tripoli. A narrow dark passage lined with coat hooks led from the front door to the back of the house and her private quarters, all in a very compact space.

I had never before studied so intensely or with such great enthusiasm as in those early days in Florence under the guidance of this gifted teacher. I was determined to produce some work worthy of showing Annigoni and was spurred on by some talented colleagues. The most precocious at that time was the young Antonio Ciccone, a hitherto untutored teenager, son of poor parents in southern Italy where he had worked as a shepherd, but with an innate talent for observing and drawing with a precision and sensitivity far above his years and background. It was his drawing which Annigoni had shown me at our first meeting in London and that had led me to this studio where he was an inspiration to us all. In the ensuing years he developed into a considerable and prolific painter in his own right. His fascinating life story is recorded with illustrations of the quality and variety of his work in his own biography published in 1991.

Nerina Simi's byword was good drawing, and she pursued it assiduously with all the never-ending stream of pupils who flocked to her studio. Many of them appeared initially to have little grasp of what it meant, but after three months their progress was remarkable. Simi often said that anyone can learn to draw but that to develop and succeed demands perseverance, persistence, concentration and patience – and a lot of hard work. Painting followed later. She was a stern but constructive critic, and I am eternally grateful to her.

I must have walked for miles in those early months, not merely to and from her studio every day, but also discovering the wonders of Florence and capturing some of its magic. October was a wonderful month, the mornings bright and crisp turning into warm and mellow sunshine by mid-day. Best of all, on the walk back home, which I took along the River Arno, some of the most beautiful sunsets I have ever seen filtered through the arches of the bridges, transforming the usually torpid water into brilliant pink, flame and purple, mirrored from the sky and totally breathtaking.

The glorious golden days of October passed and the leaves fell from the silver-grey-barked plane trees lining Via Tripoli, covering the pavement with a multi-coloured carpet of 'cornflakes' which I shuffled through on my way to and from the studio. November crept in with sudden sharp mornings and early damp evenings, veiling the river in a pearly mist as the sun set like a huge golden ball – reminiscent of Turner's 'Sunset at Rouen'. At other times the sun was a flaming red in a pale silver-grey sky, reflected in a mother-of-pearl glaze on the water, more evocative of Monet's 'Sunset on the Seine'. Such natural beauty was sheer magic and so transient that I could only assimilate it

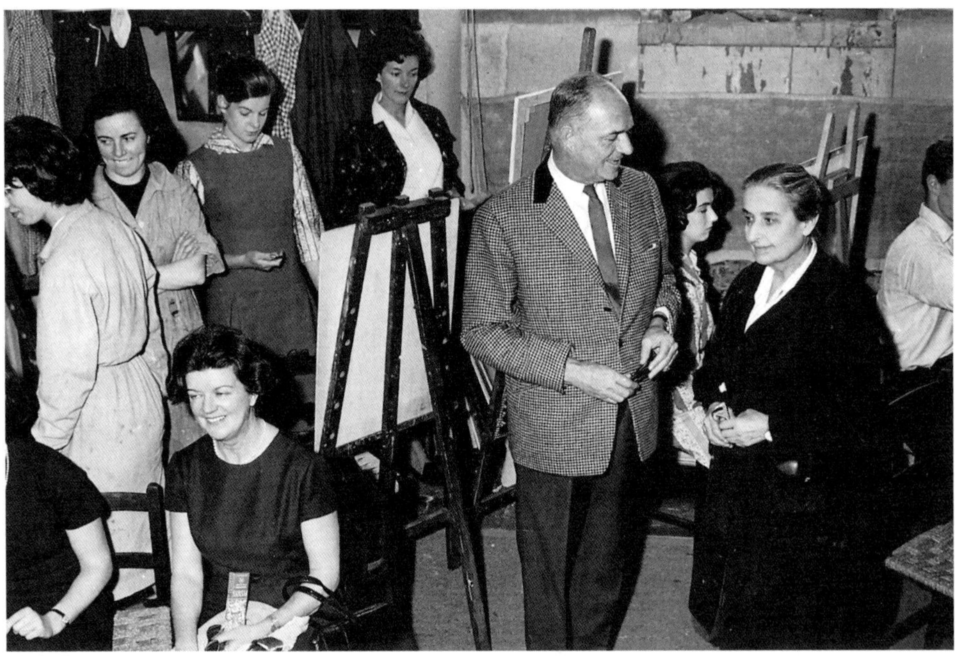

The crowded Simi studio with a visiting American gallery owner

with my senses and mentally record it, being then totally inexperienced in painting land- or sky-scapes. Annigoni later taught me to appreciate the importance of trying to capture that fleeting light at sunset – 'the best hour to paint nature,' he used to say.

During the Simi period I was completely involved in portraiture and still-life. Nature was far too complex a subject to embark upon at the same time. Maybe I was not courageous enough to set off looking for subjects early on my own, and too tired after six intensive hours at the studio to have any spare energy in the evenings. Those hours were mostly devoted to writing my diaries and copious long letters home recording each day's events. Had I still possessed those hundreds of letters written over the ensuing ten years, this book would have been produced much earlier and with far greater ease.

During the early sixties, the film of the book *The Agony and the Ecstasy*, the story of Michelangelo by Irving Stone, was being made in Rome. In order to recreate the procedure of painting the ceiling of the Sistine Chapel, skilled artists were sought to execute a life-size copy of that great masterpiece for scenes in which Charlton Heston as Michelangelo played the artist at work on the painting. It is significant that four of Signorina Simi's most talented male pupils were selected to undertake this onerous work, much to the pride of the studio.

Meeting Annigoni again

16 October 1957. This was a significant date in my diary because, quite by chance, I ran into Annigoni on my way to the studio. He seemed surprised to see me and when I told him that I was already studying with Signorina Simi he was pleased and invited me to call at his studio later that morning. Fate had intervened again, and I was one step nearer my goal. I arrived punctually at noon. Annigoni's man servant Annibale answered the bell and let me in: up a further short flight of steps to a narrow landing from which, to the left, was Annigoni's private apartment comprising a book-lined study with bureaus and cupboards and a large open desk under a jumbled pile of papers and correspondence, as well as his bathroom and bedroom. To the right of the landing a door led into his vast studio, wonderfully lit from a large north-facing window which stretched to the high ceiling and occupied most of one wall. It looked across to a maze of the backs of houses in the adjacent street, pan-tiled roofs and chimneys.

This interview was cordial and brief. Annigoni was a busy man and was due to return to England shortly to complete his portrait of HRH Princess Margaret. He said he would see me again after his return, and in parting gave me three reproductions of his paintings to encourage me with my studies– a most unexpected and kind gesture. Then, with what I later knew was his familiar farewell, said, *'a presto, forza, coraggio e arrivederci!'* I ran down those 100 steps, re-fired with a sense of purpose and determined to persevere at all costs. So my weekly routine continued, my work under Simi's stern criticism progressed and I could see notable improvement.

The other pupils were of all ages and both sexes. Many were young English girls attending finishing schools in Florence with art and/or music as part of their courses. Then there were a few Americans. One of these was a young, very attractive, talented and fun-loving girl from a wealthy Philadelphia family who later gave up a promising career as a painter to become a nun, much to all our surprise. She joined a Carmelite order of complete seclusion, which greatly concerned the Signorina. The most constant and devoted male American pupil was Nelson Holbrook White, the son and grandson of two American marine painters from Connecticut. He became a 'professional student', attending the Simi studio for many more years than all the others, coming from the States repeatedly. He later developed into a fine and sensitive land- and sea-scape painter.

In those years that I studied with Simi, a constant stream of students was always waiting on a list to be accepted when a space was vacated, but there always remained the regulars, in the main Italians and mostly Florentines, with some of whom I forged friendships that have endured across the decades.

Friends and Food

I had many Italian friends from Milan and Bolzano. Nearer to Florence my first and longest-lasting was Professor Brunero Bernardini, whom I met in my home town in 1951 when he came over with a group of scholars on a cultural exchange with Birmingham University. I was then reporting for BBC Midland News and was sent to interview them, being able to speak Italian. That early acquaintance led to a long and enduring friendship, later also with his wife Anna and their two daughters. There were many others, including not a few *corteggiatori*, between whom I had to tread cautiously. In fact, far too many distractions, temptations and late nights dining out were not conducive to early mornings at the studio – but then, 'all work and no play', as the saying goes, is almost impossible in Italy, and one is only young once.

One of the simple pleasures that I relished most was shopping in the open markets and little stalls all around the back streets of the centre. Every morning as I left Via Pandolfini I would take a circuitous route passing a *torrefazione di caffè* just to smell that pungent bitter aroma of roasting coffee, the faintly blue smoke that wafted through the door as all blends and types of beans were weighed, ground, sold or served at the counter all day long. Then there was the wholesome aroma of baking bread, produced in dozens of different types, shapes and sizes. My favourites were *cazzotti*, crusty and rolled in flour, or the long, thin and even crustier *stecchini* or *ossi* (literally sticks and bones), specialities of Florence. There were also huge rough loaves of country bread with a hard crust and dark dough, eaten daily with every meal. All these varieties were produced at small bakeries all over the town, at least twice a day so that they could be bought fresh for breakfast, lunch and dinner. They had to be as there were no preservatives or additives in those days, and deep freezing was not widely available, if at all. There were none of the sliced, wrapped and flabby loaves which in England last for days and taste of nothing.

As for the fruits and vegetables, which nowadays are available and exported everywhere, they were displayed on barrows in such a violent palette of colours that I frequently bought a selection to paint for still-life before they shrank and shrivelled and I finally cooked and ate them.

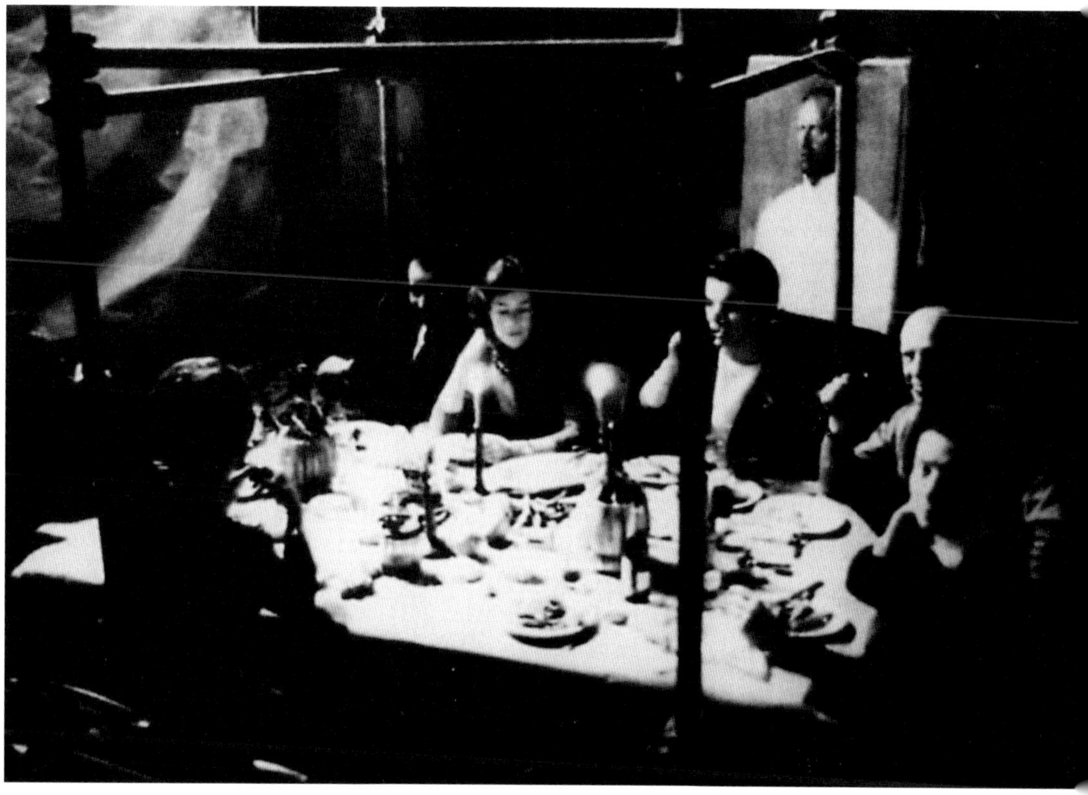

Supper party of friends in the studio

There were many individual *pizzicherie* or delicatessen-cum-grocery shops, with very high counters above sniffing and touching level, behind which the vendor served the delicacies of wafer thin hams, salami, mortadella, fresh pasta and an infinite variety of cheese from all over Italy. Oh, those daily joys of food shopping, however long it took waiting for attention! The looking and the tasting of samples added to the pleasure of being served with courtesy and a smile. Compared with that, the anonymity of today's super- and hypermarkets, all self-service and still a long queue at the checkout, is impersonal and dreary. Maybe for commodity and convenience supermarkets are superior, but for pleasure and individuality, give me those former days.

As well as cooking, eating was an occasion over which much time was taken. The lunch hour was from two to four according to the season, and dinner could spread over several hours from eight in the evening onwards. I had to eat out quite often and was frequently invited by and to friends. I became a regular customer at my favourite trattoria, but in those days a girl eating alone was rather vulnerable, as I soon learnt.

Signora Giunti kept a sharp eye on my return and was always sitting by the stove in the kitchen, with the door open, long after her husband had retired to bed. As I let myself in stealthily she looked up from her knitting or dozing with *'ben tornata!'*, a barely veiled admonishment if it was after 11 o'clock, in which case it meant 'high time!'.

'Good night, signora,' I would reply, avoiding any further enquiries or comments and dropped thankfully into my bed, sometimes to find a thoughtfully placed old stone hot-water bottle (a war time relic) to warm me. I soon bought a more comforting rubber version.

Some cold winter evenings, returning home from the studio too tired to venture out to eat, I was permitted to improvise a hot pasta supper in the Giuntis' kitchen, and on one of these occasions, the old husband was listening attentively to their antiquated radio on the kitchen table.

'Do you like music, signorina – I mean real music?' he asked.

'I love it, especially classical and opera,' I replied.

'Well then, come with me to see *Aida* this evening.'

I was surprised that this simple old carpenter would go to the opera and if so, where in Florence in mid-winter, but he assured me that we only had to go down to the little bar on the next street where that opera was to be transmitted 'live' on television. Somewhat disillusioned but with no excuse to decline, I accepted and we tottered downstairs, the old man hanging on to my arm and puffing on his habitual cheroot. We entered a little bar crowded with all the locals – mostly men, and very curious. To my amazement Signor Giunti appeared to know every movement of the opera. He nodded to the music, his hands keeping time, and occasionally joined in the chorus – slightly off-key and much to my embarrassment, and the amusement of the clientele.

Daily Life – Getting to know the City

November passed all too quickly as I actively pursued my work with alternating enthusiasm and frustration. When not studying, I was discovering and learning more about the city on foot, and with the help of friends with cars and scooters travelling further out into the nearby countryside of beautiful olive groves surrounding the hills of Settignano and Fiesole. I walked for miles at weekends, visiting every famous church, museum and gallery until I had almost reached saturation point. I recall the padre at the Anglican church of St Mark, telling me that he had lived for over 25 years in Florence and was still discovering. 'Look up when you are walking down an old street and you may well find a

Della Robbia base relief you had never noticed.'

I was also enjoying some of the social life that was opening to me through my extending contacts, and was beginning to feel *fiorentinizzata*, observing the habits and mannerisms of the people I met, and unconsciously even picking up the local accent when out shopping or talking to the Giuntis. Fortunately, I also met the other side of a very class-structured society in which titles of every sort had great importance. Very few people, it seemed to me, were simply *signore*, *signora* or *signorina*. There were the *principi e duchi*, *marchesi*, *conti e baroni* of the nobility, who were international, and then every professional or businessman was either a *professore*, *dottore*, *avvocato* or *maestro*. The ubiquitous *cavaliere* I never quite defined. It appeared that the further south one went, the more likely it was that anyone of the slightest importance would bear a title. I was surprised to receive a letter addressing me as *illustrissima pittrice* – need I translate? This did not delude me into any sense of self-importance, but I was rather amused when the postman thereafter always greeted me with, '*Buon giorno pittrice*'. So even I had gained a title and a certain caché.

Accepted into Annigoni's Studio

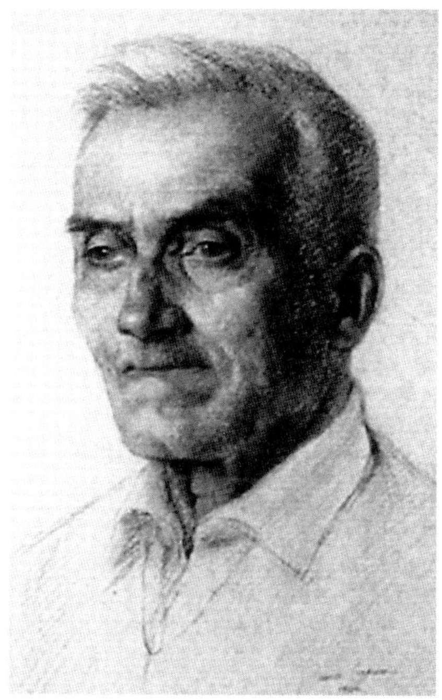

My drawing of Annibale Vanucci

Christmas 1957 was approaching fast, and I returned home to my family with some portrait commissions in prospect in the early new year. It was not until the beginning of April that I returned to Florence, full of hope and expectation.

On 12 April I picked up my courage and returned to Annigoni's studio carrying my portfolio of latest work. Annibale, like one of the porters in a Shakespeare play, again popped his head out of the little window above to enquire my business and then let me in announcing, '*C'è una signorina straniera*' ('There's a foreign lady here') as he ushered me into the studio.

'*Venga pure*' ('Come in') replied the now familiar, deep, husky voice of Annigoni, looking round his easel. 'Ah, it's you again!'

Not very encouraging, I thought. Then opening my portfolio I said, 'I've brought some more recent work to show you, Maestro.'

'Well, there are signs of some improvement here since I saw you in London.'

'I've been studying with Signorina Simi as you advised, and I'm sure that there would be much more improvement if you would allow me to come and study here,' I said in English, noting that I was being observed with some suspicion by two male pupils who were peering at me from behind their easels while yet another popped his head round the door to view this intruder. I then produced an oil still-life painting rather apologetically, admitting to having problems with half-tones.

Annigoni interrupted me: 'If you come here, you will not paint until *I* say. You'd better start on Monday. You can work in the attic and only drawing, remember. There are plenty of subjects up there. *Va bene?* Understood? *Allora, arrivederci a lunedi alle nove.*'

Blunt and brief as usual but I was *accepted* and I could hardly believe my luck. The day I had dreamed of had come at last! I was so excited that I ran down the stairs and wanted to hug someone, but as there was no one to hug, I decided to celebrate with lunch at Frizzi, not exactly the Ritz of Florence, but the nearest trattoria up the road. That day I was on cloud nine and anxious for Monday morning to arrive.

So, on 14 April 1958, a new routine started for me at nine a.m. precisely. Having decided that I was going to maintain a very low profile, on entering I gave a brief '*Buon giorno, Maestro*' and scurried up the rather perilous staircase to the attic. The walls were covered to the roof with *gessi* (plaster casts) of all shapes and sizes: anatomical parts, death masks and pieces of Greek and Roman sculpture. One large door-window led out to the roof terrace. It was very cold outside, and not much better inside with all the draughts penetrating from under the bare pantiles of the roof. I selected a cast of a man's hand and settled down to draw it for the next three hours, at the end of which I crept down the stairs and attempted to let myself out quietly to avoid disturbing the main studio. But that was not missed by Annigoni, who bade me *arrivederci* from within.

This silent routine continued for a couple of weeks until one morning I heard heavy footsteps on the stairs and Annigoni entered the attic to see what I was doing. I was getting rather tired of drawing that lifeless caste of a hand and thought I had gone as far as I could with it. He looked at it and said to me, 'You must try to imagine that this is a living hand and to feel every bone, muscle and tendon, and the blood flowing in the veins,' illustrating as he corrected a section. 'Life is the greatest experience and the most important thing is how you live it,' he told me. 'Remember that to face the truth and to try to draw it faithfully and honestly is very difficult. To know that to begin with is the only way to know yourself and discover what is within you. *In bocca al lupo, forza avanti*' (very roughly translated as 'be strong, press on and take the bull by the horns'). These were two of his many maxims, often repeated and forever remembered.

The Documentary Film

Shortly after my arrival an unexpected event disrupted the routine of the studio and led to my involvement in a documentary film about Annigoni, his painting, the studio, the pupils and the local environment. The director, Campori, a very handsome Roman, and his daughter, who acted as stage manager, arrived with their camera crew, lights and all the paraphernalia to start shooting inside and outside the studio. I remained upstairs out of the way trying to make a foot come to life. Then I was unexpectedly called downstairs to be included in the studio filming. This was to show some of the pupils at work, including at that time the then leading Italian pupils, Romano Stefanelli and Antonio Ciccone, and two young American boys: David Flackman (who also played Flamenco on his guitar and whom Annigoni nicknamed 'the blond gipsy') and Nelson Holbrook White. Annigoni's first and foremost pupils, Luciano Guarnieri and Fernando Bernardini, were already advancing in their careers and established in their own studios as professionals. There seemed to be a constant flow of painters – all male at that time.

We were filmed at work in various parts of the studio while Annigoni was engaged in painting a striking life-size portrait of the very attractive Paola dei Conti Veneroli Pesciolini, of a noble Florentine family. It was a far from formal portrait: she was depicted standing in a field of maize in glowing autumnal colours, a pullover casually tied across her shoulders. Then there were the outside shots, all in the nearby countryside and along the River Mugnone, showing Annigoni painting small quick oil sketches and walking in the city as he always did.

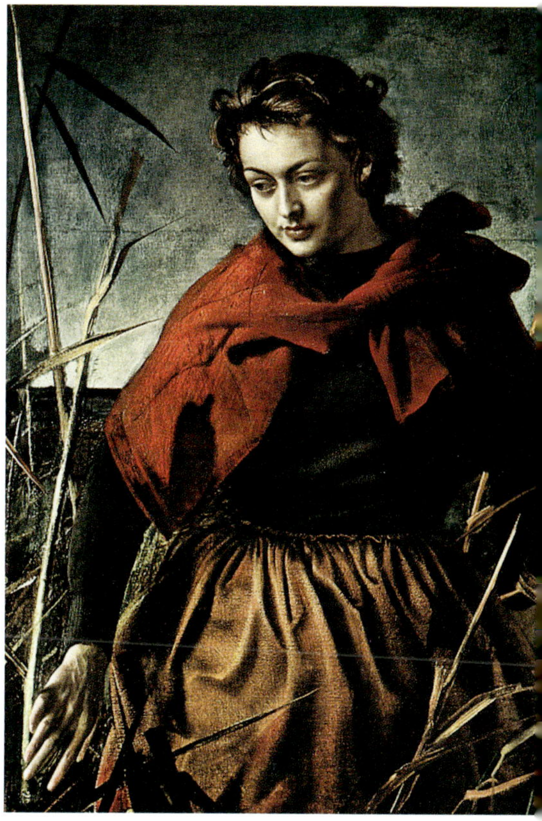

Portrait of Paola dei Conti Veneroli Pesciolini

During this disruptive but enjoyable invasion, normal studio routine work was abandoned and we were kept hanging around for takes and retakes until the director was satisfied. Lunchtime came and Annigoni suggested we should all go out to eat: 'You too, Marlene Dietrich,' he teased me, for my small part in the film. So we set of with the crew to walk across the river to the well-known Trattoria da Angiolino, which for Annigoni and his pupils was a favourite haunt at that time.

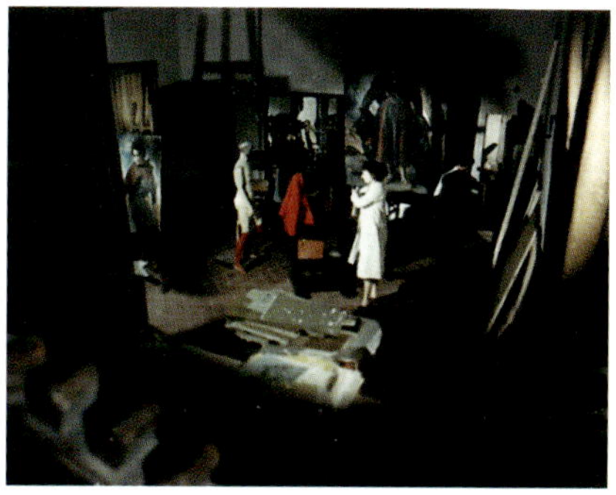

The studio during the filming

The Trattoria da Angiolino was and remains in Via Santo Spirito, a narrow and perilous street in the San Frediano artisans' district. I became a regular client for many years. It was a family business: Angiolino, the affable and hard-working owner, his wife who served the desserts and made out the bills at the counter and their son Peppino, a young man who hurried about constantly taking orders, as well as a couple of cooks in the open kitchen at the far end of the restaurant and two waiters who rushed about balancing plates up their arms, calling '*Subito, subito*' to the impatient customers at tables which lined either side of the long room. The walls were decorated with some fine mural paintings by local artists, including some of Annigoni's senior pupils. It was characteristically Florentine and very *casalinga*: good, plain home cooking.

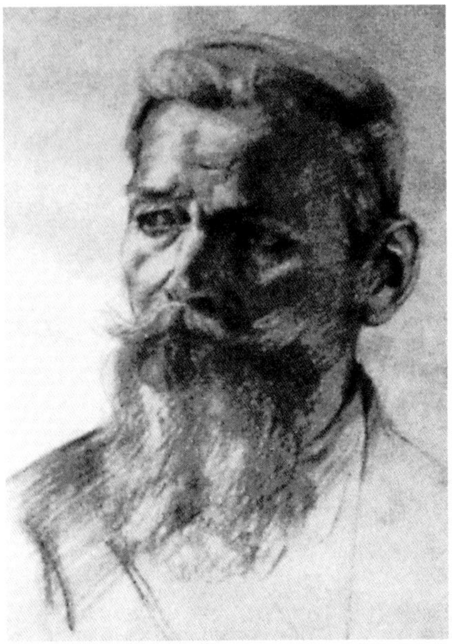

My drawing of Annibale de Rosa

The atmosphere was convivial and noisy, with vociferous Italians enjoying their food and talking demonstratively as only Latins can, constantly calling to the waiters, who in turn shouted the orders to the cooks who prepared the many dishes in a haze of smoke from the open grill and steam from the boiling pans of pasta. A palate-tempting titillation of delicious odours combined with a cacophony of clattering plates, clinking glasses and above everything, voices. Few Italians, it seemed to me, talked quietly when eating out in company, and all seemed to talk and occasionally listen at the same time.

The general bonhomie was infectious, making a meal an occasion to be savoured, and which could often last for hours, especially in the evening. When dining out with Annigoni and his entourage, as I was soon to experience, dinner could often last until after midnight, and we were usually the last to leave. The poor, tired waiters were already piling chairs onto the cleared tables, the kitchen was closed, the floor was swept, and all the staff were anxious to go home, yet waiting with infinite patience for our party to depart and bidding us goodnight with smiles and thanks. Customers were valued and treated with courtesy and respect, which occasionally they did not deserve by their behaviour.

The filming episode had brought me more easily into the company of the male pupils. And, being English and speaking Italian had other advantages when I was required as an interpreter to help translate the Italian script into English or to explain certain words and meanings. So this temporary diversion from the attic was welcome as was participating in the film.

The weather was still cold for April when I returned to my studies up the stairs, wrapped up from head to foot. Dear old Annibale took pity on me and each morning brought up a bucket of hot cinders which he raked out of the large iron stove in the studio. I balanced my poor frozen feet on the rim and some heat penetrated up my body, but not for long. I had to resort to mittens for my numb fingers.

I had 'graduated' from drawing the hand to a foot, and finally to a death mask of Bismark, with even less hope of feeling the blood in *his* veins. As the weather began to improve, several of the pupils decided to combine resources to hire a model. Down in the little Piazza dei Mercanti we found an odd, little old man with a long beard, wearing a battered old trilby hat who, at the prospect of earning a few lire for sitting still, willingly agreed to be our model. He sat still but stank atrociously of smoke (a cheroot was almost stuck to his lips) and sweat. He was quite a character, also called Annibale, and with the surname de Rosa (would he had exuded a scent as sweet as his surname). Our own dear Annibale did not approve of him. I still have portraits I drew of both of these old men.

By early May, it was becoming very hot and the attic changed to an oven. Annibale de Rosa was exchanged for a nude model, infinitely more appealing in every way.

Secretarial Work

Annigoni began to call for my help frequently with some of his English and American correspondence. As the pile of unopened mail on his desk increased daily, I suggested putting it into some sort of recognizable order, at which he glowered at me, but then to my surprise handed me several letters telling me to answer them.

'How can I possibly do this without knowing your wishes?'

'Well, I'll tell you briefly and you can translate them into good English when you are at home.'

'But even if I had a typewriter, my typing is appalling.'

'Well, your handwriting is excellent, so what is the problem?'

I gave in and opened some of the letters long past their date: invitations to several functions and private dinners – the easiest to answer, requests for interviews and applications from would-be pupils.

'I don't want to accept any of them,' he said.' Explain that I am far too busy, or say that I have been abroad or whatever. You'll know exactly how to say it. Just use your initiative and rid me of all this tedious business. Make apologies where necessary and decline all the social invitations that I have not the time or inclination to accept.'

So I had my work cut out that evening, writing for several hours in English, French and Italian. I felt that at least I had gained a position of trust and reliance in being delegated this task, as well as an opportunity to do something useful for him. Next morning I produced the replies on his printed note paper for his approval and signed simply 'pp Pietro Annigoni'. I could see he was pleased.

Then there were the constant telephone calls, mostly answered by Annibale. Many came from abroad and could not be understood by the old man, who would call to me, '*Down,*' (very few could pronounce my name correctly), '*venga al telefono, c'è straniero*' ('come to the phone, it's a foreigner'), and the rest was left to me to deal with. I was getting into the familiar routine: the door bell below would ring, Annibale would pop his head out of the little landing window, call 'Who's there?' and when informed of the name, disappear into the studio to see if the Maestro wished to be interrupted at his work. Frequently he did not. Annibale would return to the window and call down to say that, 'The Maestro is in Bergamo' – a diplomatic white lie that was often repeated. I wondered if so many 'visits to Bergamo' from behind his easel were believed. However, an artist must work in peace and concentration, and most people who knew Annigoni well only called between noon and one o'clock, which was the official visiting hour. Otherwise, there would have been no peace at all.

During my ensuing apprenticeship Annigoni was travelling and working abroad for long periods at a time. The studio was very empty without him, despite our daily individual work. During these absences, he entrusted me to check over his mail, sorting out the social from the business letters. The latter were dealt with by Riccardo Noferi, his oldest and closest friend and constant companion, who worked in a bank and was therefore a great help to Annigoni. He was a most *simpatico* man: good-natured and full of humour, enthusiasm and dynamic energy. He called frequently at the studio with messages or for a brief chat, dealt with business matters and became a good friend and support to me, which I needed and appreciated. Riccardo was a friend to us all, but to Annigoni more like a brother.

During Annigoni's absences the mail increased and the conglomeration mounting on his desk provoked me into initiating some order and a filing system, despite his instructions to deal only with the post and not start tidying up or he would never find anything. First, I created some space and then sorted, labelled and segregated items needing attention from those to be filed. On his return, despite remonstrations of mock fury, he was not displeased to find an orderly and visible desktop and an armchair free from months of accumulating clutter. He really needed a full-time, experienced secretary, as I often pointed out to him. 'I can rely on you and that is enough,' he replied.

Much later this post was to be filled by Palmiro Meacci, who was a friend of many years from the Bar Daria below the studio and who served as a contact and private agent for Annigoni. Then later, following the tragic death of Riccardo Noferi, Palmiro became an invaluable aid, friend, secretary and companion for the remaining years of Annigoni's life.

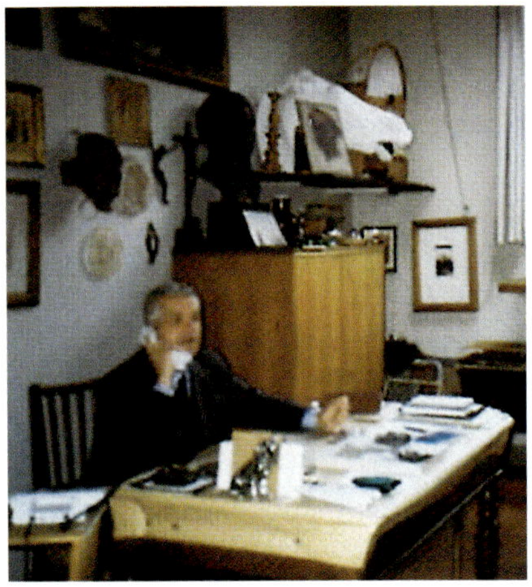

Palmiro Meacci at his desk

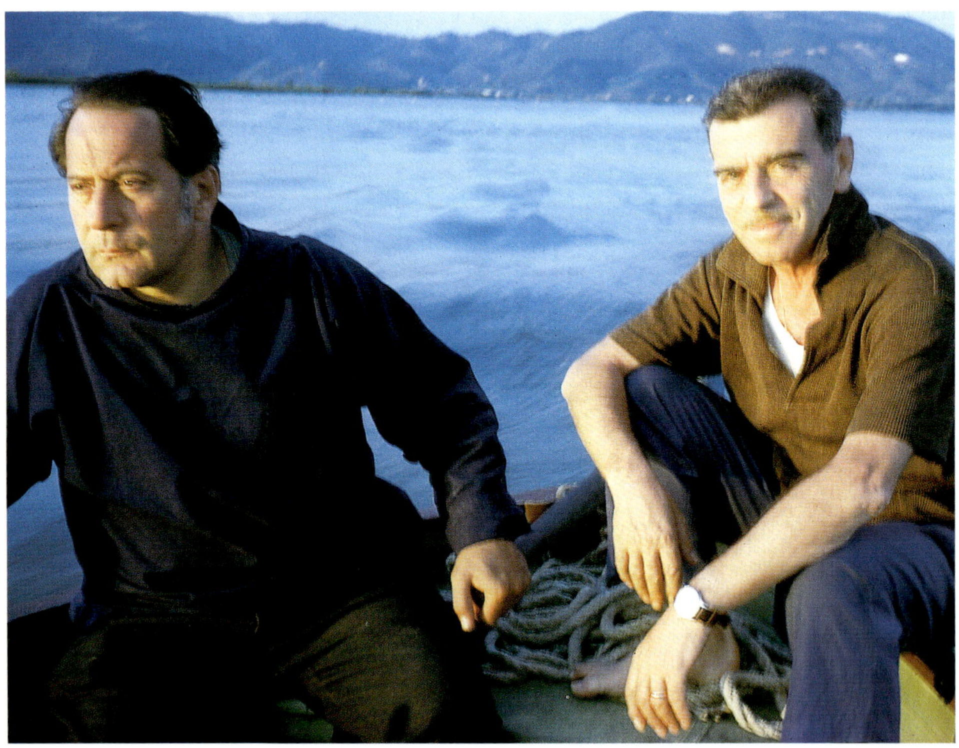

Annigoni with Riccardo Noferi

The Bar Daria

The Bar Daria, named after the owner, Daria Bartalesi, a plump and amiable woman and great admirer of Annigoni, was his favourite bar. Daria, her son Bruno and Palmiro Meacci, all worked in this family business, which was frequented by an assorted clientele of local stallholders, shopkeepers, artisans and painters. In this atmosphere Annigoni felt at ease.

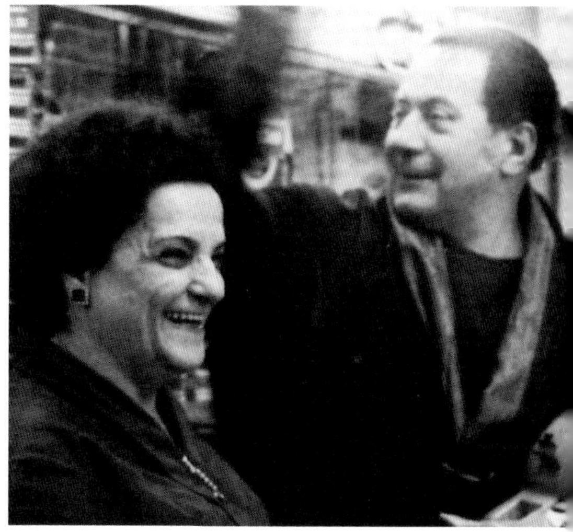

Annigoni with Daria Bartalesi

Daria had opened this very small bar in 1943. A passionate lover of art, she had created a meeting point for many artists, who collected there over a glass of wine or a coffee to talk painting and exchange views, and often to sell their paintings. Daria allowed them to hang their work on the limited wall space of the very narrow bar and all down the stairs to the basement kitchen. Annigoni described her in a dedication as 'the queen of the Florentine Montparnasse'.

Like most Italian bars, Bar Daria was open all hours and often until very late at night. It was always the place for us to meet up before going out to dinner and to return to much later after an invariably lengthy meal, with much wine often provoking some high-spirited horseplay between the men. On one occasion Annigoni, who was engaged in a noisy argument with Bruno, suddenly grabbed a soda water syphon from the bar and, imitating a machine gun, drenched poor Bruno. Fortunately, the latter took it in good part and everyone, except the soaking Bruno, ended up laughing. Annigoni's patronage was valued, as were some of his paintings on the walls, so Bruno tolerated with equanimity the antics which often took place after much imbibing.

The bar also produced delicious canapés and patisseries which gave me an idea later when I was learning to mix tempera colours (of which more anon). I noticed that many whites of eggs were discarded down the sink during the process of mixing emulsion for the medium. This wastage of useable foodstuff irritated me, so I brought a large plastic container to the studio and as the whites were separated from the yolks I collected them – often as many as a dozen. I took them downstairs to the bar together with caster sugar and asked Daria if they would make some meringues for me after their baking was over and the ovens had cooled to the low heat necessary. Next day I collected a large tin full of delicious meringues, bought some whipped cream to fill them and handed them around to my colleagues. Nobody refused them except Annigoni, who never ate sweets, and nobody wasted egg whites after this. Fortunately, colours were not mixed very often, because one can have a surfeit of meringues.

Daria was always pleasant and welcoming to everyone, especially to Annigoni and his old friends and pupils, greeting us all by name and often with a kiss.

Occasionally I ventured downstairs for a warming *cappuccio* during the cold winter months, hoping Annigoni would not see me, but he always heard my footsteps and the clicking of the door lock. 'And where do you think you are going?' he would ask.

'Only for a quick coffee. I'm so cold and empty,' I would reply.

'A serious painter should not be distracted by such material feelings,' he would admonish me from within the studio.

Feeling guilty, though I think he enjoyed teasing me, I would say that I would only be ten minutes. Even he, I had often noticed, telephoned the bar for a coffee to be brought up to the studio, by which time it must have been chilled – but then, he never felt cold anyway.

Many years later, in 1993, five years after Annigoni's death and also after the death of dear Daria, Bruno put on a small show of Annigoni's sketches done in the Bar: *una piccola rassegna di curiosità del Pittore*. There was a little collecting box for tips on which was written *Se non avete il core, come le pine verdi*. Included in this strange collection of mementos were wine labels depicting Tuscan landscapes, printed from paintings by the Maestro and also Romano, illustrated books, medals, etchings and drawings of familiar faces. There were also dedications such as 'to Bruno, the rescuer', recalling when Bruno had repaired the lock on the door of Annigoni's apartment after forcing an entry to enable him to get into his own apartment one night when he had mislaid the key.

For Bruno, Annigoni may have been a painter of royalty, but he was at the same time a man who enjoyed the simple, unaffected life of ordinary people, café life, la *fiorentinità*. It was exactly this that made him loved by simple people and too often criticised by affected intellectuals. Bruno commemorated the Maestro with this small and intimate exhibition, a long overdue recognition sadly lacking in other more illustrious quarters.

Throughout the past decade on my frequent returns to Florence I have always visited the Bar Daria and am always welcomed with the same friendliness.

A night out with Annigoni, Riccardo Noferi and others

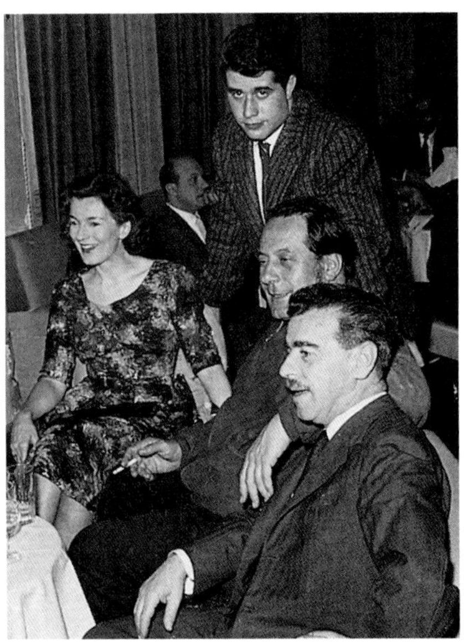

Eating out with Annigoni

Annigoni never owned or drove a car. He walked wherever and whenever he could. As a youth he had walked the length of Italy. He had many willing friends and companions to drive him anywhere and everywhere and usually sat out of sight in the little private backroom of the bar while waiting to be collected for meals further away from the city. He was a familiar burly figure to everyone in his heavy black winter jacket, beret, corduroy trousers and dark red scarf wound around his neck, much later to be replaced by his 'Mao Tse Tung' jacket and cap.

In those days his favourite restaurants were da Angiolino, Buca dell'orafo and Sostanza. He was never alone but would be accompanied by his special

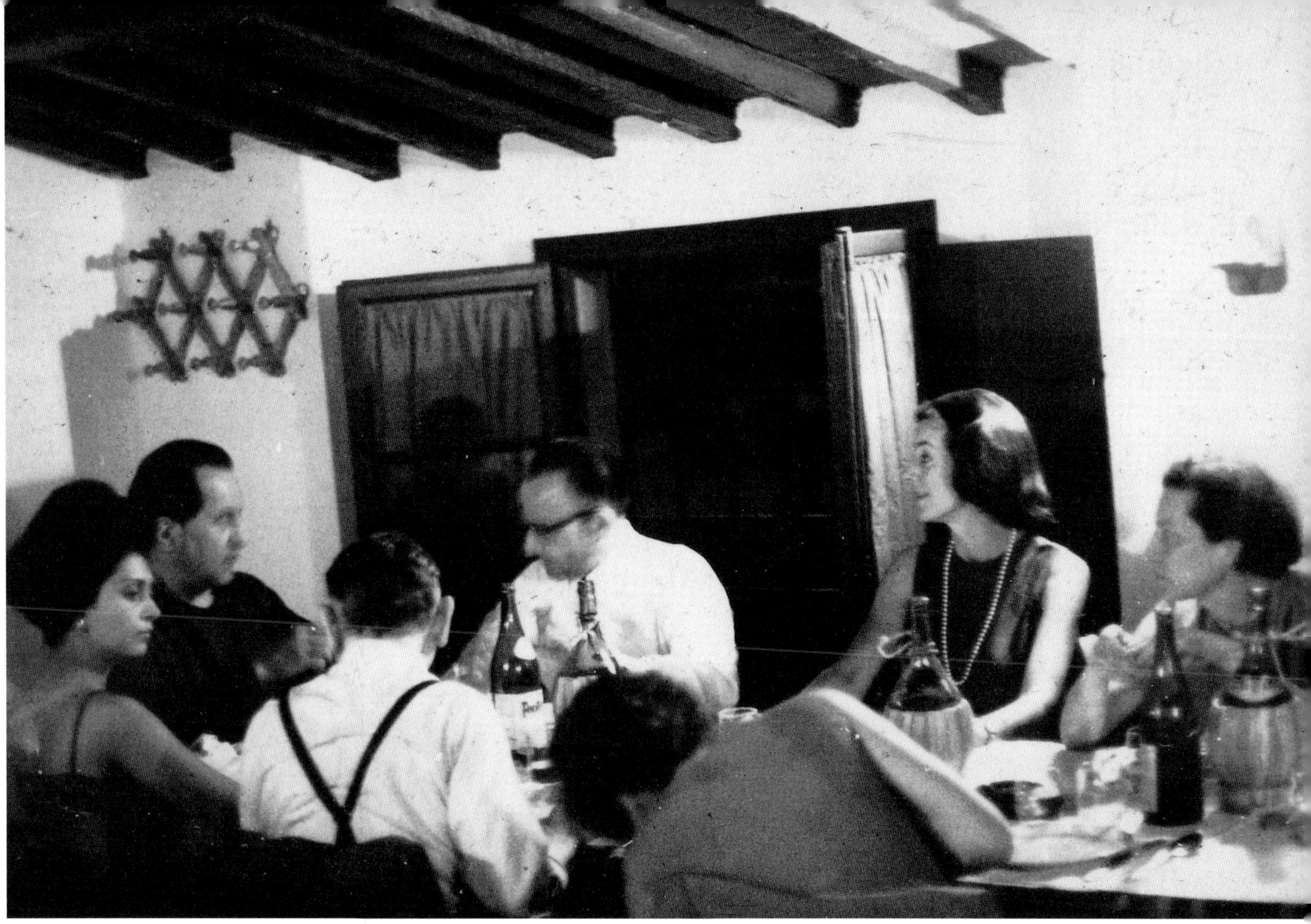

With Annigoni and friends, dining out in the country

friends, occasionally by clients, and often by pupils. I was one of the lucky ones most frequently included. His generosity was without measure. The company was never less than four, and more often three times that number. The larger gatherings were usually for supper. We were expected to be at Bar Daria punctually at eight o'clock. He detested unpunctuality or excuses, as I was to learn to my cost and his annoyance. 'One should always allow time for any unforeseen eventuality,' he often repeated when I was only a few minutes late. On one occasion I was unavoidably delayed by a telephone call at my apartment and was literally running down the Corso to the Borgo Albizi to meet the deadline. I was wearing a coat with a long silk scarf that was trailing behind me in my haste. Suddenly a car pulled up alongside, a window lowered and a hand grabbed my scarf pulling me to a halt. Annigoni was holding me in his grasp. 'You are five minutes late!' but before I could explain or apologize he continued, joking ironically, 'Remember how Isadora Duncan died, throttled with her own scarf by a passing motorist. It might be fatal next time, Dawn!' And he pulled me into the car to the amusement of the other passengers and to my acute embarrassment. I was never late again, though often breathless from hurrying. I was consequently referred to as *la signorina sempre di corsa*.

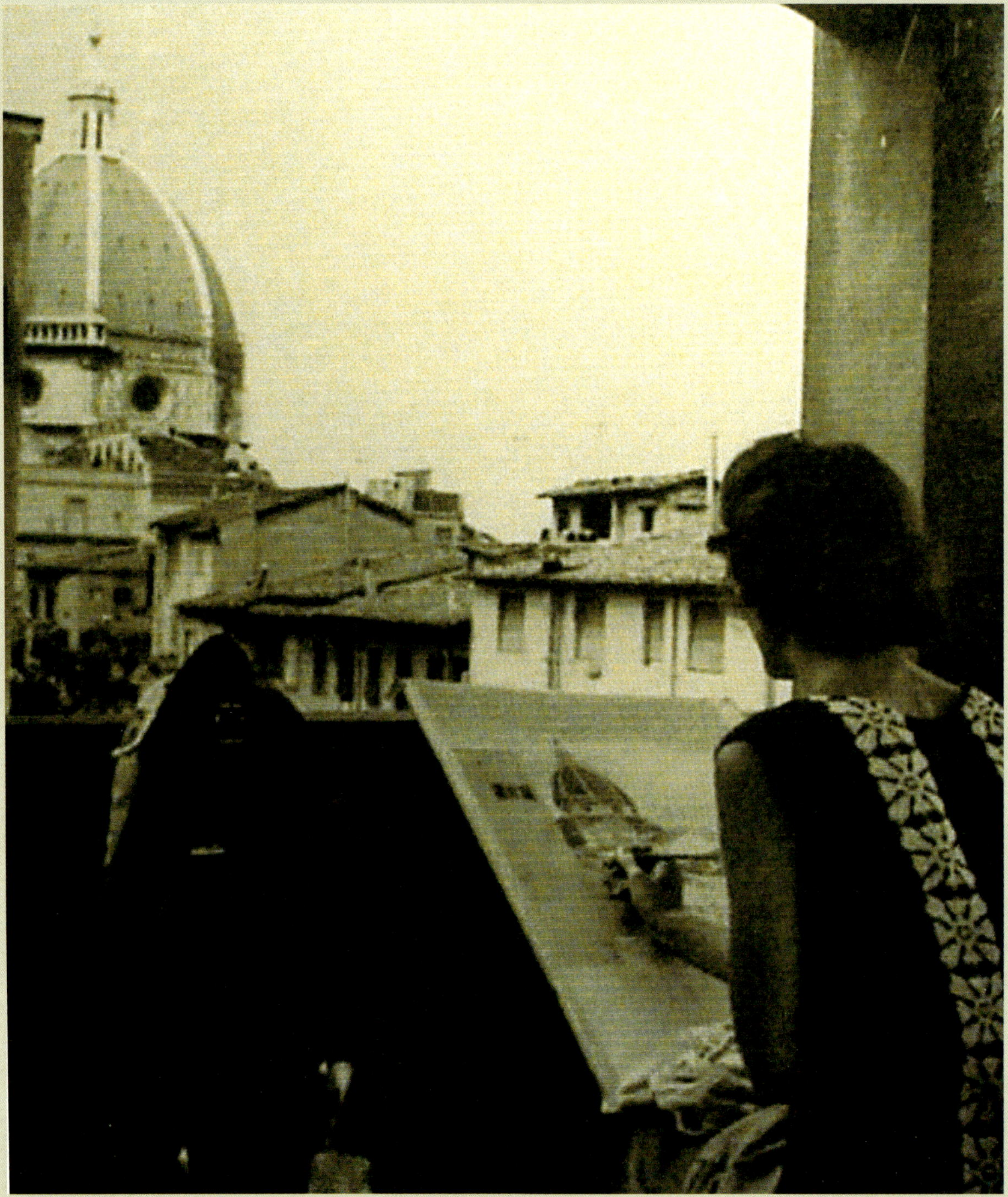

STUDIO LIFE

After several months of drawing daily in the attic, the temperature under the roof became almost unbearable as, in May, spring suddenly exploded into a hot early summer. I found it only slightly cooler out of doors on the terrace, where I was partly protected from the sun by an open-sided veranda with a tiled roof under whose shade I sat to tackle one of the most difficult views of the city: one dominated by the great Dome of Brunelleschi that crowned the cathedral of Santa Maria dei fiori.

It took me many mornings of careful observation to draw the complicated construction and the perspective while allowing for the continual opening and closing of shutters, distracting washing lines of clothing and so on. Pigeons nesting in every nook and cranny and swallows and swifts fluttering under the eaves added to the general clutter of domesticity. To paint the scene in watercolour was quite ambitious.

At noon the great bell of the *Duomo* struck, its deep and sonorous tone heralding the hour, by which time tantalizing odours of cooking were emerging from the kitchens below, whetting the appetite which three hours of concentrated painting alone produced. It was time to pack up to go home for lunch. This I bought on my way, often too hungry to wait to shop at the fruit and vegetable stalls, bakery and grocery in the little piazza below for my basic meal of salad, bread and cheese. I was almost ravenous by the time I reached my lodgings, and there were more stairs to climb before I could prepare and eat my food.

After that there was an even longer walk to Simi's studio where I had to be by 2.30 p.m. It was all go and no siestas after lunch for me, but lunchtime was a little interval of peace and quiet in my room, sitting at my window in the

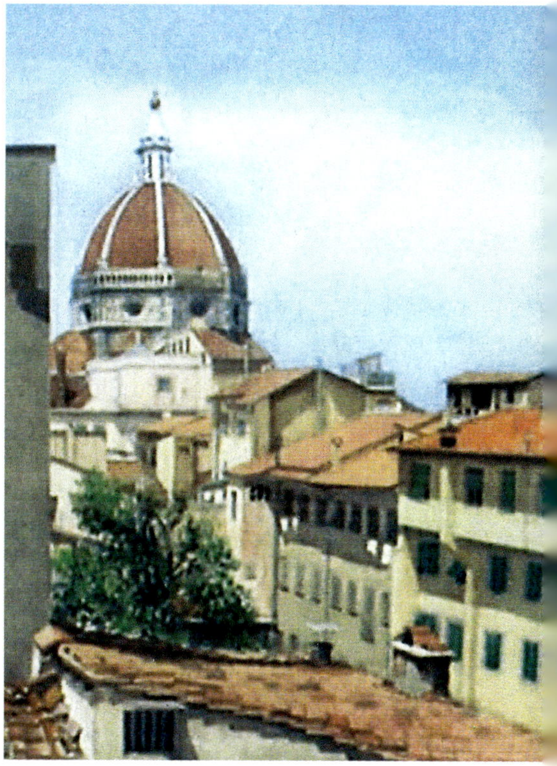

Opposite: Painting the Duomo

sun enjoying my simple food before the afternoon session.

There were many more intimate suppers. Eating out in noisy restaurants was not always restful and congenial, so occasionally the Maestro would suggest having supper *alla buona* at the studio. The kitchen was only basically equipped for culinary purposes, possessing an old gas cooker and a few saucepans and plates – just sufficient for a simple meal of pasta, bread and wine.

Annigoni made his own special sauce of hot chillies and tomatoes which brought tears to the eyes and eruptions in the stomach. But he insisted it was good for the digestion when washed down with a good deal of local red wine. 'Remember Dawn,' he used to say frequently, 'you must always drink a lot of wine but it must be *vino buono*.' This, consumed with crusty, delicious *pane di campagna* and followed by cheese, fruit and strong black coffee, was as good as any feast. We enjoyed many convivial evenings over those studio suppers, often by candlelight and to the strains of Vivaldi on an old record player, in the good company of Riccardo and Adriana Noferi, Annigoni's closest friends, and Danish friends Else and Bodil Steen, along with any of the unmarried pupils, who were glad to share such a homely evening of good food, enjoyable company and stimulating conversation.

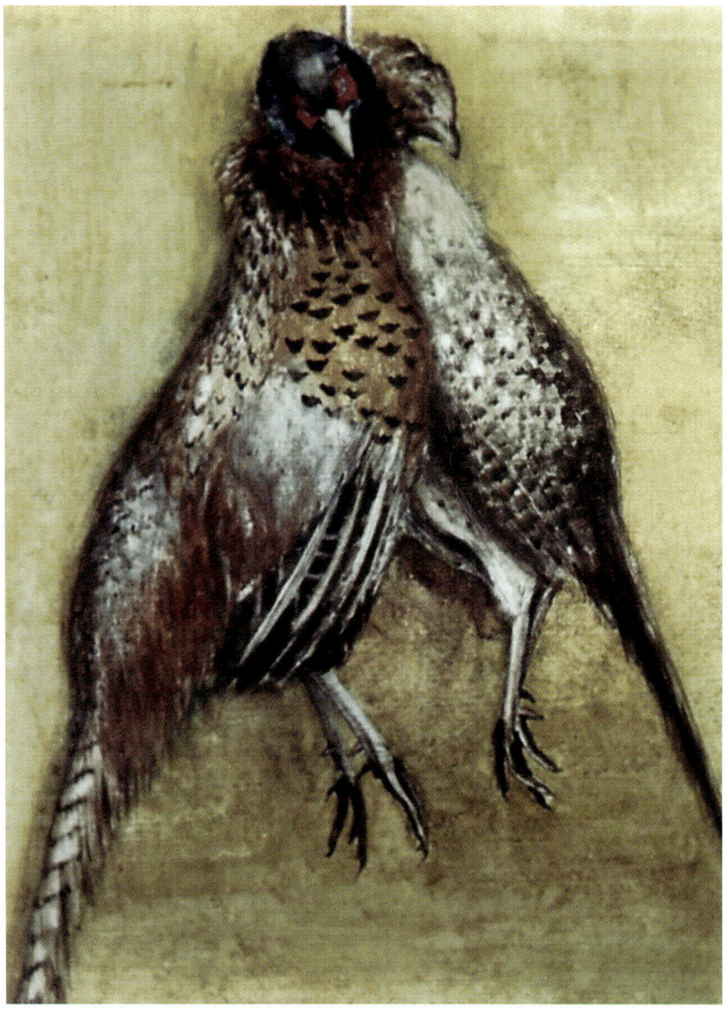

On one occasion, a shooting friend brought a gift of a brace of pheasants, newly shot, which Annigoni hung up for us to paint. After hanging for several days in an increasingly warm temperature, they were becoming rather high, so I suggested that I cook them for a supper party. Annigoni was diffident, although I assured him that I could cook. After the tedious job of plucking the birds, I decided to take them to the Noferis' home to prepare them in a better equipped kitchen and cook them in a more suitable oven. My own method is to simmer the rather dry pheasant slowly in red wine with onions and herbs for about one hour the day before eating, and then tenderize them by leaving them to marinate overnight The next day, you remove the pheasant from the marinade (which makes an excellent gravy) and then roast them in the oven with chestnut stuffing. The company in the Noferis' kitchen that evening was apprehensive about my ability as a cook but all applauded the meal, even accepting the oddity, for them, of the accompanying redcurrant jelly. Annigoni declared that the *fagiano alla Dawn* was the tastiest he had ever eaten. High praise indeed!

A Change of address and eating venues

I had meantime changed my lodgings because old Signora Giunti had become frail and was in poor health. With much regret I had to move further away from both studios to find a room in a much less favourable area, near to the railway station in the busy Via Nazionale, with another elderly couple, the Signori Poggini. They already housed two other foreign girls, a minute and voluble Italian teacher from Lybia, and a German-speaking Swiss, with neither of whom I had anything in common. Luckily we only met early morning and evening when dodging one another to occupy the one combined bathroom and lavatory.

Fortunately, my room was spacious and overlooked a quiet inner courtyard. It was so hot at night that I either opened the windows for some air and was the target for a murderous attack of mosquitos with a persistent hunger for my blood, or shut both windows and shutters and nearly suffocated. So my sleep was very turbulent. I soon found out that Via Nazionale was full of cheap *pensioni* and the haunt of prostitutes – consequently not a desirable area to be out alone at night.

I enjoyed walking to and from Angiolino's for most of my evening meals for which, as one of the regulars now, I ate at a fixed price of 500 lire. This meal consisted of a half pasta, which was ample for me, a main course, bread and a quarter litre of wine – amazing value, even in those days. Moreover, the food was good and satisfying, the ambience *agréable* and I felt no embarrassment eating on my own there. In fact, I soon became known to other regular evening diners, including several foreigners like myself. Among these was a Dutch girl who was a blood analyst at the big Hospital at Carreggi, and two delightful and attractive Danish girls who were buyers and exporters in the fashion world centred around Florence. They later became drawn into the intimate circle of Annigoni's female entourage and referred to him always as 'P.A.', which thereafter became a habit. In reference to the allure derived from Camay soap, they nicknamed him 'the Baron von Camay', because of his attraction to beautiful women and vice versa. This name they often called him good-humouredly to his face.

The foreign contingent meeting at Angiolino's was further increased by two Swiss girls who worked as multi-lingual secretaries. Our conversation was often in several languages. We met at Angiolino's at different times and adopted our own table in a secluded corner of a quiet inner room, causing some curiosity from the other, mostly male, diners.

One of these was a slightly built, impeccably dressed, good-looking middle-aged Italian, an eminent professor, surgeon and consultant, a bachelor with an attractive voice, and a roving eye, who was also an inoffensive womaniser. Being highly intelligent and a good conversationalist, he often joined our table and was most entertaining company. Whenever one or other of us was eating alone, he used all his charm and persuasion to offer a lift home in his eye-catching sports car. One then had to be prepared for fireworks, as I found out when tempted to accept a lift rather than face the long walk back to my lodgings late at night. After his various attempts at mild seduction (always with charm and a sense of humour), I decided that in the end the walk, however tedious, was the only way to avoid entanglements! However, there was one encounter that was somewhat disconcerting and which I recounted in my diary. I now recall it with amusement.

An evening encounter with an eccentric

15 May 1958. Eating my usual supper at Angiolino, I had a strange encounter with an extraordinary little gnome-like man with piercing brown eyes, a mane of white hair and without a natural voice – he spoke in a rasping whisper directly through a tube in his throat. He was staring fixedly at me from across the trattoria all through the meal and made me feel most uncomfortable. Then he sent a glass of *vin santo* (a strong fortified liqueur wine) over to my table by the waiter, who told me that the *professore* sent his compliments and hoped that I would accept this wine, together with a card on which was printed *'Prof. Vittorio d'Aste, Dottore in Lettere e Critico d'Arte della Nazione'* (*La Nazione* was the newspaper of the city). As I lifted my head in puzzled embarrassment, he silently raised his glass to me with a broad smile to which I could only respond with a polite one. With little enthusiasm, I indicated my thanks with a suitable gesture while secretly wishing I could avoid the inevitable encounter.

I prolonged my dessert as long as I could, hoping he would leave before me, but instead he got up and advanced towards my table, a diminutive little figure in an ill-fitting suit and enormous bow-tie, carrying a large fedora hat in his hand, which he pressed to his chest in a courtier-like manner. He picked up my hand, and before I realized what was happening he had pressed it to his lips. Then he promptly pulled out a chair opposite me and sat down, never taking his eyes off me. I noticed that all the waiters seemed to know and respect him, so I could hardly rebuff him, but I felt most uneasy. I politely thanked him and rose from my seat saying that I was late and must return home. He immediately rose too and said he would accompany me, as a girl alone should not walk the streets at night, whereupon grabbed my arm and propelled me out of the restaurant (all five foot, four inches of him), donning his enormous hat and gripping my arm like a vice. All the while he rasped out in a torrent of Italian his love of all things artistic, poetic and musical, and especially his love of beautiful women.

I kept up a brisk pace wondering all the while how I was ever going to free myself before I reached home, the whereabouts of which I had no intention of divulging to him. We headed towards the Piazza Republica and he told me he lived in Via dei Ginori, which led off from it, insisting that I should see his painting collection then and there. I tried to disentangle myself from his grasp to no avail as he gripped my arm even tighter and rushed me at great speed towards a large *portone*, pressing a bell which opened it onto a dark inner courtyard from which a dimly-lit staircase led up several floors. The door closed heavily behind us and I feared that my fate was determined with no hope of escape.

Never letting go of my arm, he talked all the way to the apartment in unintelligible noises and then whisked out a huge key to another vast studded door, which opened into utter darkness. I was on the point of screaming and running as fast as I could back down the stairs, when suddenly the whole entrance was flooded with light, revealing walls covered with wonderful paintings, together with signed photographs of well-known artists, singers, musicians and politicians all dedicated to Vittorio d'Aste. Eventually he released his grip on my arm, stood back, raised his arms (whether in welcome or triumph I will never know) and said 'Now you can see my little world and I can share it with you, adorable creature.' I managed to pull myself together, glancing round and making some suitable comments, and with my excuse of it being far too late finally persuaded him to let me go, much to my relief.

Next morning at the studio a messenger delivered a small package addressed to *'ILLUSTRISSIMA PITTRICE DAWN'* which Annibale handed to me with a broad smile, arousing some curiosity from my colleagues and causing Annigoni to suggest teasingly that a romance was blooming. While hardly able to contain my own curiosity, I refused to open it there and then to keep them guessing. When I reached home I found that it contained a small book of poetry entitled *L'Asino Poppetano* by Vittorio d'Aste and was dedicated inside to *'La bella Aurora, pittrice sensibilissima in cammino verso la bellezza, cangiante e sirenica da mille occhii'* and signed *'con festato cuore, Vittorio d'Aste, 15.5.1958'*. Well, I must say it was the first time I had received a book with such a romantic dedication and of the author's own verse – even if he was already in his eighties!

A few days later my admirer unexpectedly called at the studio. On hearing him announced by Annibale and not wishing a further encounter, particularly in front of everyone, I hastily retreated to the kitchen, urging Annibale to keep silent if he enquired about me. Annigoni greeted him warmly as an old friend and colleague, and the professor complimented him on his painting with poetic eulogies. I realized how stupid I had been to react as I did, feeling embarrassed at my ill-founded but understandable reaction to a total stranger. I wrote him a very nice letter thanking him for his gift, but to avoid further encounters I kept away from Angiolino's for a while.

Suppers at Sostanza

Meals and eating out were an integral part of the lighter side of life. One of Annigoni's favourite restaurants at that time was Sostanza in Via Porcellana (known by a coarser name to the locals). Here a regular group of us gathered frequently for supper at his invitation, almost always comprising Riccardo and Anna Noferi, myself and Else and Bodil Steen, and sometimes also studio colleagues or the current portrait sitter. The party frequently also included visitors from abroad.

Sostanza consisted of a long and very narrow room extending from the street entrance to the kitchen at the other end, with small and long tables on either side of the single passageway. The *padrone*, Mario, was a tall, handsome, swarthy southern Italian. He would only take bookings provided that customers arrived by eight o'clock, otherwise they had to queue, which was then a rare sight in Italy. They often had to wait a long time. The menu was limited but the quality and the cooking were excellent. You had to expect to share a table for six or eight as space was very limited. Only the Maestro's table at the very end of the room, next to the kitchen, was reserved for him whenever he wanted it. The place was invariably full by 8.30, with others waiting hopefully outside; however, Italians take a long time over a good meal in congenial surroundings. The arrival of local strolling musicians, who played their way around the most popular restaurants at peak time, added to the entertainment and the din. They often improvised local Tuscan *stornelli* (ditties of three lines) about any particular well-known individual in raucous voices while the hat was passed around.

The speciality was beefsteak *alla griglia*, accompanied by very fresh vegetables and salads, excluding potatoes. According to Mario, only the Germans demanded potatoes, and he was not fond of Germans and did not encourage them, so that was reason enough for the omission of that vegetable. But there was plenty of dark solid country bread to mop up the delicious juices of the meat and as an essential blotting paper for the wine. Annigoni was an acknowledged *intenditore* of wine and would only drink the best quality – and a lot of it!

The walls on either side of the room were adorned with autographed photographs of many famous clients from all over the world, postcards in every language and, of course, paintings. One in particular always fascinated me. It was a very unflattering portrayal of human beings with animal heads guzzling plates piled high with food while the dignified figure of the waiter, impeccably dressed in a tailcoat, stood aloof with a look of disdain for the gluttonous group. This satirical interpretation of gourmands, wittily painted by Annigoni with tongue in cheek, caused some amusement.

The King and Queen of Denmark dine at Sostanza

There was one special evening that I remember. King Frederick and Queen Ingrid of Denmark were visiting Florence and called to see Annigoni at the studio. It was a very friendly and relaxed meeting, and they admired his paintings. Before leaving they asked him to recommend a good and, more especially, informal restaurant. The trattoria was duly telephoned on their behalf and a table reserved for their Majesties. 'We are fully booked tonight,' Mario replied bluntly, presuming that someone was playing a practical joke on him.

'Even if their Majesties arrive before eight p.m.?' persisted the enquirer.

'Then they will have to take pot luck,' replied Mario, unconvinced.

That evening Annigoni had invited his usual friends, including me, to join him for dinner, meeting at Daria's bar at 7.30 prompt. Five of us set off by car for Sostanza. On arrival, Annigoni told Mario, 'I want to keep two places at my table for my guests tonight.' Meanwhile two *fiaschi* (2.5 litres) of the best Tuscan wine were ordered. On the dot of eight o'clock the royal couple arrived, quite unrecognized by anyone other than ourselves and Mario.

Annigoni rose to greet them, kissing the Queen's hand, while Mario looked on, open-mouthed in amazement. They sat down on either side of him and we were all introduced, including Mario, who, hastily rubbing his greasy hands on his apron, gave the King and Queen a hearty handshake, beaming from ear to ear.

Despite this breach of protocol, their Majesties, who were known for their liberal and friendly behaviour, were immediately relaxed and informal with everyone. Their English was impeccable but their Italian minimal, so much translating of the various dishes ensued, while Mario hovered over them, strongly recommending his speciality charcoal-grilled beefsteak, gesticulating with his hands and pursing his lips to extol the delicious quality of the meat as if they had never tasted such steak before. The orders were placed and the conversation flowed with great conviviality and good humour. Annigoni was naturally experienced and adept at conversing with royalty. Adjacent diners were already aware that some VIPs were being entertained in a tri-lingual conversation (two Danish compatriots were present, Elsa and Bodil Steen). Mario never usually left the open kitchen other than for a quick glance to make sure that all the clientele were happy. He was continually occupied in a haze of blue smoke over the charcoal grill, but on that evening he kept a special eye on the 'royal' table.

At the conclusion of a memorable meal, with a car waiting to collect the royal couple, Mario came forward, now on top of his form, to say goodbye and to thank his eminent guests. Then, placing a clean corner of his grease-stained apron on the table and producing a ball-point pen, he asked the King and Queen to sign their autographs. Their Majesties complied with good humour, despite this further infringement of etiquette. Mario held up the apron with a look of utter delight, vowing he would never wash it. I should not be surprised if it were later framed to join the rogues' gallery of celebrities on the wall.

One of the most amusing evenings I can remember was when the famous English actor James Robertson Justice joined our table and entertained us with hilarious anecdotes. We were well entertained again when the brilliant cartoonist Giles of the *Daily Express* shared his experiences over dinner with Annigoni, who in turn congratulated him on his humorous caricatures of very believable human beings.

Eating out at the Buca dell'Orafo

Another then favourite venue was probably the smallest trattoria in Florence, the Buca dell'Orafo (the goldsmith's cavern) – aptly named, as it was near to the goldsmiths' quarter, only a few steps from the Ponte Vecchio, down a narrow alley named the Volta dei Girolami.

Florence has always been a renowned centre of craftsmanship, and especially for its jewellery, which is displayed in the many fascinating shops that cover the Ponte Vecchio. A lot of it is made in the honeycomb of workshops contained on three floors of the ancient *casa dell'orafo*. Presumably the little trattoria was once frequented by the jewellery-makers and local shopkeepers but eventually it was almost taken over by tourists. The room was miniature with a low ceiling and very compact seating. The owner greeted his guests from a high counter at the door. He took the orders and collected the bills. One elderly, affable and very flat-footed waiter served everyone. The food was excellent but patience was necessary.

One evening we were dining at the Buca dell'Orafo with the usual company of friends when a man approached from another table and introduced himself to Annigoni. 'Maestro, as a humble artisan to a great artist, may I show you my latest creation for your appraisal?' And taking from his pocket a small leather case, he removed an exquisite diamond brooch. It was in the form of a budding rose suspended on a spring from behind a platinum mounting so that it gently quivered at the slightest movement, making the many-faceted diamonds scintillate even more brilliantly. It was a creation of great skill and artistry. Annigoni, although not a lover of jewellery, congratulated the jeweller on his work as it was passed around the table for all of us to admire in turn.

On another evening at the Buca, among our company was a famous soprano, currently performing the title role in Verdi's *Aida* at the amphitheatre in Verona. At the end of the long evening, one of the guests asked if she would sing for us, whereupon she started an aria from Puccini's *La Bohème*, at first quietly just for our table. Within seconds the whole room was hushed and the full strength of her beautiful voice reached a crescendo which, in the limited space, actually shattered a glass that was being held up to toast her. Someone came to the table, obviously a lover of opera, and told the singer, 'Your voice is too great for this room.' So with everyone's agreement we walked outside to the nearby Piazza Signoria, by now deserted. It was a moonlit summer night after midnight, and there under the Loggia dei Lanzi she sang the whole aria. The sound reverberated around the piazza as we stood enraptured by the magic of her voice in such a perfect setting: the climax to an unrepeatable evening.

My brief sojourn in Via Guicciardini

15 May 1958: *Festa*, a public holiday for Ascension Day on which there is a local and rather strange custom that children carry wicker cages containing crickets about the town, usually towards the Cascine, a wooded parkland on the outskirts of Florence, where they gather with friends for picnics. The days were getting hotter, but luckily it was cooler in the evenings.

I had found another lodging on the far side of the River Arno, which divides the city, in the more respectable area of Via Guicciardini. It was a room in the apartment of two elderly spinsters which looked onto an inner courtyard and so was quite light and peaceful. The two old ladies soon informed me that their late father was an admiral in the Italian navy. They were of a good family and had fallen on hard times and so were *obliged* – they emphasized the word – to take in a lodger, which was not their custom.

I had misgivings about their pretensions, but I could not find anywhere more central and urgently needed somewhere to move into. I enquired about the bathroom facilities and access to the kitchen, at which they seemed perturbed.

'How often would you require a bath? We would have to heat the boiler, and that uses a lot of electricity, so we would have to charge you 300 lire for a bath.'

'Well, maybe twice a week?'

'Impossible!'

'Surely, if I am paying for it!'

I explained that I was accustomed to regular bathing, especially in hot weather. They were adamant. One hot bath on Saturday night and a cold shower mid-week, no cooking in their kitchen and only cold food in my room. Had I not already wasted so much time hunting for accommodation, I would have walked out there and then. I soon wished that I had, as I then noticed that the telephone in the hall had a padlock attached to the dial. They must have read my thoughts because they hastily explained that the reason for locking the phone was to save themselves from the temptation of using it unnecessarily.

Fearing that they were going to lose me as a lodger, they assured me that I had only to ask and they would remove it whenever I needed to make a call. They would work out the cost and note it down to be paid separately with the bill for the laundry. However, whenever there were incoming calls for me, they always kept the door of their living-room ajar, giving me no privacy, so I made all my calls from a public telephone box at great inconvenience. Even the bed sheets were turned from top to bottom before they were replaced by fresh ones. I had never encountered such meanness and pettiness and decided to be out of the house for as many daylight hours as possible. At least they conceded me a key, with strict instructions.

I awaited my one weekly bath longing for a good soak. After producing only a few inches of tepid water, the tap ran cold and then spluttered to nothing, with ominous noises emanating from the tank, so even this small luxury was denied me. I cleaned my teeth and gargled with TCP to counteract the very nasty smell from the pipe and banged the bathroom door behind me in angry frustration. Out came one of the sisters, to whom I complained in my strongest Italian, whereupon she went in to inspect and I showed her the little cold puddle of water in the bath. She gasped and, pinching her nose, accused me of the bad odour (the antiseptic) that had made the whole place smell like a clinic.

Next day I started to look elsewhere. I was determined to find an apartment of my own. Despite previous pleasant memories, I had had enough of rented rooms. The domestic privations and lack of freedom and privacy in the home of these 'old witches' was more than I could stand.

My new apartment

This time, shortly after giving my landladies notice, I was lucky in finding a minuscule flat – more of a cupboard with compartments – right in the centre of the city, in Via Condotta, number 14. It was on the topmost floor, literally under the roof, a tiny garret bathed in light, with a splendid view over the roof tops of the opposite side of the street, and beyond towards the Piazza Signoria with the great bell tower, *il Campanile*, of the Palazzo Vecchio surging into the sky.

There was one small bed-sitting-room with just enough space for a single divan bed and a table under the window, a chest of drawers and barely two chairs. The 'entrance hall', as described by my landlord, was no more than a small ship's galley with cupboards on one side, a sink and just room for an electric hot plate. Above and below were more shelves and drawers for kitchen utensils, cutlery and tableware, all compactly fitted to utilize the last inch. To one side of this corridor was a built-in wardrobe. Opposite this a sliding door revealed a tiled area containing the shower, washbasin and lavatory, so close together that you could almost use all three at the same time.

The apartment was all newly decorated and simply furnished, and I knew that I could add to the happy atmosphere with rugs, cushions and pictures. It was easily heated with a tiny electric fire, and, luxury of luxuries, I had a telephone! I signed a contract with the foxy-looking, red-headed landlord for six months to begin with, at 20,000 lire per month. That was quite a high price for such small accommodation in 1958, but it was cosy and cheerful, in the centre and all my own. I called it 'my cupboard', and it felt like heaven.

To add to my pleasure, my nextdoor neighbour, Nelly Bühler, was one of the Swiss girls whom I met at Angiolino's. Indeed, it was due to her that I had found the apartment. There was a third door on our little landing which hardly ever opened until one day on the stairs I met an Italian girl called Maria Teresa Iannucci. She told me she was from Rome and kept the apartment above Nelly's as a pied à terre (which she rarely used). She invited me in to have a look.

The door opened directly onto another steep staircase, which led up to a long and very narrow attic room of different levels. A shallow strip of glass directly onto the eaves of the roof let in light but with little view other than sky and the top of the *Campanile*. There was only room for a large double bed against the wall, with barely space to move, and being literally under the roof the apartment was freezing cold in winter and baking hot in summer. I preferred mine, but I liked her and we became good friends. In subsequent years, when I returned to Florence for less frequent visits of shorter duration, she loaned me this attic. Maria and I have maintained our friendship ever since, like so many friendships formed in Florence in that decade.

Learning to paint in tempera

After weeks of study in Annigoni's attic, I came down into the small kitchen where the colours were prepared by one or other of the pupils as the need arose. Here I watched one of the most experienced, Fernando Bernardini, preparing up to 18 colours, a procedure that he patiently taught me.

Annigoni had evolved his own special medium of *tempera grassa* (oily tempera), which involved fresh eggs, very dry white wine, stand oil and mastic varnish, the addition of oil giving the medium more flexibility and the pigments greater expansion. This medium takes much patience and time to prepare. Very simply explained, the process requires 18 to 20 powder colours, scales to measure them, an electric mixer, a chemist's glass cylinder into which to measure the proportions of the emulsion, a slab of marble (we used porfora, which is very cold) on which to mix the powder colours, sufficient dry white wine to form a paste, the appropriate number of plastic bottles for each colour to be kept in, and at least a day to complete the mixing of pigments with the emulsion (each colour requires a different proportion). A nearby sink into which to thoroughly wash all the implements used between each colour is also necessary.

This method involves a lot of washing up as you go along. The procedure has to be watched in order to understand each stage of the process, and that is the way I learnt, observing Nando. Thereafter I was able to prepare my own colours and recorded each mixing in a book, as the quantities varied according to the size and number of the paintings. I found this an invaluable reference and time saver.

Maintained in a large ceramic or plastic bowl containing damp sand these colours keep fairly well in cool weather, usually for about four to six months, provided the bottles are vigorously shaken each time before they are used and well sealed afterwards. All this is not as easily portable as a box of oil paints, and nor is the support wood panel on which to paint. This is, ideally, a board of well-seasoned poplar wood, although I have since worked on blockboards, suitably prepared. In either case the board needs to be covered with a fine canvas well glued down with animal size (i.e. rabbit's foot). Finally the canvas must be given two coats of gesso to obtain as smooth a surface as possible.

Up to and including the eighties, I continued to prepare and use this medium but in subsequent years it has become more and more difficult to obtain reliably seasoned wood and good, fine quality canvas. Added to this is the complicated and time-consuming mixing procedure. I have therefore turned to oils, pastels and mixed media.

Tempera is not for the hasty or impatient, nor for the *alla prima* painters used to using loaded brushes, and least of all for beginners. The technique for handling the application of the colours has to be learnt step by step and requires skill, restraint and the right temperament. I had the best possible master to watch and learn from. I also became a cleaner of palettes, every morning replacing the colours and thoroughly washing the brushes afterwards, especially the fine and expensive sables.

I was eager to try out this fascinating medium for myself. My panel and colours prepared, I considered what subject and where I should be allowed to paint. Annigoni told me to get hold of a mirror and try to paint myself. 'The model won't cost you anything; it will test your ability, concentration and humility, and it is possibly the most difficult subject to tackle.' I could hardly have felt more humble, but I was determined to show him that I could do it.

At least I was now down in the main studio, albeit up a few steps on a small mezzanine area which housed the big *torchio* (printing press) for lithography along with a second press for etchings. This space I was to share

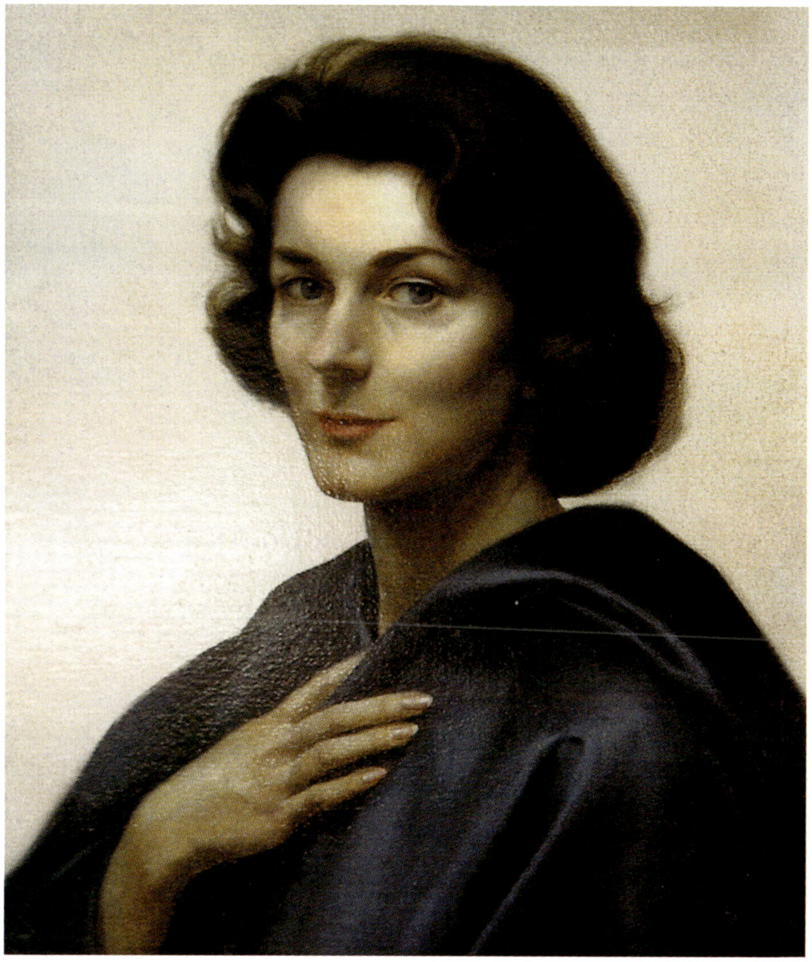

My self-portrait

with Antonio Ciccone, the youngest pupil whose drawing had so captivated me at my first meeting with Annigoni. I'd made it so far; I had been accepted, and now here I was with Antonio, both of us painting our self-portraits from mirrors attached to our easels. I must have worked on my reflected image for a month, with diminishing enthusiasm and increasing frustration, directly under a skylight which during the cold winter months cast a very unflattering light on my already pale face.

Occasionally the Maestro came up to see how we were progressing, gazing with critical approbation on Antonio's work, and on mine with a look of hopelessness. Although I am not a very temperamental person, I am highly sensitive, and I *was* doing my utmost. I asked Annigoni for constructive criticism, knowing that I was going wrong but not able to correct my mistakes.

'Well, if you can't see it for yourself, what can I tell you?' he said, and with that he took one of my larger brushes, dipped it into a mixture of dark tones on the palette and then boldly washed over my entire image, obliterating every detail. I looked on dismayed as it disappeared under a translucent haze. 'Now start to construct the form again and ignore the details,' he said, continuing with those familiar words, '*Forza, coraggio.*' As he turned to go he muttered something like, 'Women shouldn't paint, no staying power,' adding for a final sting in the tail, 'You would make a much better actress, Dawn, and it's never too late to change.'

That was the last straw, even if it was a teasingly back-handed compliment. I looked down to avoid showing my tears of frustration and disappointment at his rebuke.

Antonio smiled at me reassuringly and consoled me somewhat. 'Don't you see that he is testing you, otherwise he would ignore you and that would be much worse. Go on and rise to the challenge!'

Partly in despair, and not a little angry at this humiliation, I took the painting into the kitchen, covered it with detergent and washed it immediately under a running tap, watching my image slowly dissolve in streaks, literally down the drain, while tears ran down my cheeks. I blotted off the excess wash of very muddy colours to reveal a nebulous image which looked back sorrowfully at me. By now more composed, I carried it back to the studio, showed it to Annigoni and asked him, 'Is that better?'

Smiling, he replied, '*Brava!* Now start again seriously and try harder,' adding a few consoling words: 'Well, *some* women can paint.'

This woman was determined to do so, and from that first of many crises, I gradually began to climb the ladder again, step by step. (If at first you don't succeed then try, try, try again!)

After several more weeks of hard and persistent study, a very much stronger face with greater depth and character was emerging, and I was including in the composition my left hand holding up a shawl of blue silk to my throat. This was much more interesting after all the weeks of eye-to-eye contact trying to avoid a blank stare. At last I was getting some encouraging approval from the Maestro, and I felt better about myself.

Much later I was to sit for Annigoni, at the request of my mother, when he kindly agreed to do a drawing in pen and wash in his spare time. I felt very honoured and was also intrigued, especially as he evidently found my face difficult to portray. In fact, he destroyed the first drawing without even allowing me to see it. I had two or three more sittings for the second one, and I hardly moved. The result was a very sensitive likeness which delighted my family and which I greatly treasure as the decades pass and I look back at that young woman with what he described as *una bocca etrusca*, although why I should have an Etruscan mouth I never could quite understand.

Those brief sittings with the golden afternoon light flooding the studio were so relaxing and peaceful, and in a way formed a bond between teacher and pupil – and now sitter – which made me appreciate the importance of co-operation and the essential rapport between painter and subject. Occasionally, Annigoni allowed a recording of Vivaldi's Four Seasons to be played, one of his particular favourites which I shall always associate with him and those sittings. It must have produced the meditative expression that he captured so subtly.

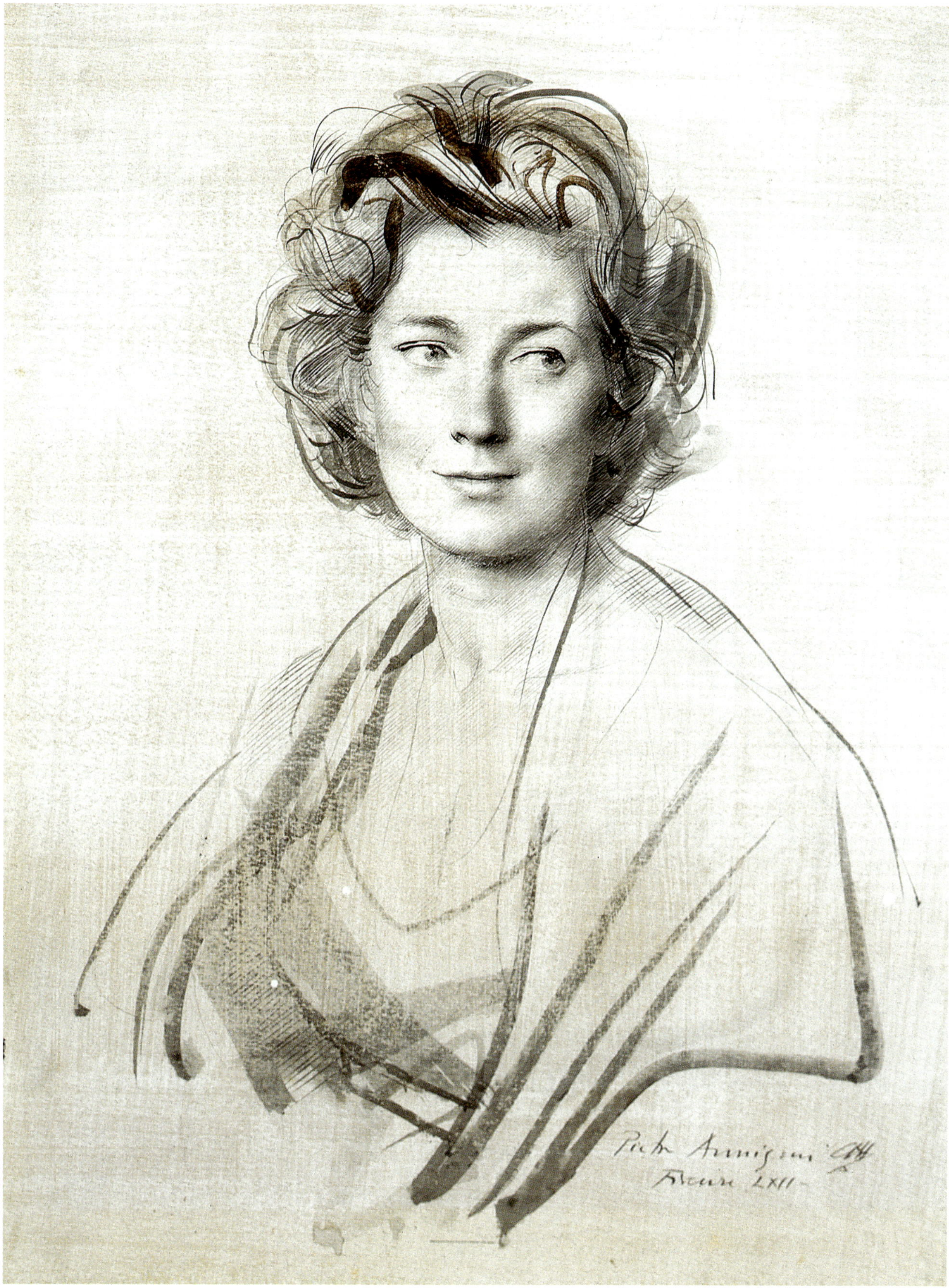

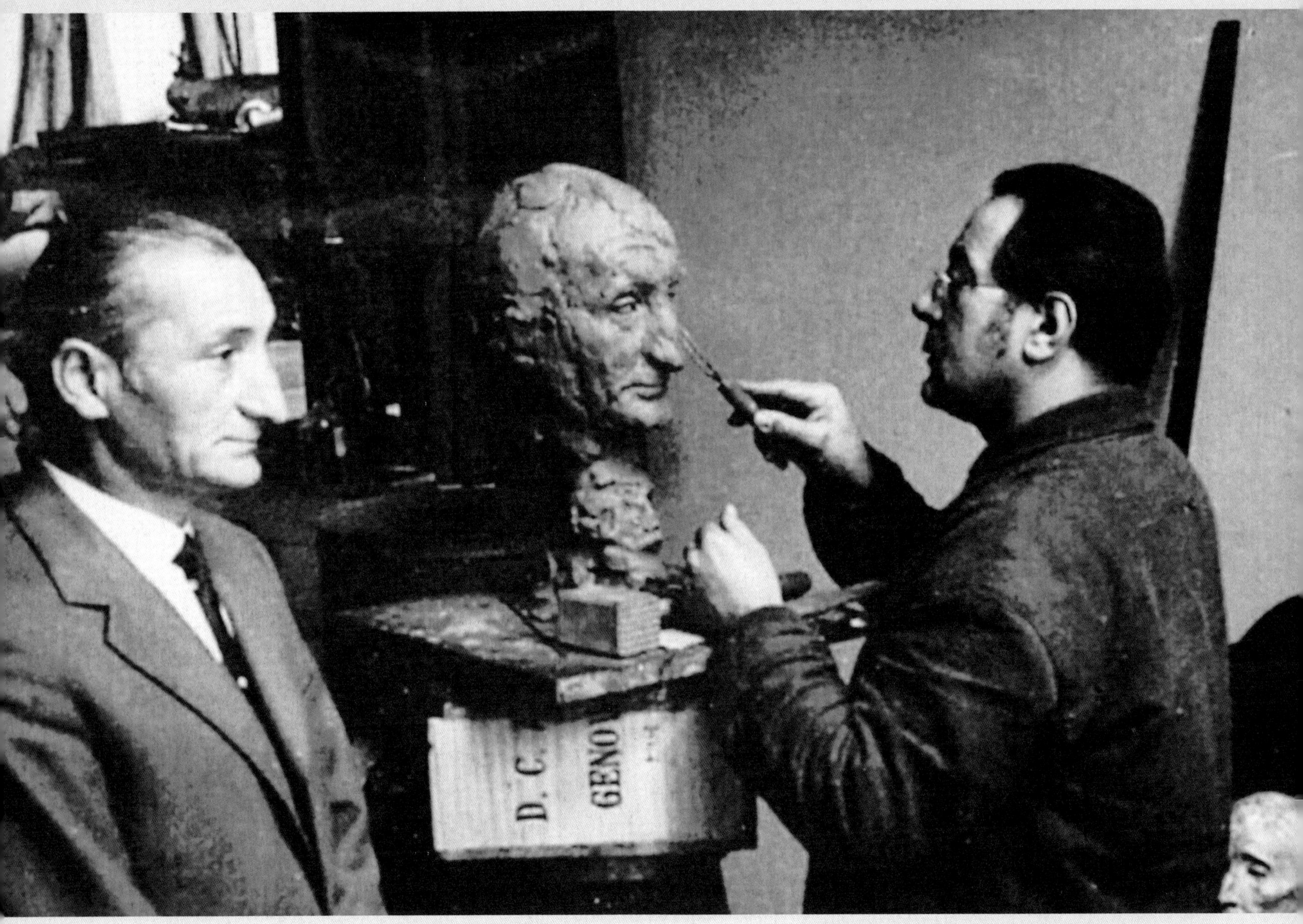
D. C.
GENOV

VISITORS TO THE STUDIO

Two American ladies

One morning during the visiting hour, two middle-aged American ladies had an important appointment. They were announced and were obviously rather overwhelmed as they entered the studio and announced themselves to Annigoni.

'I am Iris Hoffenbaker and this is my friend Caroline Wagner,' said one of the women, adding in hushed tones with emphasis and as if to impress, '*a very distant relative of the great man*. We are from California,' she continued, 'on a tour of your lovely country, and an artist friend of ours said that we must include Florence and call on the artist who painted Queen Elizabeth and our president. So here we are! We have read *The Agony and the Ecstasy of Michaelangelo* of course, and we are dying to meet this present-day Renaissance artist.'

On and on she gushed, hardly drawing breath, much to Annigoni's embarrassment and my amusement. Mrs Wagner produced an autograph book and requested him to sign, with a dedication to her. How, why or by whom they were sent and why Annigoni had agreed to see them was intriguing, for their limited knowledge of painting was based on films and books, and I imagined he was another tick on their Italian itinerary: 'been there, done that and now met *him*'.

From my vantage point, hidden behind my easel putting the last touches to my self-portrait, I could hear all the banal comments about feeling the 'vibes' of the Renaissance and the effusive compliments and ingratiating remarks that were beginning to irritate Annigoni. Although he did not show it, he was anxious to get rid of these time-wasters. Then the talkative Iris caught sight of me and asked if she could see what I was doing. She climbed the short staircase to the upper floor where I was working. 'Oh my! Are you a pupil? Aren't you just lucky to be here with this great artist! What a lovely, lovely portrait, and *who* is your model?'

Opposite: Annigoni modelling the head of a friend

The expression on my face must have communicated to her and, realizing the blatantly obvious, she put her hand to her mouth in embarrassment. 'Oh, my goodness, do pardon me! Every time I open my mouth I seem to put both feet in it. You must excuse me, dear. I really know so little about art. I can't even draw a straight line' (the worst of all clichés) 'but I do know what I like and I *do* like that.'

Out of the corner of my eye, I caught Annigoni looking up at us with barely concealed amusement. As they departed with even more gushing remarks, I exploded with indignation. 'It surely can't be that unrecognizable!'

My still life of the studio

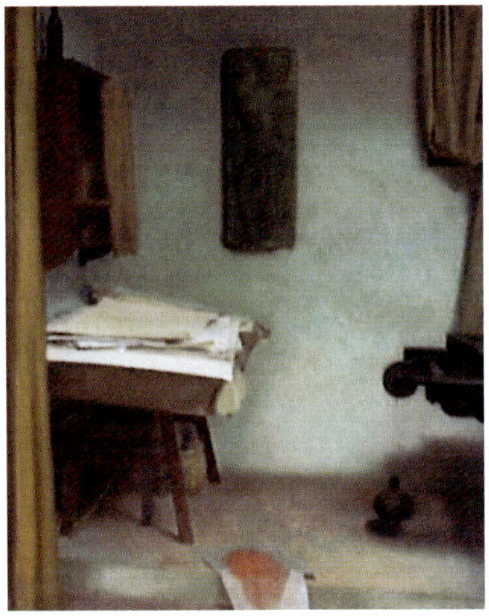

He was still laughing but replied, 'Well, it's not exactly disgusting!' I learnt later that from him this was quite complimentary and that he rather enjoyed my over-sensitive reactions.

When, some time later, my portrait was accepted on my first submission to the Royal Society of Portrait Painters' exhibition in London, I was so delighted that I could hardly wait to tell him. He merely commented, '*Bene*, good, now get on and do something better.'

My next subject was much larger. Annigoni suggested the corner of the studio where I was working with the two old printing presses, a table littered with papers and shelves above, a timeless and fascinating subject but difficult. This met with his approval, and he later selected the painting along with other works by his pupils for his first big 'solo' exhibition in London in 1961, held at the Federation of British Artists' galleries, then in Suffolk Street.

Royal Visitors

From my fortunate vantage point overlooking the main studio, I was able to see Annigoni at work on many different subjects, and this taught me a great deal. I also saw many of the wide variety of visitors who came from all over the world. Almost every day someone would call at the official receiving time. After lunch, the Maestro worked alone or with his models in peace and quiet.

Annigoni was never 'in Bergamo' when the charming Helena, former Queen of Romania, called on him. She had lived in exile in Fiesole for many years and was a great admirer of his work. She also showed great interest in his pupils' progress and often chatted to me.

Another royal visitor was Prince Albert and his beautiful Italian wife Princess Paola (née Ruffo di Calabria). The Prince's brother was the then King Baudoin of Belgium. The Prince told Annigoni that he would very much like to have a portrait of his wife but doubted if he could afford Annigoni's fee, which caused a little amusement. The three of them then retired to his private studio, so I never heard what eventually transpired, but I do not think that portrait ever materialized.

A similar enquiry came from Queen Juliana of the Netherlands, but the portrait was never painted as she could only give him three sittings and Annigoni therefore declined the commission.

Some time later Annigoni went to Denmark, where he stayed for some time in order to paint Queen Margretta and her consort Prince Henry, who succeeded King Frederick and Queen Ingrid. Their earlier visit may well have influenced this commission. These two fine portraits, which remain in the private royal apartments in Denmark, were little publicized.

ROYAL PORTRAITS AND OTHER FAMOUS PEOPLE

The British Royal family portraits

The first, foremost and most famous of Annigoni's portraits was of course that of our Queen, who gave him the hitherto unprecedented number of 16 sittings at Buckingham Palace for his first great portrait of her in 1954. This caused him considerable travail, anguish and emotion, with the added stress of the press, who besieged his Kensington studio. Their banal questions, inaccuracies and distortions displeased him.

The portrait was an outstanding success, received with great satisfaction by the royal family and with general acclaim by the public. This in turn led to subsequent private royal commissions for portraits of HRH Princess Margaret and HRH Prince Philip, the latter again commissioned by the Worshipful Company of Fishmongers, to accompany the earlier portrait of the Queen. I cannot imagine that any of these sitters enjoyed the tedium of having to pose standing still for up to one-and-a-half hours on many occasions. But whereas the portrait of the Queen bore a serene and tranquil expression, Prince Philip looked very stern. I dared to comment to Annigoni that the Prince looked 'almost fierce', to which he replied, 'He can be a rather fierce man.'

I realized myself what a great responsibility such portraits can be when in 1993 I had the honour of painting HRH The Princess Royal, who posed for me in the yellow drawing-room used frequently as a studio at Buckingham Palace, and before the easel used by many famous portrait painters. That is quite intimidating to start with. One is alone with a blank canvas and, pressurized by very limited time, unable to waste a precious minute. With the expectation of producing a successful likeness of a very well-known face and

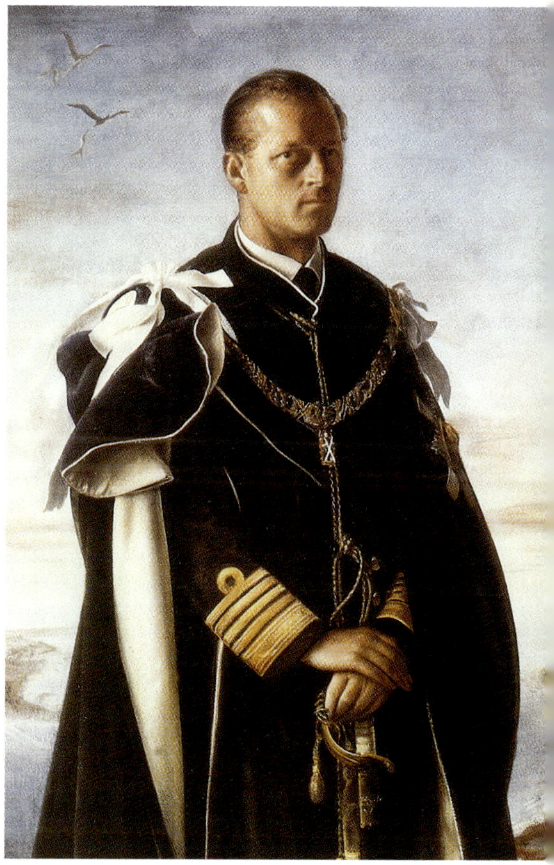

The first portrait of HRH Prince Philip

a good painting one is unable to relax. Princess Anne selected pastel for a change of medium, which pleased me.

When Annigoni came to paint the Queen Mother, I think he found her more responsive and certainly very entertaining, although, like the Queen, she did not keep very still and talked a great deal. She apparently enjoyed the sittings and amused him with her sharp wit and mimicry. That portrait was commissioned by the University of London, of which she was chancellor, and she posed in her academic robe. Her Majesty suggested wearing the mortarboard instead of holding it in her lap, and placed it at a jaunty angle on her head. The university authorities were not too pleased with the result and little has been seen of that portrait by the public.

In similar robes but without the controversial cap, the Duchess of Kent sat for her portrait in Annigoni's Kensington studio in South Edward Square. I saw the portrait in the course of painting and thought he had captured the soft and gentle expression perfectly.

Teheran: meeting and painting the Shah of Persia and Empress Farah Diba

Annigoni's *capolavoro* was undoubtedly the great dual portrait (270 x 150 cm) commissioned by the Iranian Oil Corporation for the coronation of the Shah and his Empress, Farah Diba.

In October 1967 Annigoni arrived in Teheran to start the preliminary sketches for this great undertaking. He had to wait a week before his first meeting with the Empress, undergoing all the heavy protocol, bureaucracy and security procedures from the highest government minister to the lowest valet. He arrived at the gates of the palace in a chauffeur-driven car sent to take him to his 3.30 p.m. appointment. The guard on duty asked his name and business – all in Iranian – and then telephoned through to the palace to verify the authenticity of this visitor from abroad. There were several more requests for identity and further telephone calls, while Annigoni had to wait, sharing an inadequate umbrella with the guard. Finally someone came from within the armour-plated interior waving a permit of entry to the residential palace and Annigoni was allowed to enter, followed closely by the man with the permit. He looked for somewhere to deposit his rain-sodden coat while two or three footmen walked between the pillars totally indifferent, and a European woman tidied up something on a table before disappearing – only to reappear 10 minutes later to enquire who he was and the purpose of his visit. Again he repeated his name. He was finally shown into an enormous salon, still closely

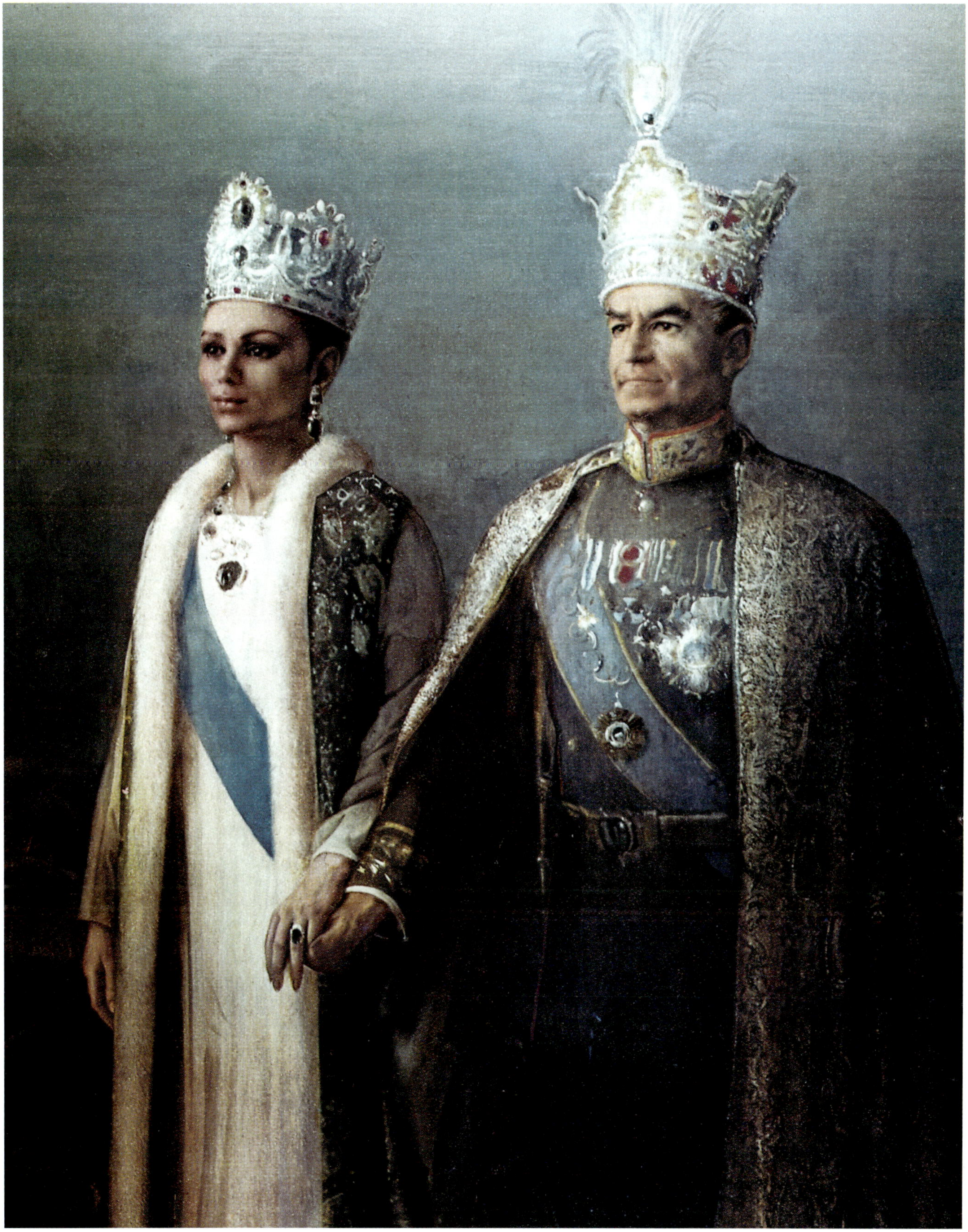

followed by the 'bloodhound' holding the permit.

Annoyed by this behaviour, Annigoni threw his wet overcoat purposely onto a beautiful armchair, from where it was quickly retrieved by the eldest of the footmen who, grumbling and with a look that would penetrate a wall, carried it off. He was then offered some tea at the end of the long hall, and the 'bloodhound' finally disappeared to be replaced by the Empress. Annigoni bowed as she offered her hand. He found her charming, very slim and even more striking than her photographs, especially her stupendous and penetrating dark eyes. She spoke easily and pleasantly in English. Evidently, until that morning no one had mentioned anything to their Majesties about the portrait, much to Annigoni's amazement. One month earlier the president of the Oil Corporation and the court minister had assured him that all was arranged. The Empress explained that in fact he had been expected for a portrait commissioned by the Iranian Bank but evidently due to the floods in Florence he had been obliged to decline that commission. Whatever the misunderstanding, she seemed pleased with this second opportunity and assured Annigoni that the Shah would be delighted.

Annigoni wished to paint the Shah and the Empress standing together in one portrait, dressed in their coronation robes. This would obviously require many sittings. The Empress replied that they would try to do their best to comply and then showed him the room allocated for the painting. This had a good north light, which pleased him. Next day was to be the first pose with the Shah.

Annigoni took his leave, but the departure through the gates entailed the same fuss and palaver as before. The car did not arrive. Four or five different 'types' appeared, talking among themselves animatedly then staring at him without a word. After about another 20 minutes with no sign of a car, he indicated in sign language to the silent group that he would walk. They grinned broadly, communicating nothing. After about two hours of walking aimlessly in the fog and then in almost darkness, he managed, fortunately, to catch a passing cab, which took him to the Hilton Hotel.

Next morning the first pose with the Shah took place, evidently the engagement requiring some arranging on the Shah's part. Annigoni found him natural, polite and intelligent, if not as linguistically gifted as his wife. Annigoni had decided to do only two detailed preliminary head and shoulder studies in pastel and ink at the palace. From these he could later paint the life-size portraits in his usual medium of egg tempera in his studio without pressure of protocol or other problems. The panel required would be very large and heavy, needing the support of his sturdy oak easel.

From the studies – brilliant portraits in themselves which he later gave to the Shah and Empress when he personally consigned the completed portraits – he produced a magnificent painting. As all the accoutrements of the royal regalia, crowns, medals and jewels had to be accurately portrayed, he had requested photos of these as an aide memoire. In due course not only these but a large parcel arrived via diplomatic channels containing exact replicas of the Shah's ornate medals and the Empress's crown of diamonds, rubies, pearls and emeralds, and her diamond and emerald jewellery. These fakes must have represented a considerable cost on their own. The Shah's medals, sashes and orders extended from his shoulder epaulets to his waist. Their fabulous high jewel-encrusted crowns – the Shah's even taller than the Empress's, with a peacock feather at the peak and described by Annigoni as a *torta Siciliana* (wedding cake) – must have been a headache to support and a challenge to paint. Realizing the necessity to underplay the overpowering effect of all this jewellery, Annigoni succeeded in portraying the brilliance of these essential emblems of a great and ancient dynasty without distracting the attention from the heads that bore them.

I was fortunate to be in the studio to observe this fascinating painting develop into a truly magnificent portrait of the heads of a dynasty so soon to come to a violent and tragic end with the Iranian revolution. The royal family fled into exile in the US, where not long after the Shah died of cancer.

Some years later, I asked Annigoni what had eventually become of the portrait that had taken him more than 100 hours to complete over a period of five or six months. He told me he had heard that when the palace was overrun by the military, much of its treasure was looted or destroyed, and, apparently, the portrait was used as a table at which the soldiers ate, a final insult and outrage to a royal family and to a great work of art.

Other famous people

Annigoni had originally established himself in London in 1950, exhibiting an early self-portrait, evocative of Renaissance painting, at the Royal Academy Summer Exhibition. This caused a stir and swiftly drew commissions, including a painting of the Duchess of Devonshire, who apparently spread the word around aristocratic and social circles, leading to the commission to paint the Queen. And as one good portrait will always lead to another, there followed an avalanche of commissions – from the nobility, rectors of colleges, chancellors of universities, directors of institutions, American and European presidents, international socialites and famous names of stage and screen including Julie Andrews in her role as Eliza in *Pygmalion*. Another sitter was Margaret Rawlings (Lady Barlow in private life), whom I met when I was painting a portrait of her daughter who, like me was then studying with Signorina Simi. I saw this small and very striking portrait of her mother at their home and remarked on the strong resemblance. She pointed out to me a hardly noticeable detail: Annigoni had painted a tiny devil nestling in her earring alluding possibly to her personality. It was a habit of his to include some small significant reference to the personality or background of the subject. She was amused by this but not by the inclusion of a falling leaf in the background. As she commented, 'I may well have said farewell to my youth but I was certainly not saying hello to old age!' It was a characterful portrait of the actress.

Commissions followed from all over the world, many of which involved much time in travelling from one continent to another with large amounts of luggage. Setting up his easel in unfamiliar surroundings and climates which were not necessarily conducive to peaceful painting, Annigoni nevertheless managed to fill sketch books on all his travels and did many landscapes when time permitted and a car was at his disposal.

In February 1957 Annigoni travelled to India to paint the Maharani of Jaipur. In July 1966 he was in South Africa to paint the very forceful looking Mrs Oppenheimer, wife of the diamond magnate. Ten years earlier, on one of his many London sojourns, he had painted the ballerina Margot Fonteyn between performances in a wonderfully romantic pose expressing all the grace and fragility of the great prima ballerina. She wore the flowing national costume of Panama for which her husband, Roberto Arias, was then Ambassador to Britain. After he was shot and paralysed, she gave up dancing to nurse him but later developed cancer. I wonder what became of that lovely painting after their subsequent tragic deaths?

Early Fresco Painting: Castagno and Florence

Annigoni's output in portraiture was prolific by any standards, starting with the drawings, paintings and etchings of his youth, and two self-portraits of 1932 and 1936. However, his fresco paintings, mostly of religious subjects and also painted from an early age, brought him considerably more satisfaction and fulfilment and, moreover, gave him the freedom to use his imagination to express himself in the highest and most enduring form of art.

The critics who attacked him as a fashionable royal and social portrait painter had no conception of his range and versatility in creating ecclesiastical works on a vast scale, nearly all of which up to that time were confined to his native country and had to be visited to be appreciated. What inspired him to paint so many religious subjects? Was he a religious man? I have often been asked this question. I would say that he had a deep sense of an almighty being, which he describes in his autobiography:

> "I am, as many are today, a man without the gift of faith, but I am nostalgic for God... I believe (in spite of being the son of rabid anti-

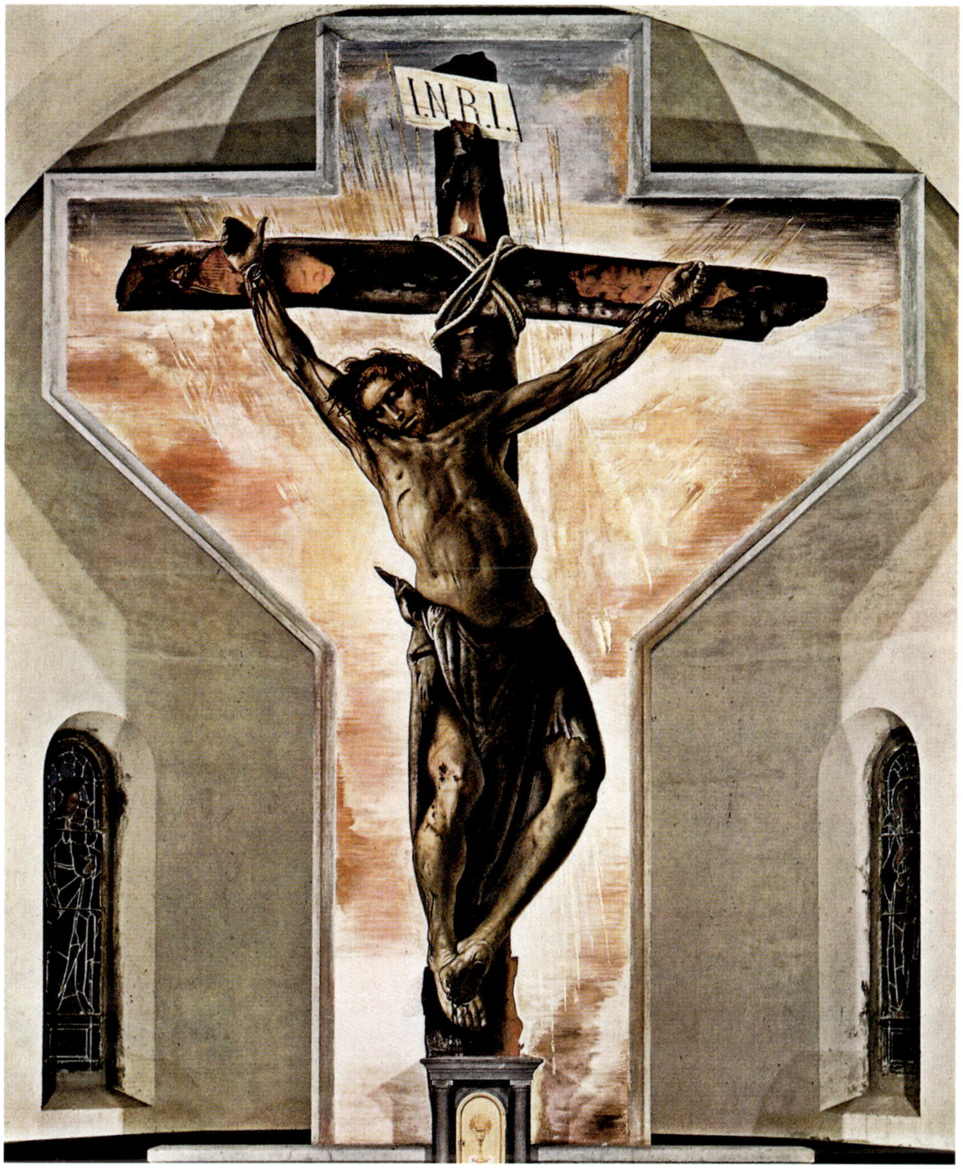

Fresco of the Christ of Castagno

clericals) that the longing for a certain and revealed faith in the divine has deep roots in my spirit and determines one of its essential, if contradictory, traits which does not fail to be reflected in my actions as man and artist.

On the other hand, the spiritual anarchy of our time often arouses in me a furious sense of rebellion that tends to reinforce this longing which is above all, then, the nostalgia of one who is not in accord with the epoch and society to which he belongs ...

In the end I can accept the idea only by thinking of God as something completely beyond the scope of human comprehension, like space. I can only say, with whomsoever said it first, I believe because it is unbelievable. But I believe in a 'great' design, that one day after death I will have a revelation in which I see how everything takes its place in that design.'

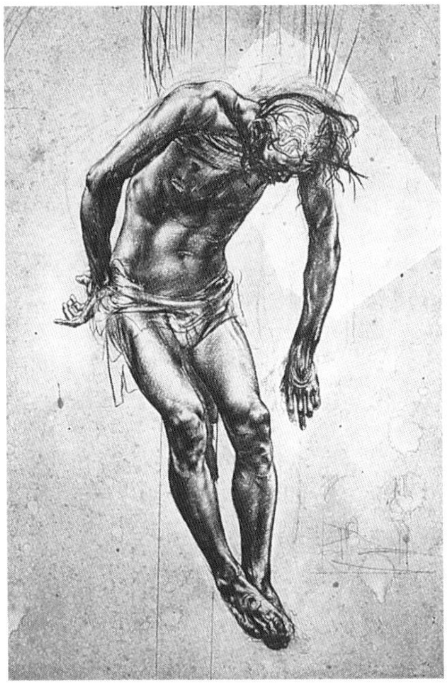

Study from life for the Deposition of Christ. (San Marco, Florence)

These feelings were already manifest in two of his earliest paintings of the crucifixion. The first was executed from 1937–41 from a study of a deposition which subsequently became a painting for the Convent of San Marco in the centre of Florence. This dramatic work depicts Christ hanging in death. So meticulous was Annigoni in the detail of the anatomy that he used a live model, looped under the armpits with cords, hanging from a cross in the studio. Despite appeals for a rest while Annigoni drew rapidly lost in concentration, the model was urged to 'hang on just a moment or two longer'. Finally, with the model almost on the point of fainting, the artist was able to capture the sense of weight of an inanimate body, before quickly resuscitating the poor model!

Annigoni used this work as the basis for his second crucifixion fresco, in the ancient church of Castagno, a small hill town in Tuscany made famous by the fifteenth-century painter Andrea del Castagno. Annigoni worked on this, assisted by his leading pupil Luciano Guarnieri, the young Antonio Ciccone and the plasterer Vannucci from December 1957 to March 1958. He noted in his diary that these were 'days of fervent work and great peace'. Along with other friends and pupils at the time – Luciano Guarnieri, Romano Stefanelli, Fernando Bernardini, Antonio Ciccone and Nelson White – as well as most of the village, I attended the dedication of the completed work, which was donated to the parish to commemorate the five-hundredth anniversary of the death of Andrea.

From the preparation of the large panel to the completion of the life-size painting, involved many journeys to and from Florence (about 50 miles) and many hours of work on scaffolding during the coldest winter months. A fresh layer of plaster had to be applied to the wall each morning in order for it to remain sufficiently moist to absorb the tempera paint. This allowed the painter to work on only one section a day. The work had to be swift and accurate, as the colours amalgamate immediately with the plaster and once dry cannot be altered. The work demands great dexterity and concentration and is therefore very tiring. This form of painting is the most durable, as has been proven by the survival of examples in the medium through many centuries.

With colleagues following the Service of Commemoration at the Church of Castagno

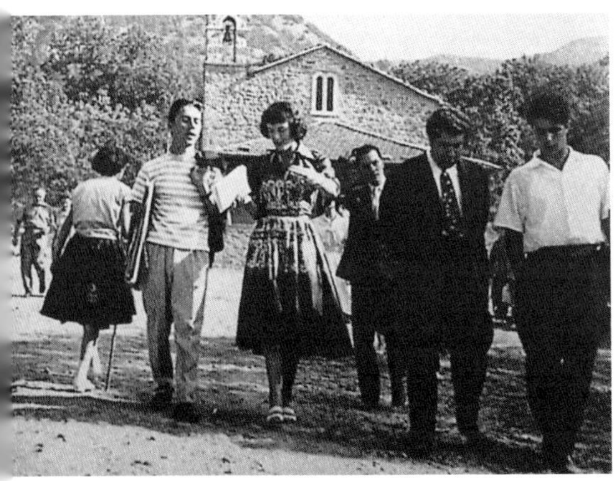

The Christ of Castagno shows the tortured figure of the dying Christ in the last moments of agony: his legs broken and bruised, his side pierced, the weight of his sagging body tearing the skin of his hands where the nails have pierced through the flesh into the wooden cross. Looking up to contemplate this awesome figure gasping his last breath from a broken body, one realizes fully his torture and suffering so that even an unbeliever cannot but be deeply moved. Annigoni's interpretation of the sacrifice of a human being and, more importantly, the Son of God was full of depth. How many crucifixions have been painted over the past centuries by great masters, from the stiff and aloof figures of the early Sienese painters through the tortured contorted figures of Mannerism to the grandiose depictions of Rembrandt and Rubens! However, of this century I have seen few depictions of this tragic offering for the sake of mankind that have moved me more than Annigoni's.

'The Sermon on the Mount'

No concept was too large or demanding for Annigoni. In his early years, from 1938–53 (at protracted intervals due to the intervening war years) he had devoted all his skill, creative imagination and energy to 'The Sermon on the Mount' (300 x 400 cm), a vast and complex work in tempera on canvas, producing a modern yet timeless interpretation about which several books have been written. This is a masterly composition of countless figures, each one an individual character expressing a different reaction, some withdrawn in meditation, others in concentrated discussion or violent argument. Every figure was carefully placed to lead the eye of the viewer through a maze of people and storm-twisted trees onwards into the far distance dominated by an awesome and atmospheric mountain. This painting was owned by an old friend and admirer, Commendatore Luigi Bresani, after whose death it was donated to the Collegio Ghislieri in Pavia.

The Sermon on the Mount

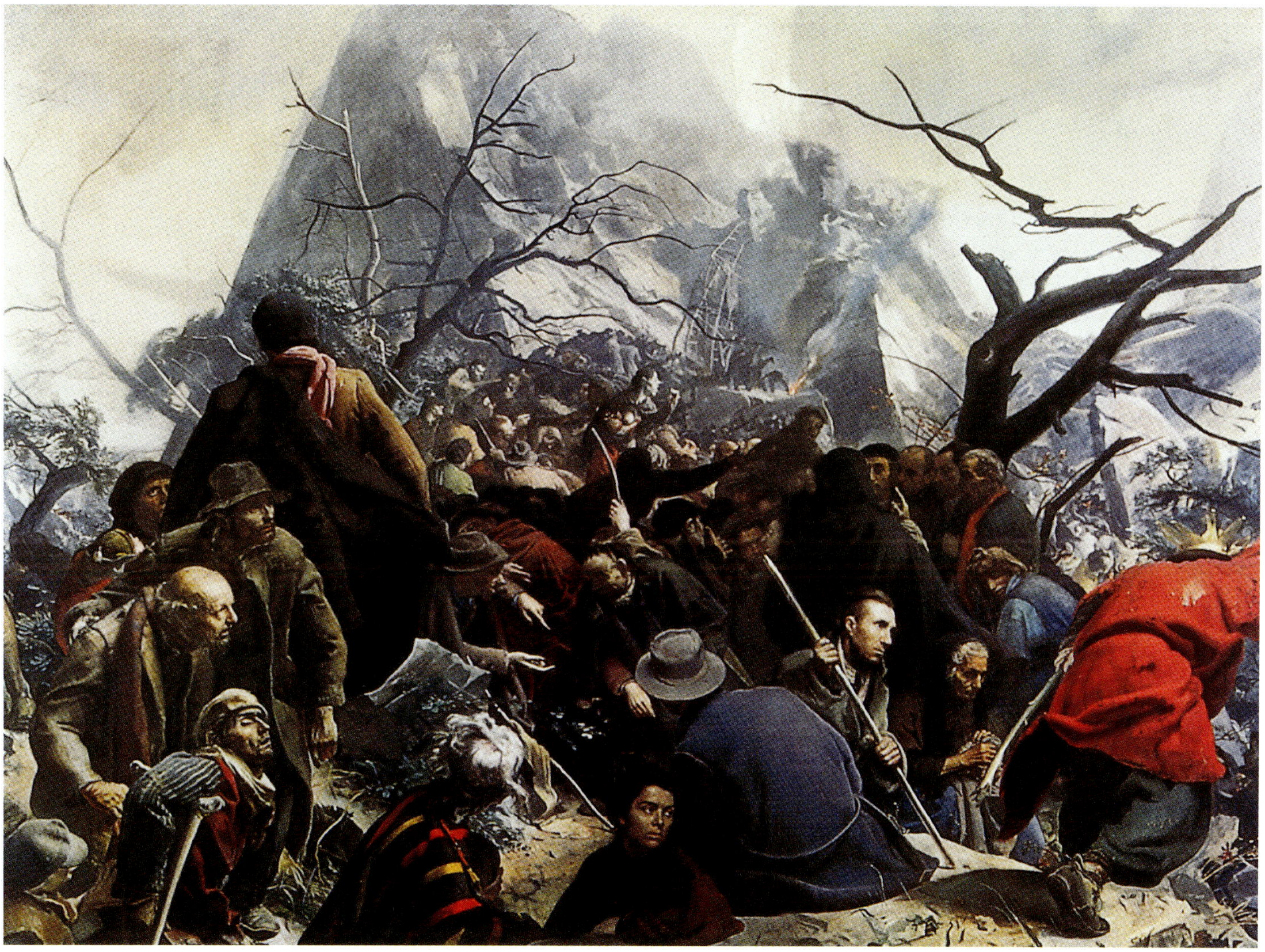

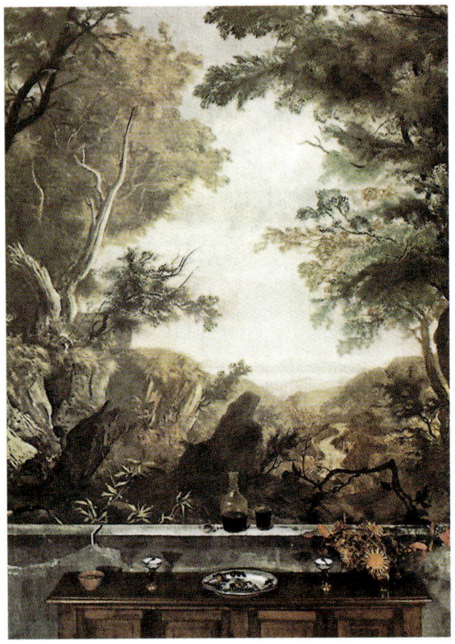

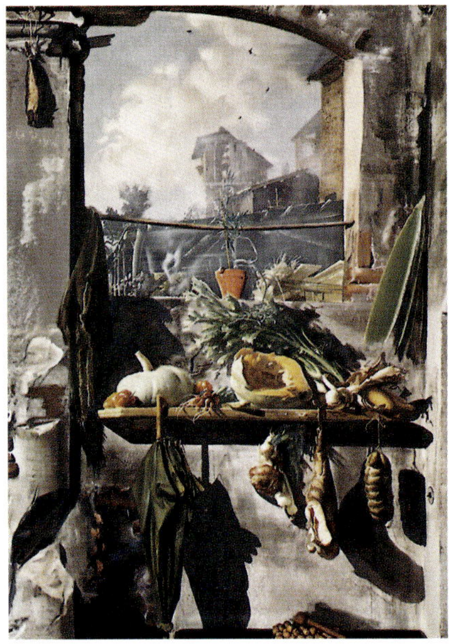

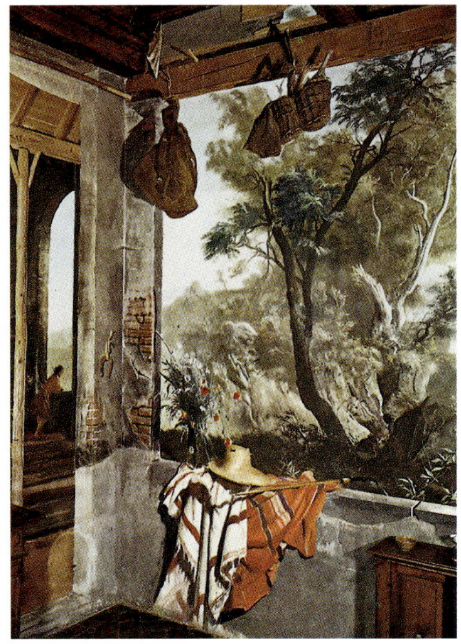

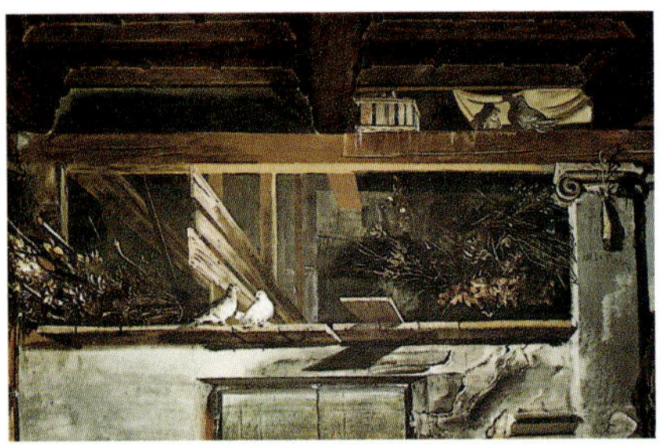

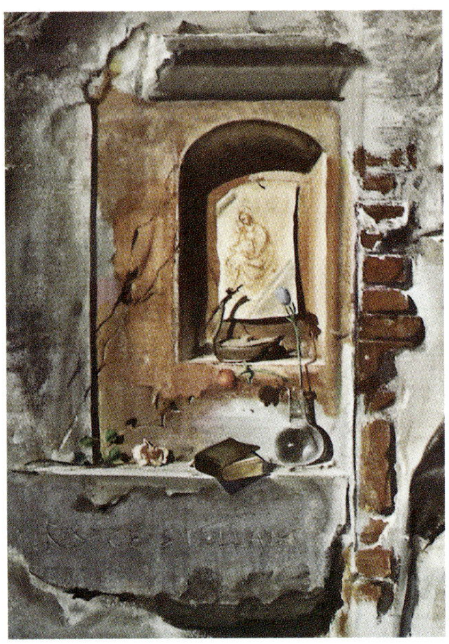

An unforgettable visit to a private treasure in Florence

I was taken one day by my friend Adriana Noferi to visit the home of a charming Florentine lady, the Contessa Margherita Veneroli Pesciolini. She had known Annigoni since his early days as a painter, then established in a studio in Piazza Santa Croce. She asked him if he would like to paint a mural in her house when he had some spare time. It was a very old house on the outskirts of Florence with a very dark interior, especially one small internal room with no windows. 'Come and see what your Maestro did for me,' she said.

She opened the door and turned on the light. I gasped in amazement as my eyes traversed the four walls from door to ceiling, transformed with great imagination and skill into a complete *trompe l'oeil* of windows opening onto idyllic landscapes, framed by window sills, shelves and cupboards filled with still-life objects of everyday domestic use: fruit, vegetables, salamis and hams, bottles of wine, books, hats on shelves and umbrellas propped against the wall. The three-dimensional dexterity of the painting defied the eye: a cobweb across a corner, two doves perched on a ledge high up near the ceiling. Here was a fantasy of imagination painted with such realism that one could not resist the urge to touch and feel its substance.

'He must have spent many, many hours developing this,' I said.

She smiled. 'Yes, from 1950–59, and he would not accept a fee. He was a good friend.'

The Painting of St Joseph the Carpenter

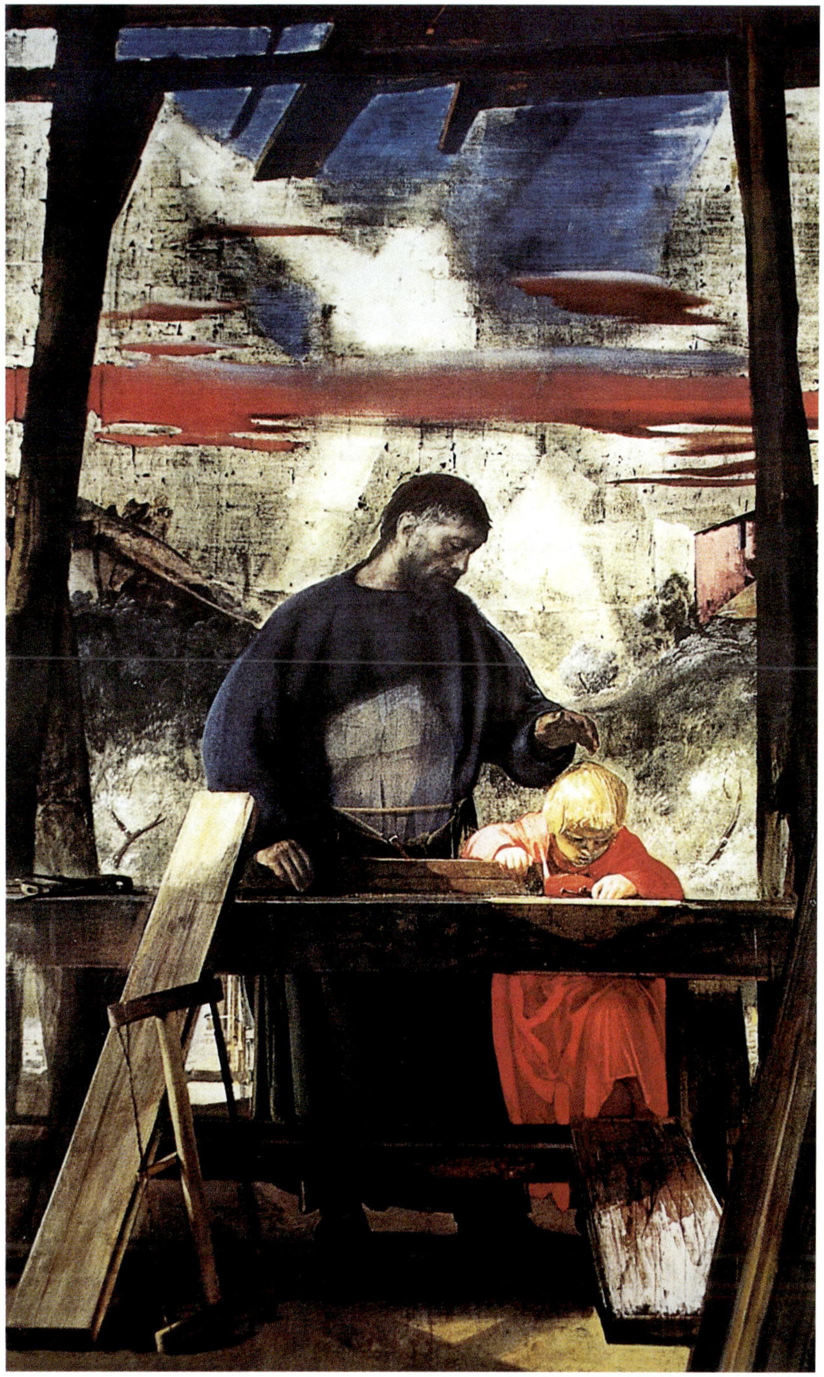

St Joseph the Carpenter

This was an unusual conception depicting Joseph with Jesus as a young boy learning the trade of carpentry at his workbench under an awning, against a background of the Tuscan countryside. Joseph looks down on the Christ-child, depicted at the age of 12, intent on helping his father, who bends over his tools, wood shavings at his feet. The father stretches out a hand lovingly as if to protect the child, but without touching him.

The panel painting was intended for one of the side chapels in the Basilica of San Lorenzo in the heart of Florence. I recall its progress vividly because I watched Annigoni develop it in the studio. I remember the boy who posed: the flaxen-haired son of a friend and a perfect child model.

As usual, Romano and Nando assisted Annigoni with the background area. Much of the sky was gilded, adding luminosity and brilliance to the composition. The technique of gilding fascinated me and I asked to be allowed to try my hand at it. To my great surprise Annigoni agreed to concede a small top corner of the sky, with the threat, '*Guai, se rovina il mio quadro!*' ('Woe betide you if you ruin my painting!').

Following Romano's instructions, I held my breath (essential) as I lifted the first wafer-thin sheet of gold leaf with a wide soft brush, flicking it onto the painting successfully, thank goodness, and then burnishing it.

On 21 June 1962 at six p.m. the painting was dedicated following a solemn mass attended by the pupils and a few close friends but without Annigoni. I felt very honoured to have contributed one square foot to posterity.

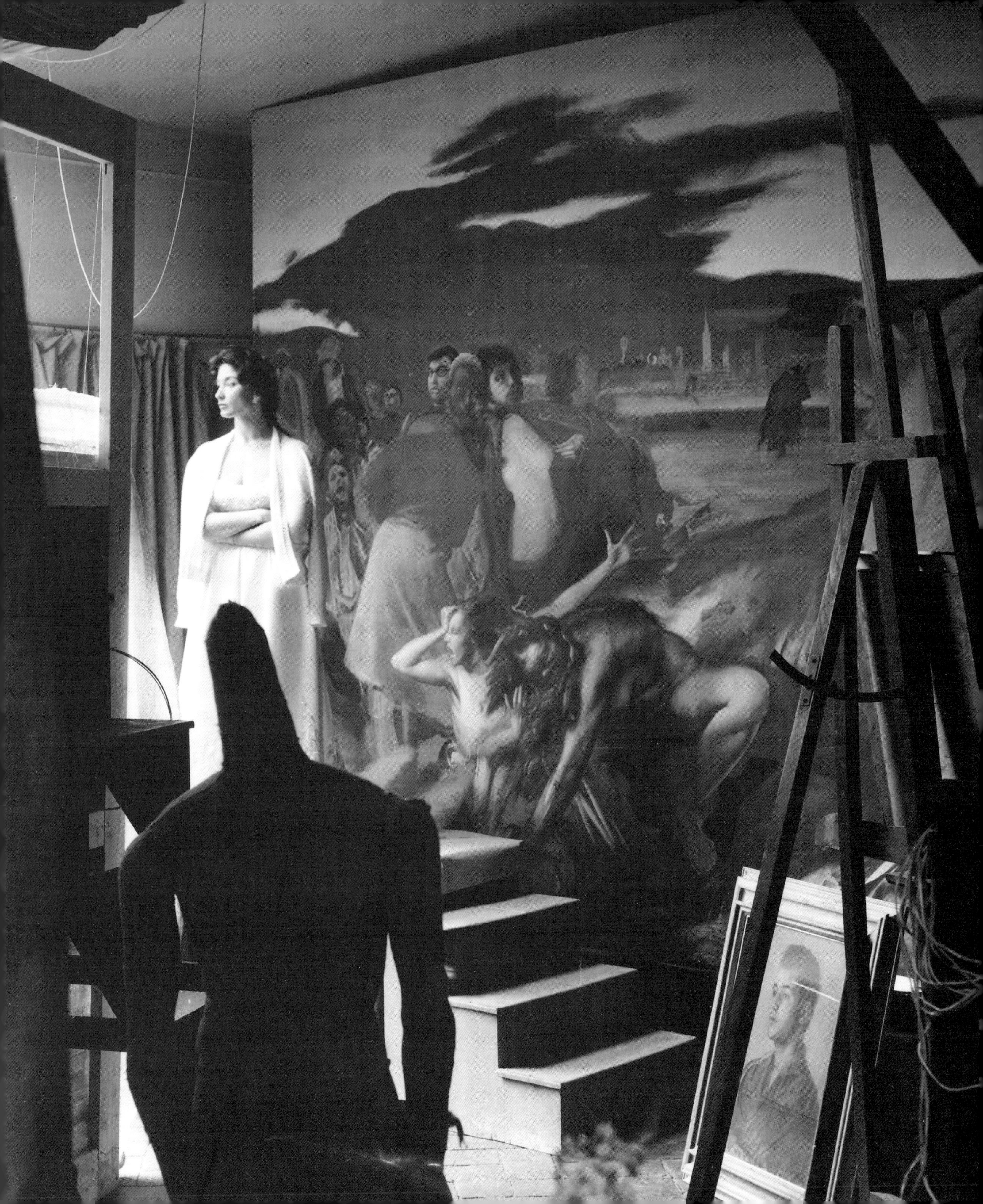

ANNIGONI'S SITTERS

The glamorous Baronessa

One of the most fascinating aspects of the studio for me was Annigoni's sitters and many visitors, famous and occasionally infamous, unusual or ordinary. Many of them came to pay homage to the Maestro, others came for advice or desiring to be pupils of his elite school. Most of them came to be recorded for posterity in portraits.

All Annigoni's countless portraits vibrated with life and with great insight into character. He caught the essence of the individual as well as a striking likeness which rarely failed to please the person concerned although it was often denigrated by the so-called intellectuals and critics, most of whom cannot themselves paint. Annigoni stood alone and single-minded in his vision and was true to himself. His talent far outreached the portraiture which made him famous. His mastery of composition, landscape, etching, lithography and sculpture (the latter which few knew about) made him an indisputable and highly accomplished master of arts.

I used to arrive at the studio soon after nine a.m. Three rings on the doorbell was the 'password' for Annibale to let us in without the usual enquiry. Annigoni was normally in his private study at that time, dealing with the mail and selecting letters for me to attend to on his behalf, or he was already down at Daria's bar having his early morning coffee. He would call me into his study whenever there was some correspondence or other matter to deal with.

One particular morning he dangled a blue envelope towards me and said, 'Smell this!' It was heavily scented and addressed in bold handwriting, with a Paris address under a coronet embossed in white on the reverse side of the white tissue-lined envelope.

'Impressive,' I remarked.

'Well, read it. You can read and speak French perfectly well, so I want you to answer it in my "imminent absence".' He watched with a bemused

Opposite: The Baronessa rests between poses

expression as I read the contents.

'She wants you to paint a full-length portrait of her very soon, apparently, and suggests dates. She seems to be very self-assured and knows what she wants.'

'Well, write and tell her briefly that I am going away soon and cannot undertake any more commissions for some time ahead. Write it now and post it today.'

I duly complied and after his approval signed the letter 'pp Pietro Annigoni'.

Not very long afterwards one mid-morning the bell rang. Annibale was absent so I had to open the window and ask who was there. I looked down onto a dazzling vision of elegance, from the top of her head, crowned with a white mink Cossack-style hat matched by a luxurious full-length fur coat, down to her slender ankles and feet in black crocodile high-heeled shoes. (How had she ever climbed all those stairs in such footwear?) She looked up at me with a radiant smile on the most paintable face an artist could wish for, announcing her name and an appointment with Annigoni.

'She's here!'

'Who is?'

'The Baronessa. She is waiting below, and just wait till you see her!'

He came out onto the landing as I opened the door for her. She entered, a little breathless after the steep climb, and mounted the final further steps inside the entrance. She was dressed to conquer and was aware of it. She announced herself; the impact was dramatic. '*Bonjour, entrez s'il vous plait,*' was all Annigoni said, but his expression said much more.

'I don't take no for an answer so I decided to come to Florence and meet you. That is why I telephoned to make sure you would be here.'

She had not wasted much time. Annigoni showed her into his private study and closed the door. I could see that *this* portrait was not going to be bypassed.

Following their private discussion, I called a taxi for the Baronessa and she left smiling, revealing dazzling teeth, with an 'À bientôt.'

'What a beautiful woman!' I said in sheer admiration.

'Yes, I think she will make a very interesting portrait,' was all Annigoni said.

The sittings, or rather standings, for it was a full-length portrait, started soon afterwards. Meanwhile the Baronessa settled into her suite at the Excelsior Hotel for an indefinite stay. As usual, Annigoni made preliminary sketches, first of her head – and what a head she possessed! – well-defined bone structure and strong features framed with a mane of glossy dark chestnut hair which she normally wore swept back into a chignon. But at the removal of a few hair pins, it fell like a shimmering cape onto her shoulders and down her back enhancing her pronounced Latin characteristics (she was of mixed blood, predominantly Latin American and Spanish). She was married to a German and spoke four languages, though not Italian, but with all her attributes and charm that was hardly a problem.

When she arrived for the first sitting, she was more suitably attired in casual clothes and her mass of hair was tied in a pony tail. She adapted easily to the studio and was immediately friendly with us all. She conversed in fluent French with Annigoni and easily in English with me.

Having decided on the pose, it was then the apparel. She had brought a beautiful white satin ball gown with a low neck-line which showed off her bare shoulders and revealed a voluptuous bosom. She stood radiantly on the dais, looking over her shoulder and through the window into the far distance with the assured poise of a woman proud of her physical attributes and their effect upon others, yet without any conceit.

The rapport was immediately established and she posed well and kept quiet until the rest periods – a good start. Later when Annigoni invited her to dine, as was his custom with sitters he found congenial, she responded with delight to this unaccustomed bohemian way of life, turning up at these relaxed and entertaining suppers in jeans and sweaters (designer of course), her long hair loose, in complete contrast to the jet-set international socialite who was whisked off at weekends by unseen admirers in Maseratis or Porsche sports cars to Milan for the opera, or flown to Gstaad for skiing between poses. We never met her husband or knew if she was still married, but she brought her mother to share her suite and her young daughter was installed at the elite boarding school at the Poggio Imperiale. A rather strange Middle-Eastern-looking man sometimes appeared, whom she introduced as her lawyer (we nicknamed him her 'protector'). She was complex, a personality of contrasting moods and tastes, living in the fast lane between her various houses in Paris, New York and on the Côte d'Azur according to the season and social events. But for all her apparent wealth, beauty and zest for living, this facade veiled an emotional vulnerability and insecurity. She was a lonely woman searching for happiness and isolated from reality.

The portrait proceeded well. I watched it develop daily from start to finish and learnt a great deal about perception and interpretation, of which Annigoni was a true master. The Baronessa responded wittily to his often provocative quips and used all her feminine skills to beguile him.

She had a generous nature, inviting me several times to visit her at her suite. On one occasion, hearing street musicians playing below, she opened the window and emptied the entire contents of her purse down over them, much to their surprise. She possessed fabulous jewellery, some of which she brought to the studio with the intention of wearing it for the portrait. Annigoni flatly refused, telling her that she needed no adornment. However, he finally conceded one item, an incredibly large uncut solitaire diamond ring of such proportion and brilliance that it scintillated with light. This one jewel encapsulated her personality and attracted almost as much attention.

The poses extended over a long period during which she was flown or

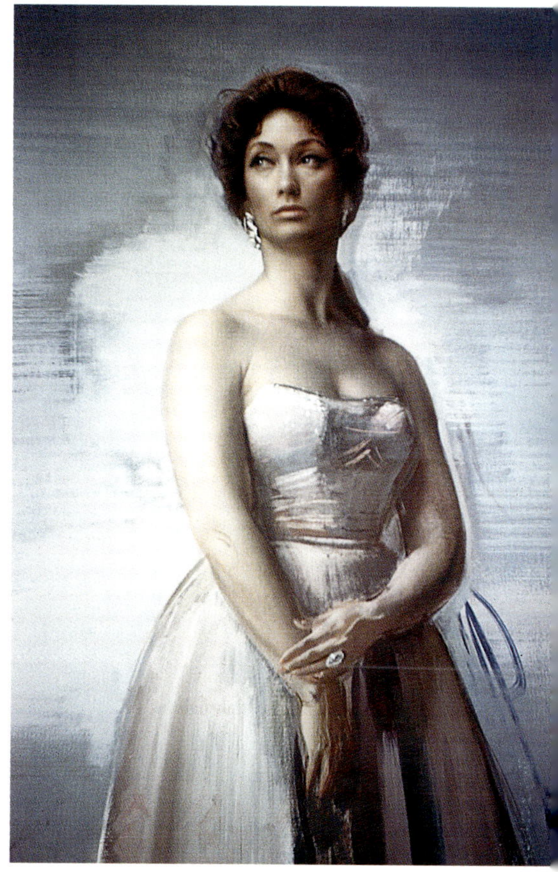

Unfinished portrait of the Baronessa

driven to whatever was filling her life at the time. During her absence, Annigoni developed the background of the painting. She was depicted standing on a tiled patio with a house on fire in the far distance. I asked Annigoni about this image.

'Don't you see?' he said. 'She inflames everything in her path.'

It was his usual final touch, symbolic of the character.

It was a very arresting portrait of an enigmatic woman. The size of the panel required the dexterity and strength of two men to manoeuvre it through the door down the first steep flight of stairs and the further four flights to street level. From there it was sent on to the packers who were responsible for shipping it abroad. These specialists were well accustomed to dealing with the many large paintings sent from the studio all over the world.

It turned out, in this particular case, that when the painting arrived at the intended residence, it was too large for the wall and was consequently transferred to the Baronessa's second home in another country. I heard that she even requested Annigoni to paint a smaller head and shoulders to fit into the first home, but he had no more time.

The socialite from Milan

Of the innumerable people remembered from those years, many were famous, some were flamboyant, and I recall one who was frivolous. She came from Milan.

She was an attractive and vivacious dark-eyed, dyed blonde, extremely well endowed both physically and financially, the latter thanks to a wealthy husband who was a well-known food manufacturer and who had commissioned an almost full-size portrait of one of his best assets. This small but dynamic woman burst upon the studio with all the self-assurance and determination of a politician's wife. She was attended by a 'shadow' in the form of an inconspicuous lady's maid who rarely spoke and whose sole purpose was to carry an impressive leather beauty case containing cosmetics required to adorn her mistress. A ritual was the make-up session before posing, the maid holding up a mirror for her to apply lavish powder, lipstick and mascara, followed by an abundant spray of hair lacquer before she was ready to pose.

This very voluble lady immediately established her position and requirements, telling the artist how she wanted to be painted and in what attire with the authority of one accustomed to getting what she wanted, that is, until she found out who was in control in this studio, which Annigoni soon made politely but firmly clear. He told her to stand on the dais, keep quiet and look directly at him.

She acquiesced for a while, but after about ten minutes started to chatter about herself, her home, her likes and dislikes. Annigoni, hidden behind his easel, was drawing vigorously in charcoal, increasingly irritated by her irrepressible nattering and responding only in monosyllables. When this solo conversation provoked little reaction she soon became bored and her vitality evaporated, her hitherto lively expression with it.

'Maestro, you must understand that I have to express my feelings. It's part of my personality. I am not the quiet type,' she said.

The poses were short because when Annigoni could no longer stand her chattering and constant moving, he walked out of the studio and into his study, closing the door firmly. With only the maid and I present, she turned and asked my name. As it was difficult for an Italian to pronounce, she called me 'Dolly', rather to my annoyance. She used me as a go-between when she became aware that Annigoni was irritated, though I could only explain to her the necessity of keeping as still and quiet as possible.

One morning as she chatted continuously, Annigoni's exasperation exploded and, throwing down his brushes without a word, he walked out of the studio and did not reappear. She looked across in amazement to where I was painting. 'What is the matter with him. Do you think he is angry? What can I have done to annoy him?'

I tried diplomatically to explain that painters needed peace and quiet to be able to work.

'But how can he paint my personality if I cannot open my mouth?'

I could hardly reply without offending her. She decided that enough was enough for that day and asked me to order a taxi for her and the silent maid.

The situation must have had some effect on her, because for the next session some days later, she arrived in a very acquiescent mood, her maid carrying a magnificent ballgown of heavy black satin, which was especially procured from Como, the centre of the silk industry. This contrast suited her complexion, showing off to perfection her bosom and shoulders, around which another long matching stole was swathed. A lining of white satin glimmered between the folds of the dress, breaking up the solid black. The large amount of material took some time to arrange, with the dresser fussing around her. The effect was stunning.

At the weekend the signora went home, returning on Monday to resume posing. This time she was laden with packages containing cheeses, sausages, salami, mortadella and other culinary delicacies, all part of the family firm's production. She generously distributed these to all of us in the studio, reserving a huge bel paese for the Maestro, whether as a peace offering or as a tactful way of promoting better relations I don't know. But these gifts were very well received and appreciated by all of us – not without a little amusement. We all left with enough food to last for weeks.

With her 'shadow' crouching on the steps behind her, the two women made an interesting contrast of social background and character. Hidden in the alcove behind Annigoni and his easel, I decided to do a drawing of this incongruous pair. The signora was aware of everything that went on, and after the end of the pose she came over to look at my drawing. She was very pleased with it and wanted to buy it when it was finished, but she insisted most emphatically that she did not want her maid included and asked me to erase the poor woman. I politely declined to do so as I wanted to keep the study for myself. Unfortunately, I can't recall what happened to it. It would have made an interesting illustration of the painter, the model and the maid.

The portrait grew in stature, capturing the signora's character and stance, which seemed to say, 'Here I am, look at me.' Her dark brown eyes followed the onlooker in all directions, as the subject's eyes do in all good portraits.

Towards the end, she was anxious to know what Annigoni intended to paint in the background, suggesting that the fine avenue of poplar trees leading up to her villa would be to her liking and inviting him to come and see them for himself. I expected another explosion, but with great restraint he replied, 'I have already decided the background. You will be leaning against a table with a still-life of a large parmesan cheese.' Although he said this jokingly, despite her protestations he did in fact create a still-life of fruits and cheese on the table behind her, which was after all appropriate as her husband's company produced most of Italy's best-known cheeses. In his own subtle way and with great taste, he alluded to her particular background.

This portrait took some time to complete, and one day when the signora exasperated Annigoni more than usual by her fidgeting (doubtless due to boredom), he came to have a look at my work. Hidden from her sight behind the easel he whispered to me in mock desperation, 'How I envy you!' Nevertheless, despite all the problems that every artist has to face in the course of a portrait, it was a striking painting of a very superficial woman. From my vantage point, the sittings had some amusing moments and were a lesson in patience and endurance, but I know for a fact that they stretched Annigoni to the limit of his.

The sophisticated American

The elegant and cultured Mrs C was quite another character. She was immensely wealthy thanks to two husbands, the last a banker who had left her a fortune and whose dying wish was for her to be painted by Annigoni.

She arrived one morning, a slim and soigné woman somewhere in her fifties, dressed with impeccable taste in black relieved only by a choker of pearls, her platinum-grey hair perfectly coiffed back from her face. She had pale skin and good bone structure. The only indication of her age were the delicate lines around her eyes and those more deeply etched between the eyebrows, which gave her an expression of slight disapproval. It was an interesting face which, when she smiled, was totally transformed. She did not smile often. She was a person used to authority, to being obeyed and to having first class in everything. She posed well, sitting quietly and upright, looking directly at Annigoni with a quizzical expression and attending to her correspondence on her lap during rest periods. At the end of each sitting Annibale ordered a taxi and she left with only a brief glance at the painting in progress, and without any comment.

One morning, while Annigoni was in the other room, she approached me and confided her disapproval: 'I don't like my portrait. I didn't come all the way to Florence from the States to be painted with a face as long as a horse!'

'How can you possibly say such a thing?'

'Because he's given me such a long face and such a set look, to say nothing of these frown lines. I was painted by James Gunn before this, you know, for my husband. *Quite* a different painting. Well, just look at the texture of my skin,' she said, inviting my close inspection. 'I have a massage and beauty treatment every morning, and my masseuse says I have a complexion like porcelain. But in this painting I look pale and pasty, and just dull.'

I tried to convince her that she was mistaken, but to no avail, and at the end of the sitting she left without further comment and with only a formal 'good morning' to Annigoni. He turned to me and said, 'I know she doesn't like it but I know even more that it is just like her.'

Next morning Annibale was on some errand and I had to let her in. As I greeted her, I noticed that she was wearing a triangular plaster patch on the bridge of her nose and, showing concern, asked her if she had injured herself.

'Oh you mean this?' She pulled off the patch. 'It's just one of my "frownies".'

But the frown lines remained. She had already told me that she wore an elastic chin-strap overnight, but I resisted the temptation to ask whether she had 'smilies' for the same purpose.

One day she invited me to lunch at the well-known Harry's Bar, *the* place to eat and be seen. The small party included her very attractive, Italian-looking daughter, and two well-known American guests. She hosted the luncheon and led the conversation with great charm and ease, and also invited me to paint her daughter. The fact that she was being painted by Annigoni was in itself another social achievement, whatever her own misguided personal feelings about the likeness.

The sittings were protracted as it was later decided that her hands would be included in the portrait. She was becoming increasingly frustrated and continued to show little interest in the progress. Moreover, pressing business matters necessitated her return to the States. So, giving little notice to Annigoni, she announced her departure. Then she suggested that he should come to California to complete the portrait, adding that, after all, he had to go to England to paint the Queen!

I think Annigoni was relieved to see her depart and was not anxious to proceed any further.

'What will you do with a half finished portrait?' I asked.

'I shall probably paint a wimple around her face and a nun's veil over her head and turn her into a mother superior.' This of course he had no intention of doing and for some time the portrait remained unfinished on the easel.

Later the signora sent a letter, enclosing a cheque and also a photograph taken some years earlier by the famous photographer Karsh of Ottawa, who with clever lighting and some deft touching-out of the lines around the mouth and eyes, had produced a very flattering black-and-white photograph of a much younger woman. The rather pathetic letter emphasized that Karsh had captured her likeness, which had delighted her husband, and continued that she wished Annigoni had been able to capture her in the same way. What could an artist reply to someone who could not see the difference between a painting and a photograph, however artistically taken?

In fact, while in the studio, the portrait evoked much interest, curiosity and favourable comment, most of all for the penetrating grey eyes looking intently at the viewer with such a compelling gaze. Someone remarked: 'She must be a very intelligent and interesting woman,' at which Annigoni smiled ironically and said, 'Anything but intelligent!' However, he replied to her letter and thanked her for the cheque, which he returned, saying that he had no desire for her to have a portrait she did not like, even less, understand. So he retained it as it was with the lower half unfinished and the hands only barely suggested, but complete in itself. It was a subtle and restrained portrait of a lady, although it was subsequently exhibited as 'Portrait of an Old Lady', which the sitter was not. More appropriate would have been the kinder Italian phrase *una signora di una certa età* (a lady of a certain age). The portrait thereafter remained in Annigoni's home.

I reminded Annigoni of the famous line of the Scottish poet Robert Burns: 'Oh would some power the giftie gie us to see ourselves as others see us', which reminds me of another occasion, when an English couple visited Annigoni to commission a drawing of their daughter, who was studying in Florence. She turned out to be a rather plain girl with a poor pale complexion. Annigoni decided to do a pen and ink drawing of her. When it was finished the parents came to view it. It was immediately obvious to me, painting nearby, that they were not pleased and, moreover, very embarrassed. The husband remained silent while his wife struggled for words to express her feelings. Eventually she said, 'It is really a beautiful drawing but I wish you had not given her that expression.'

Annigoni replied frankly, 'I only draw what I see, and it is there. You don't have to accept the portrait if you don't like it.'

All three then retired to his private study. Shortly afterwards the couple left rather hurriedly without the portrait and Annigoni returned to the studio, clearly irritated. I could not resist remarking on their behaviour and inability to see the likeness and asked him what he would do with the portrait.

'I shall add a scarf round her head and turn her into a peasant,' he said. This he did some time later and the drawing was immediately sold.

Problems of portraiture

If only the average layman could understand the painter's approach to revealing the character and personality that gradually emerges as a painting develops! The art is to encapsulate as far as possible a composite image from the many and changing expressions of which the camera can only capture one at a time – and afterwards, if necessary, cut out any blemishes or wrinkles. These facial characteristics are, after all, like our handwriting, part of our character, reflecting our innermost thoughts and expressing our feelings. We all like to look our best when painted or photographed, and it is said that the camera never lies, but none of us sees what others see. Even our mirror image is in reverse, and what it reveals is often very daunting and displeasing to us. This poses a problem for every portrait painter: total honesty or subtle flattery.

Flattery that produces an enhanced or rejuvenated face is false, making the artist untrue to himself even though the sitter may be delighted. The painter needs the perception of a psychologist, the tact of a diplomat and the ability to place the subject in a good light and position in order to emphasize his or her features to the best advantage. However, where the psychologist has to reason about and analyse a personality, the artist has to feel and interpret his reaction, which may not always be pleasing to others. A good rapport between the painter and his subject is essential. If there is no mutual compatibility, in my experience, the painting will not be successful. Annigoni also had these problems to face and to solve. He succeeded in making a portrait convince the onlooker of his integrity and faithfulness to the character. Holbein was the prime example of this great gift, creating faces which are timeless.

Painting is a personal and private pursuit in which one expresses one's innermost feelings about a chosen subject. Millet remarked that 'an artist must first of all feel strongly about the subject of his painting before being able to transmit those feelings to others.' In the specialized field of portraiture the artist has also to satisfy the client if the painting is a commission. Frequently a committee is involved. This is demanding and often limits the freedom of the painter, becoming inhibiting unless one is in full command of the situation. The client expects a good likeness and may not always appreciate the finer qualities of painting, or even how he or she appears to others. In my experience, if the subject does not appeal or has no strong features the commission is best avoided diplomatically. It is better safe than sorry if one's reputation is at stake.

Walker's famous portrait of Oliver Cromwell was painted 'warts and all' and presumably accepted as an unflattering likeness, whereas Graham Sutherland's controversial portrait of Sir Winston Churchill, depicting a face full of character and strength, received much adverse comment, especially from Sir Winston and his family. Yet the portrait was painted by an acclaimed, eminent and highly individual portrait painter who most certainly brought out the character of all his famous sitters. Did it deserve to be burnt after Sir Winston's death on his orders?

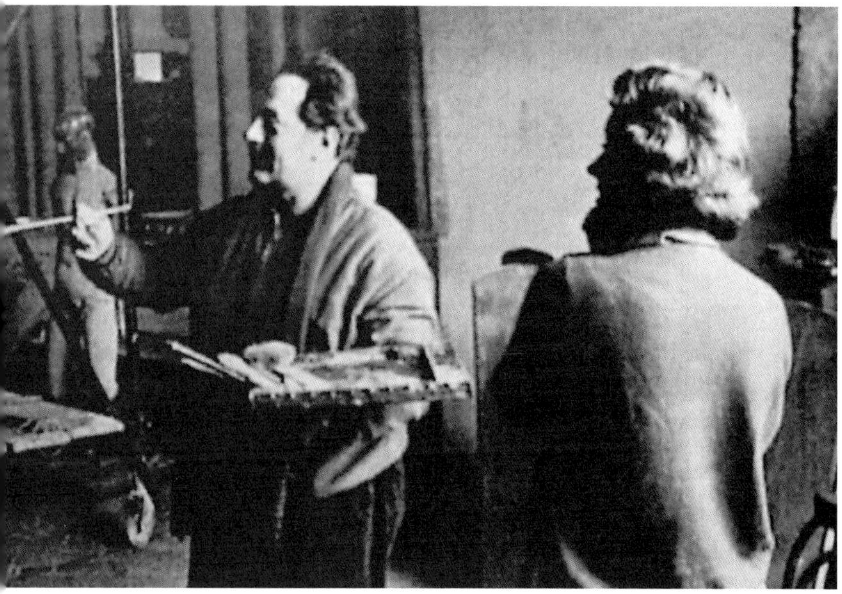

Watching Annigoni at work

The great John Singer Sargent, a supreme master of a wide range of subjects and media and especially of portraiture, combined distinction, elegance and the nobility of Van Dyck with wonderfully free bravura painting. He described portraiture ironically as the 'likeness of someone with something wrong with the mouth' – so often the critical comment of the layman. In fact, the mouth is the most mobile part of the face and expresses much of the character of the person.

Apart from these most sensitive personal feelings of the painter for the subject portrayed, there must also be a good balanced composition of colour, form and design; spontaneity of brushwork and freshness of application, and also a little inexplicable magic to captivate the beholder. This elusive combination was achieved by the great masters, such as Rembrandt, Rubens, Velasquez, Van Dyck, Titian and Holbein, and is visible in many of the surviving paintings of the Renaissance. How wonderful it would have been to watch those painters at work, from sketches to a blank canvas and throughout the development of their masterpieces.

Annigoni always urged his pupils to study the great masters, and many of their paintings and sculptures were available to us in the galleries and museums of Florence. He often said, 'I cannot teach you how to paint, only how to look and perceive. You will learn much from the work of the masters.' I can honestly say that I learned much from being able to watch him at work, but to put this observation into practice is not so easy. We are on our own and the road is long, hard and, most of the time, solitary.

Throughout the history of art, painters have been influenced by their masters as well as their contemporaries, and this was particularly pronounced in the school of Annigoni. But there is only one original, and carbon copies, however expert, are never individual. Every painter has to develop a personal style in order to succeed and be recognized.

The American general

Many years earlier, towards the end of the Second World War, the German army was retreating through Italy northwards. After a heavy bombardment of Florence by the pursuing allied forces, an American brigade under the command of General Mark Clarke was temporarily stationed near the terribly battered city.

Annigoni was already well-known in Florence as a very talented young painter with a promising future. General Clarke was persuaded to call on him with a view to having his portrait painted, albeit with very little time for sitting. Annigoni agreed to paint as much as he could in the time available. The General posed in his olive green fatigues during a lull in the fighting, but he was not able to stay long enough for the three-quarter-length portrait to be completed from life, so the painting had to be completed without him.

There was always work in progress in the studio. Finished paintings were stacked against the walls on two sides of the room, waiting to be framed, delivered or collected. A number of them were also stored in the attic. The back of one very large painting intrigued me and, turning it round, I immediately recognized the face from the many wartime photographs I had seen during my school days. It was undoubtedly the famous American general. What was it doing up there all these years later gathering dust? Annigoni recounted the story of how the General had eventually returned to Florence at the end of the fighting when Italy had surrendered and had come to see the completed portrait. He looked at it for some time in silence and then said to Annigoni very bluntly, 'I never lost a battle, but I sure don't look like a victor in this painting.'

'How could he say that? It's a wonderful likeness,' I said.

'Well, evidently he didn't think so, and I kept it,' said Annigoni. So it remained hidden, facing the wall behind a curtain.

Evidently, much later on at the invitation of a friend, the portrait was exhibited in the foyer of the Excelsior Hotel, where it was seen and purchased by Gerard Kraft, who in turn sold it to an American army officer living in Italy, after which it came into the hands of another US army general. He offered it to the West Point Military Academy, which apparently refused it because it was not the right size! However, it appears that the much-travelled painting was finally presented, after much time had elapsed, to Mark Clarke himself, from whom Annigoni received a letter enclosing a photograph of the General standing beside the portrait he had rejected so many years earlier, now looking up at it with clearly apparent pleasure.

'Isn't it ironic?' Annigoni said, showing me the photograph. 'He rejected the painting so angrily and hurriedly that he forgot his combat jacket. I found it suited me, fitted comfortably and was warm in cold weather. I even wore it at Buckingham Palace when I painted the Queen and Prince Philip. Naturally, I removed all the insignia.

I wish I could ask him now if he actually wore it during the painting, as I can remember how cold I felt in that yellow drawing-room at the first sitting I had with Princess Anne on a chilly March morning in 1993. The central heating was minimal and I was shivering in a jacket and had to ask a footman to get the room warmed sufficiently before the Princess arrived for her sitting, whereupon a small electric heater was hastily produced. It had about as much effect as a candle in a cathedral.

The Composition 'VITA', 1957–60

I was only present in the studio from 1958 and can therefore speak only of some of the many paintings I was privileged to watch in progress during that period, from which I learnt a great deal. Many of Annigoni's greatest works were fresco paintings in churches and cathedrals all over Italy and in private mansions in America as well as a few in England. Eventually, tiring of the demands of portraiture he devoted the last 11 years of his life to frescoes. These immense works made great physical and mental demands upon him but will surely remain as a permanent legacy for the future and as proof of the validity of this great painter.

One of these frescoes, arguably one of Annigoni's most imaginative paintings, expressed his deep and disquieting feelings about the society and outlook of the sixties. This was the complex and questioning composition, 'VITA' ('Life') (315 x 550 cm). It was painted in the studio during the period of my tutelage, so I was able to watch its development and occasionally participate as a model. No words of mine can adequately describe it, although its message is clear. The best I can do is translate Annigoni's own words about the feelings that motivated him to paint this disturbing picture:

> 'I believe that in everyone's life there are times when we are liable to form bitter opinions about certain aspects of the world in which we live. Day by day, scanning through any daily newspaper, we accumulate sensations of pity, horror, anger and rebellion which, even if only fleeting, contribute to a subconscious state of anxiety and distress. This sometimes develops into more generalized and meditated considerations. This allegorical picture is the outcome of these feelings maturing, having repeated themselves with ever increasing frequency.
>
> The fundamental conception is of materialism, which at some times

is blind and brutal, at others acutely selfish or accommodating, and which is infiltrating everywhere.

On the right-hand side of the painting I represent the crowd of people commonly known and recognized as 'nice', or, if one prefers, the conformists – the conventional people of every walk of life. All turn together in the same direction, each one shut up in his own little self-centred world. This group of individuals goes on in its way, following its own safe road, as if protected against vice and wickedness by the anti-conformist martyr – in the centre of the painting – a figure on a cross, crucified and reviled.

Once again this anti-conformist, in the heart of the crowd of conventionalists, has become their martyr, and at the same time their protector. Embodied in him is the need for self-criticism: the necessity of renewing or reviving spiritual values and re-establishing a moral equilibrium which has become vague and dispersed. He has rebelled against the materialistic selfishness that has gradually formed a suffocating crust over these values. As his rebellious outcry against the selfish interests and habits of the majority was too violent, he has been condemned by them, sacrificed, and later, as always, erected as a symbol of the eternal and invincible forces of the spirit.

The strong figure of a young woman in red advancing against the tide represents the new conformist who, with absolute faith, makes her way towards the martyr, determined to overcome the resistance of the massive figure of the cleric robed in black, his head sunk into a book, who here represents allegorically the formidable negative power that even a cleric can assume when he betrays the high spiritual office entrusted to him, crystallizing it around the temporal security attained.

On the left-hand side of the painting are depicted the 'bad' people under a stormy sky: a prostitute debased to the lowest form of human depravity, a delirious drug addict and a rent boy. Here is a violent and bestial explosion of horror and crazed fear, into which the figure of Death unexpectedly breaks, the sharp and menacing blade of his scythe, seen emerging from the edge of the painting, on the point of enveloping the debased people. From behind this group emerges the bespectacled face of an intellectual of arid and destructive mentality. Below him, almost veiled in obscurity, some blind figures, ignored by everyone, follow one another hopelessly and precipitously towards an excavation in the midst of steel scaffolding. Further still in the distance the profile of an anxious, noble, young girl represents the aspiration towards the good that can still free itself everywhere, against all odds. In the centre foreground of all this confusion is the solitary figure of a young boy who has to face life but turns to face the onlooker, bewildered and frightened, to ask why, how and where to go.'

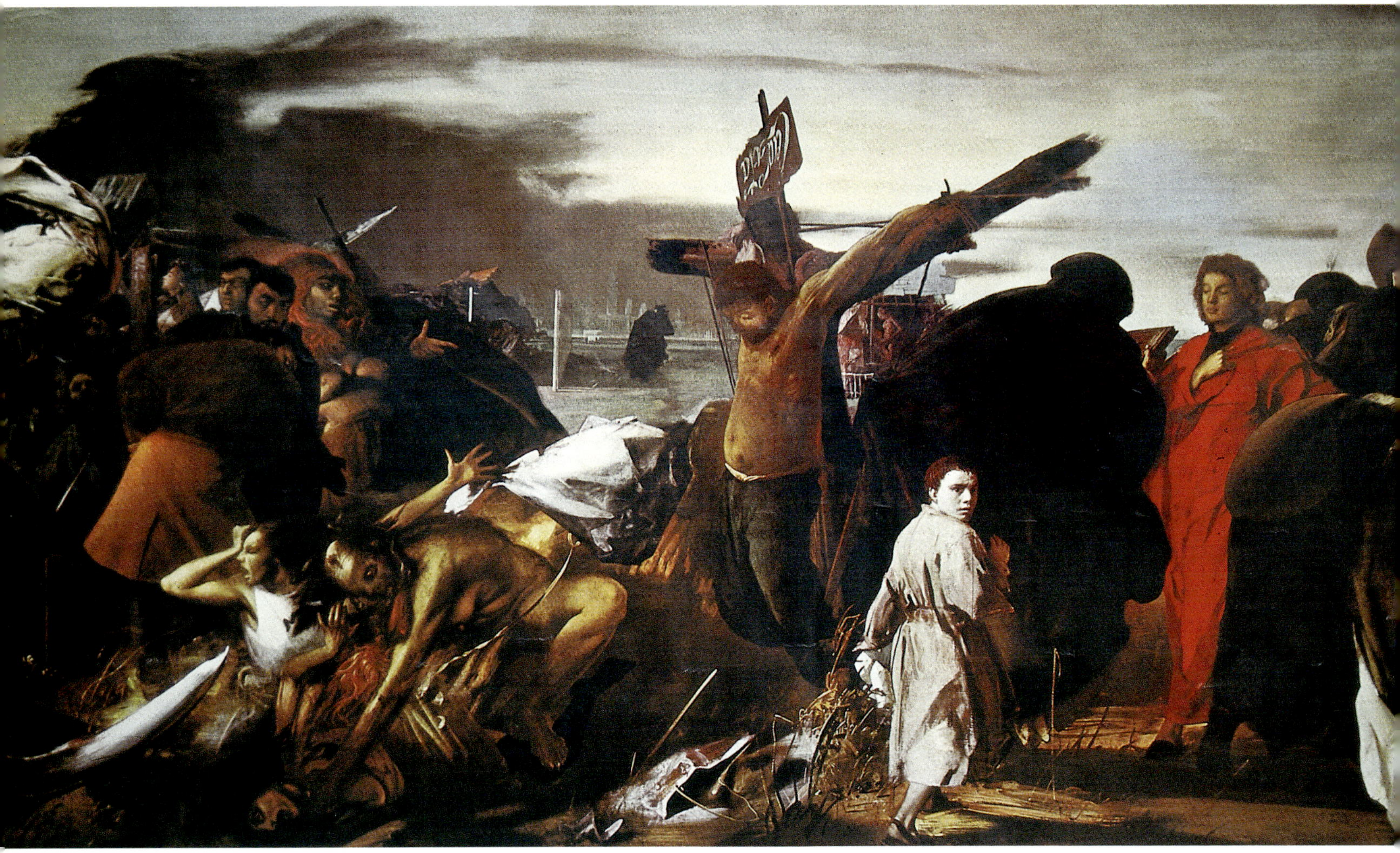

'Vita' at the Accademia D'Arte, Montecatini

This painting demands attention and analysis. It cannot be passed by without a strong reaction either of revulsion or depression. There are many questions to answer, many imponderables. On the far-distant gloom-laden horizon, for instance, a city of skyscrapers emerges from under a cloud of pollution, then fades and merges into a lighter and brighter prospect towards the east.

One morning, when Annigoni had been painting the martyred figure, the centrepiece of the subject, I came into the studio and noticed an addition from the previous day. Above the head on the rough wooden cross he had painted a battered metal sign on which was written an inscription in what appeared to be oriental calligraphy. 'Whatever does that say?' I asked.

'Can't you read Arabic?' he replied mockingly.

Still puzzled, I tried to interpret the connection between the title over the head of Christ at his crucifixion and these incomprehensible words. Annigoni told me to look at it upside down, which revealed the worldwide familiar logo of Coca Cola.

'Isn't that rather blasphemous?' I dared to comment.

'It is intended to be,' he replied. 'After all, what sign is more instantly recognized throughout the world. Remember this martyred figure is also being reviled.'

These words had a very sobering effect upon me.

I mentioned that I had modelled for one of the figures, that of a monstrous hermaphrodite with a grotesque head bending over and strangling a terrified woman. Posing for some time with arms outstretched and leaning towards the floor, I had no idea of the portrayal that was to face me the following morning. My bare back had been covered with black hairs, my head was almost bald and my skin was sickly green!

'Maestro, what *have* you done to me?' I asked in horror.

'I've turned you into a monster,' he said. And from then on he nicknamed me, albeit with tongue in cheek, 'Monster', which he said was a term of endearment.

In April 1961 Annigoni presented 'VITA' to the public in his first major one man show at The Federation of British Artists' gallery, then in Suffolk Street. He was generous enough to include the work of some of his past and present pupils. The eldest was an old Swiss friend and contemporary, Ponziano Togni, who was a superb draughtsman and exponent of pen and wash drawings very much in the style of Annigoni. Also showing were his three leading English pupils, Denis Ramsey, Douglas Anderson and Tim Whidbourne, and his first and only other woman pupil, Hungarian Zsuzsi Roboz. Only Tim Philips was absent. All these extremely talented painters were already establishing themselves professionally on their own but the mark of the master upon them was apparent. Included from the Italian school of the time were Fernando Bernardini, Romano Stefanelli and – the youngest – Antonio Ciccone. The American Nelson Holbrook White, a Simi pupil who became a close companion of Annigoni on many of his later travels to the States, and I completed the line-up which was photographed for the *Daily Express* on 27 April and described, not altogether accurately, as 'Annigoni Class of 1961' (four of us having already left the class).

Two years later 'VITA' was exhibited in aid of charity at Selfridges in London, where it occupied an entire window of the shop and drew enormous attention. At the time Annigoni was in the States, occupied with fresco painting at a private mansion near New York and with a portrait of the Governor of Massachusetts in Boston. I was living in London, in a small studio in Chelsea, where I was currently painting a commission.

Annigoni wrote to ask me to assist my colleague Romano, who was in charge of the handling and erection of 'VITA' – no mean task. The painting had to be removed from the stretcher and rolled like a carpet into a very heavy pack to be transported from Florence. This was relatively easy to do on the large floor of the studio, but it was a much more difficult task to unroll and erect. Moreover, this had to be done after closing time and with the window curtained off from the street. Several of us had to stretch the painting on the floor onto a wooden support and then erect it in the narrow window. Unrolling, stretching and mounting the painting was a difficult and lengthy job! I shall never forget that long evening into late night with Romano giving instructions in Italian, which I translated while helping with the enormous mounting operation under hot spotlights and in limited airless space.

Annigoni could not have had a greater public exhibition. The painting was seen by thousands of passers-by in Oxford Street, who crowded the pavement drawing attention to and raising funds for Oxfam, in aid of which it was exhibited. Later the painting went on exhibition in America, where it received some adverse criticism, probably due to the message it contained. It was then returned to Florence and put into store, which almost led to its destruction. In November 1966, when much of Florence was submerged under the flooding River Arno, which swept through the city in a huge wave causing widespread and enormous damage, the painting remained for several days in filthy water, mud, slime and other materials that had been stored with it. When the canvas was finally lifted out of all this sludge, it appeared to be in such a disastrous condition that it defied all prospects of restoration. The fine layer of Japanese paper fixed to the surface of the canvas, which held the material substance of the painting, had become detached from the underlying canvas and shrivelled into twisted pieces. Nevertheless the layer of colours had remained glued to the paper, due largely to the protective film of varnish applied upon completion.

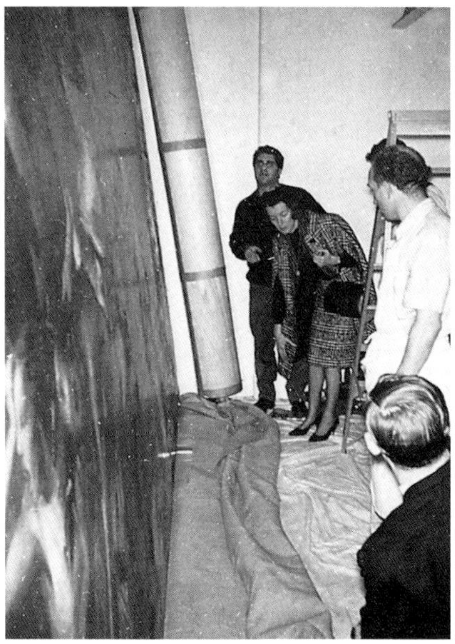

Erecting the large canvas of 'Vita' in the narrow space of a window in Selfridges store

Annigoni was working in New York at the time, while I was painting portraits in Cambridge, Massachusetts. On hearing the awful news bulletins on radio and television, I immediately telephoned him to see if his family and our colleagues and friends were safe. Fortunately, none of them had suffered personally, but Annigoni was greatly concerned for his beloved city and in constant touch with Riccardo Noferi and others for news of the disaster as the waters rose higher. The most unfortunate were those living near to the city centre, particularly those living on ground floors and in basements, where hundreds of craftsmen and artisans had their workshops and stores. Many lives were lost, especially among the poorest. Lifetimes of work, materials, tools and stocks were all washed away in the muddy, oily, polluted torrent which engulfed the city overnight, the waters rising in many places from four to six metres. For us, so far away across the Atlantic, it seemed unimaginable and we felt utterly helpless and constantly anxious.

After the floods had receded, the painting was retrieved, and with careful cleaning, drying out and pressing was miraculously restored. Thousands of other works of art had to be salvaged in galleries and museums including the National Library and underwent arduous and painstaking restoration. Major damage was suffered to paintings, sculpture, books and ancient manuscripts not only from water but – even worse – from the many oily substances, such as paraffin and

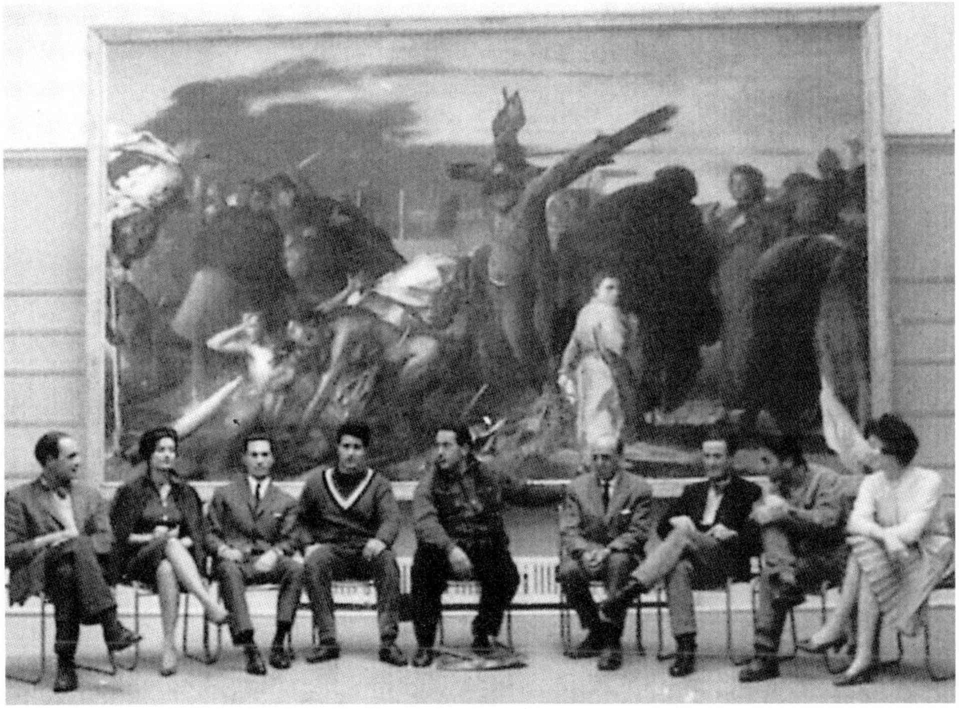

Past and present pupils at the exhibition of 'Vita' at the Federation of British Artists Gallery, Suffolk Street, London. April 1961

kerosene, which leaked from heating installations and floated on the water.

Thanks to hundreds of volunteers (students from far and wide and the indomitable Florentines), the local services (police and army) and anyone able-bodied who could help in the mammoth months-long cleaning up operation, Florence was eventually restored, albeit with the loss of many irreplaceable treasures, to its former glory. I only wished I had been able to join in the restoration of the city to which I owed so much.

Sunday painting around Massaciuccoli

Some of the greatest pleasures for me were the Sunday trips to the lake of Massaciucoli on which I was frequently invited along with a few colleagues and always Riccardo. We joined Annigoni on his boat *Onda Seconda*, on which there was just about enough space for five painters to work on the ideal subjects surrounding this quiet and beautiful lake just inland from Viareggio on the coast. Except for the villa where Puccini lived and composed much of his wonderful music, the lake had not at that time been exploited as a tourist venue but was remote and isolated, a haven of peace and an escape from humanity. There was a haze of blue mountains on one side, reminiscent of certain areas of Scotland, and quiet lagoons and canals leading towards the sea. Fishermen's huts were the only buildings, and fishing nets extended across

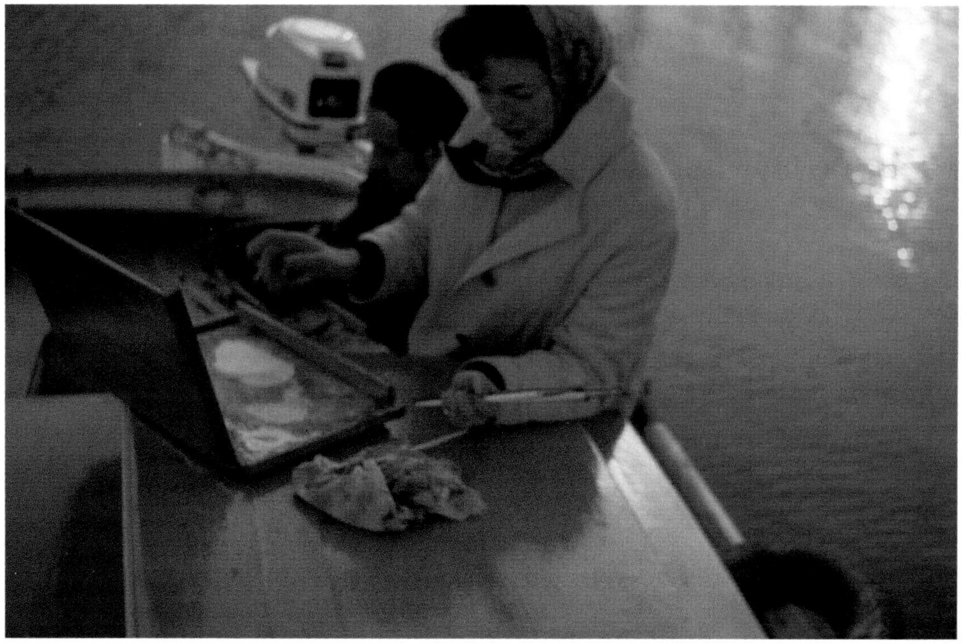

Painting with Annigoni 'on board'

the narrow reed-lined inlets. The only noises to break the silence came from the wildlife in the reeds.

The lake could be reached conveniently only with a car, which Annigoni did not possess. So we had to rise very early to be at Florence railway station soon after seven a.m. to catch the first train to Pisa. From there we went on by taxi. The meeting place was always at the station buffet, with strict instructions to be punctual.

During the winter months it was a cold start at that early hour, and on an empty stomach, so strong black coffee came first, to wake us up, followed by a quick shot of grappa to warm us up. I protested that I could not drink spirits at that hour but was over-ruled by the Maestro, who told me to 'drink up and shut up'. As if I was taking medicine, I gulped the fiery liquid in one go. It shot almost straight to my feet as I gasped for breath and pleaded for a cappuccino to modify it, much to the amusement of the men. We boarded the train, well-insulated against the cold morning air, for the one-hour train journey to Pisa. Our destination was Torre del Lago, where the boat was moored. On these early February-into-March mornings, with a nip of frost in the cold clean air and mist rising from the water, there was such peace and solitude that only the little outboard motor of the boat broke the silence as we glided quietly up the narrow inlets and the sun rose into a clear blue sky. The tall yellow reeds and bullrushes quivered with the unseen movements of reed warblers, moor hens and ducks breaking cover as we disturbed them. The stark and as yet leafless trees already showed signs of the advent of spring, their branches glowing a deep yellow ochre against the almost transparent sky.

When we had found a suitable anchorage and the engine was turned off, the only sounds were of nature: the ripple of water, the rustling of reeds and birdsong. No one spoke. Each of us was lost in concentration, trying to capture in paint some of the beauty all around us before the sun rose too high and bright in the sky dispelling that magic light that filtered through the early haze. We had to work quickly as the light and shadows changed almost imperceptibly.

The combination of effort, concentration and sitting still for several hours induced a ravenous appetite – unassuaged since the early morning espresso and grappa, hardly an adequate breakfast to work on. We were all ready for lunch at the only trattoria on the lake, Il Cavaliere, a simple rustic and unpretentious inn frequented mostly by fishermen and a few locals. Here Annigoni used a small private room, where a delicious and abundant meal was prepared and served for us by the proprietor. This was accompanied by far too much wine – as far as I was concerned. The two-and-a-half-litre *fiasco* of good Tuscan wine always arrived first, with baskets of crusty *pane di campagna*. It was thirstily consumed together with the *antipasti* of home-made *crostini* soaked in good stock and piled with sautéed chicken livers and capers (a piquant introduction to the first course) and steaming hot pasta shining with local olive oil, with home-made tomato sauce and dusted with freshly grated parmesan. That was a meal in itself, but then came the dish of the day, and if there was any room left afterwards, cheese and fruit and – absolutely essential – strong black coffee.

Often we were joined there by other close friends: Else and Bodil and Annigoni's son Benedetto with his young friends. He was and still is physically, vocally and intellectually the image of his father. There was a strong bond of affection between them and they both enjoyed discussing politics, arguing volubly and with passion. They also shared a deep love of the countryside, fishing and sailing and boar hunting. Although Benedetto did not follow his father's profession, he was a gifted draughtsman and I remember his talent for painting animals. He also seemed to have a predilection for teasing me in particular, always referring to me as *la perfida albione – tipicamente inglese* (the perfidious Albion, typically English).

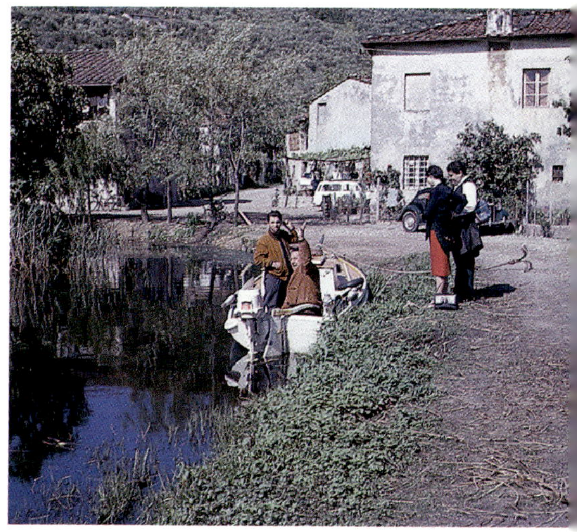

Moored for lunch at Massaciuccoli

One had to have a robust physical constitution and a quick response to keep pace with all these men, especially as I was frequently the only female in the company. On one occasion I noted in my diary:

> We had eaten and drunk too well and while they were all talking to each other, the air heavy with argument and smoke, I was nearly falling asleep (a result of the wine), so I slipped away from the table unnoticed to look for the *toeletta*. I tried every door upstairs, one of which opened into a bedroom, cool and shaded from the by-now hot sun with semi-closed shutters. There was an enormous bed with brass bedstead and feather-filled quilt. This I simply could not resist. I was longing for a nap and, as no one appeared to be around upstairs, I just dropped onto it in a postprandial stupor and must have fallen asleep within minutes. Equally

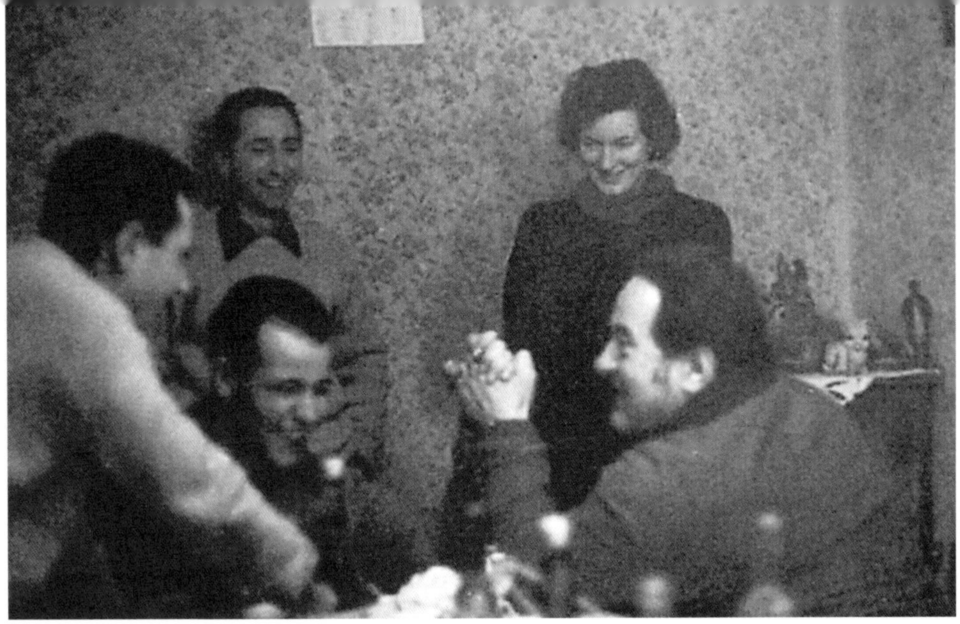

Right: Annigoni and Benedetto testing their strength

Below: Another enjoyable lunch

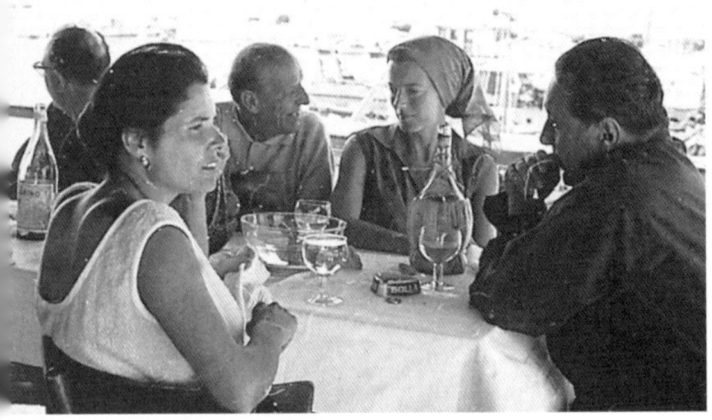

suddenly I awoke, wondering where I was and, looking at my watch, saw that it was nearly four p.m. I hastily tidied the bed linen and looked cautiously out into the corridor. Fortunately no one was to be seen. I hastened downstairs towards the dining-room from which I could hear the sound of a noisy discussion still in full spate. I had not even been missed and was not noticed until Annigoni announced that it was high time to get back to work again. 'Wake up, Dawn. You look half asleep,' he said. And I was.

It was almost approaching the magical hour before sunset – the best time of day for painting. Everywhere was bathed in mellow golden light, the sun a glowing tangerine ball shimmering on the surface of the luminescent water. I was transfixed, wondering how to transfer this rapidly fading image onto canvas. Annigoni was already working rapidly with bold brush strokes of colour, Romano bent over his canvas at the water's edge, Riccardo likewise, while I struggled to produce a few flashes of colour, feeling frustrated and inadequate. I suddenly felt two hands on my shoulders. The Maestro leaning over me said, 'The most important thing is to see, understand and remember, then slowly, with persistence, you will learn. Nothing worthwhile comes easily.' And with a pat on my head he repeated, *'Forza e coraggio!'* By the time we had packed up all our clutter dusk was falling, the boat had to be returned to its mooring and we had to crowd into someone's car to drive to Viareggio for supper. Despite my afternoon siesta, as a result of the combination of wine, the almost-sea air and the long day, all I felt like was cornflakes, milk, a bath and bed, but that was wishful thinking. The Garibaldini, a renowned fish restaurant on the sea front at Viareggio, awaited us. By this time I had been woken up by the tempting smell of *zuppa di pesce* and another substantial meal for those who could manage it. At least we could not linger over this one as our last train departed soon after 10 p.m., and that meant home by midnight with any luck.

Restful Sundays

On other Sundays it was pleasant to remain in the city, then devoid of shoppers; with the exception of the famous covered market in the centre of town, almost everything was closed. The streets were quieter and less crowded. People dressed smartly, especially the children going to mass. They then bought mouth-watering cakes and pastries from the patisseries to take home for lunch or went out into the countryside or to the nearby coastal resorts for a meal al fresco. So the city almost emptied by day and only the bars, newspaper vendors and florists did any trade. A man regularly passed my apartment in the Via Condotta calling out, '*Garofani!*' his handcart loaded with carnations. Bells rang throughout the city from every church, dominated by the deep tones of the basilicas. It was different. A wonderful day for relaxing, letter writing, visiting museums or friends and going to church.

I had another unusual encounter at the Anglican church of St Mark's in Via Maggio. I became a fairly regular attender at this high church which was the bastion of English residents. The early Holy Communion service had already started and I was kneeling in prayer when I felt a light tap on my shoulder. Looking up in surprise I was confronted by an Edwardian vision who reminded me of Martita Hunt, the British actress who played Miss Haversham in the film *Great Expectations*. Tall, refined, with aristocratic features and a pronounced aquiline nose, she wore an enormous cushion-like hat from which a veil covered her heavily made up face. She was clothed entirely in black from head to foot. After tapping my shoulder with a long ebony walking stick, she gave me to understand that I was occupying her pew and with a peremptory gesture indicated that I should vacate it. I duly obeyed but was intrigued by this theatrical performance, and by the diminutive elderly figure, presumably the lady's maid, who hovered behind her, producing a rug to wrap around her lap, moving a hassock for her feet and then scurrying back down the aisle to attend her departure.

At the end of the service it was customary for the congregation of regulars to collect at the back of the church to chat among themselves and with the vicar. I hardly knew anyone there, and so after shaking hands with the vicar I prepared to make my way out. As I did so this spectre of another era approached me and said, 'You must forgive my asking you to vacate your seat, but you see you were occupying *my* pew.' Then she added, 'Do I know you? I think not.' Before I could reply she informed me with emphasis, 'I am Violet Trefusis and *who* are you?'

After that famous name I felt like saying 'nobody in particular', but I politely told her my name.

'And what are you doing in Florence?' she persisted, with such authority that I felt I had to justify my presence. I told her I was studying painting with Annigoni. At this her imperious attitude changed immediately, as if I had said

I had been presented at court.

'You must be very good to be one of his pupils,' she said, and with that remark bade me good morning, making a perfect stage exit, her maid hovering behind her rattling a chatelaine of keys from her waist while carrying the rug and an umbrella to cover her mistress as she walked down the two steps from the entrance hall to the street. After nodding graciously to the vicar she swept out of the church and straight into an elderly Rolls Royce where a uniformed chauffeur of equal age opened the car door, letting down a little retractable step for her to climb into the back behind a glass partition. Her maid tucked the rug around her before joining the chauffeur in the front, and the extraordinary trio set off in style for her villa at Settignano in the hills above Florence. It was a little vignette of another age. Her regal bearing, bizarre attire and patrician features intrigued me.

Then on another Sunday, giving her pew a wide berth, I met her again, at the end of the service. This time she greeted me very courteously, extending her gloved hand as if to be kissed rather than shaken. She asked me if I liked music and poetry and before giving me time to answer mentioned her friend Edith Sitwell who gave poetry readings at private soirées, such as the Heber-Percys' and those of other notable English families resident in Florence. She said she would be delighted to see me on one of these occasions. I muttered some polite expression of appreciation and anticipation. Then, to my surprise, she added, 'Did you notice the brass memorial plaque on the pillar at the end of my pew?'

In fact I had, for the dedication particularly appealed to me. It read, 'To my own beloved mother, Alice Keppell, my guide, companion and own particular friend.' It was then that I realized her famous mother was Edward VII's last and most loved mistress and that she could have been their offspring. She bore a striking resemblance to the King.

In later years this fascinating and eccentric woman was to gain great notoriety for the love affair she had in her youth with Vita Sackville-West. To my great disappointment the suggested invitation never materialized, and I saw her very rarely afterwards, and then only at St Mark's church. Her health was failing and she died on 29 February 1972 following a crippling accident and a long exhausting illness. She had lived a colourful life in France, England and Italy – her final resting place. Cosmopolitan, a gifted linguist of high intellect and spontaneous wit, she was one of the last great Edwardians. I am glad to have had that brief but memorable encounter. Long after her death I read her fascinating autobiography with added interest. She was one of the great personalities of her era.

Events in and out of the Studio recorded in my diary of 1962

After spending Christmas at home in England, I returned to Florence early in January to continue my second large still-life composition in the little annexe, the only word to describe the small extrusion on the outer wall of Annigoni's studio where I had been painting since the previous autumn. It was lined on either side with deep shelves set into the walls. These were filled with old books and manuscripts and bottles of varnish and ink, all covered with dust and hardly ever touched. They had always struck me as a still-life waiting to be painted and, since there was just enough space for one person and an easel, I claimed it. At my back was a large window, very cold and draughty, a perfect still-life to the left side and to the front an overall view into the studio which enabled me to watch whatever work was in progress on Annigoni's easel. I had instructed Annibale not to touch anything on the shelves while I was away at Christmas (he occasionally had the urge to flick round the studio with his feather duster). I wanted the accumulated dust of years to remain, so I left a note on my easel saying 'not to be moved or dusted'.

I was happy to be back again and to find Nando, his friend Giovanna and Ponziano Togni all working in different parts of the studio and kitchen where colours were frequently prepared.

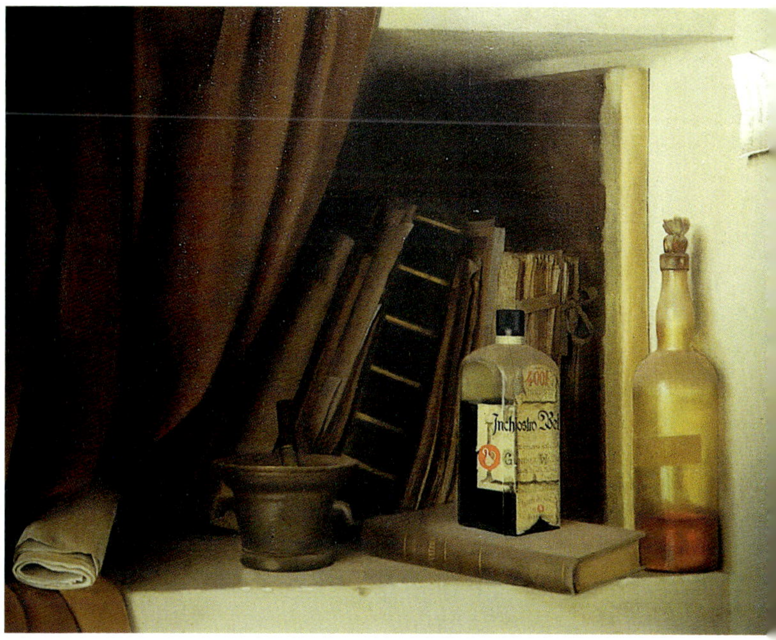

Still-life painting of studio

On 30 January Annigoni had had a pile of letters for me to answer during the evening. He was going boar hunting for a day with Benedetto and urged me to have the correspondence ready for his approval next morning. That morning there was no sign of him, but more letters had been left for me to attend to. There was also a surprise for me, a commission to paint Lady Serena Remnant, the outcome of her seeing my self-portrait at the Royal Society of Portrait Painters' exhibition.

On 6 February despite a persistent cold and headache I went over to collect one of Annigoni's oldest friends, an old and very impoverished German, Adolf Koshland, who lived alone in a seedy lodging in the San Frediano district. He was an incessant talker, rambling on about minutiae until he became boring, but loving an audience. I walked him very slowly to a supper party at Angiolino's given by Annigoni in honour of Romano's newly completed fresco painting there. Annigoni was a very loyal friend to this poor and now fragile and almost blind Jewish emigré. Koshland relished these opportunities to eat and drink and most of all talk in convivial company. He was a rather pitiful character, pale and gaunt in his large, floppy, battered, grey fedora and food-stained suit. Because he was so loquacious the meal took ages. I got home at one a.m.

I missed two days at the studio with a feverish cold, much to my annoyance, but when I returned Annigoni was full of kind solicitude and Annibale had even placed a little electric heater in my chilly 'window box'.

Annigoni was in London for the rest of February, during which time there was a lot of mail to deal with. He returned on 3 March, bringing me some fine sable brushes as a much appreciated gift. Julian Barrow, a tall and talented young English painter, had joined the pupils here and at the Simi studio. His forte was landscape and buildings and he produced some excellent oil paintings of the city and surrounding countryside, which he sold easily and for far too little, mainly to the local bars and trattorias and sometimes in return for meals. The buyers made a good profit at his expense. Annigoni said he painted Italian scenes like a neo-Constable. He certainly captured the atmosphere and sense of place. I possess two of his delightful paintings of familiar piazzas of the city. I felt sure he would become a very successful painter.

On 14 March I awoke to snow falling, a rare sight in Florence, especially in this month, and an icy penetrating wind. The studio was even colder, but Annigoni never felt it. Nando, Julian, Antonio, Togni and I had pooled our resources for a model to pose for us in the attic – poor girl! But the pressure of numbers and a bucketful of glowing cinders from the big stove in the studio helped to raise the temperature slightly. After this I needed a hot lunch at nearby Frizzi's – actually offered free in return for a translation.

On 16 March I went to the studio at 5.30 p.m. at Annigoni's request to start sorting out the chaos of paperwork accumulating in his study. This had to be done while he was away in Milano. It took me three-and-a-half hours to sort out and file, and next morning my 'spring clean' continued until a semblance of order and space was achieved – with some satisfaction on my part, and I hope eventually also on his.

On Sunday 18 March there were more letters to be answered, including one from the Rand Club in Cape Town, for which Antonio had made a copy of Annigoni's portrait of the Queen. Complaints had been sent about blemishes appearing on the painting, which was returned by air to Florence at considerable expense. Evidently none of the local art restorers knew enough about tempera to recognize the cause or the cure. When Annigoni returned he examined the painting. All that seemed apparent was an accumulation of dust and smoke fumes that had settled on the surface and which, together with the heat of a strong spot-light directed onto the picture, had adhered the dirt to the varnish. The painting was laid flat on the studio floor and cleaned carefully, inch by inch, with a sponge and pure soap and water solution, leaving the surface in its original pristine condition. 'Thank God the restorers over there have not attempted to remove the varnish, and with it possibly some of the glazes underneath!' Annigoni remarked. He was always angered by the drastic over-cleaning sometimes carried out in art galleries worldwide today which removes with the varnish the delicate final glazes intended by the artist.

It was a long and expensive journey for a spring clean but a happy return to Cape Town, with a caution about smoke and dust, and the advice that the painting should be put behind glass for maximum protection.

Two copies of the Queen's portrait were painted: one for the British Embassy in Rome by Annigoni's first pupil, Luciano Guarnieri, and another for the Star and Garter Home in London by his then pupil Romano Stefanelli. These were quite onerous commitments which were both identically executed to Annigoni's demanding standard. Annigoni and the senior pupils went to Milano to prepare for his exhibition there, while peace and quiet helped me to concentrate on my own painting. In the afternoons I was drawing several portraits, including one of Annigoni's attractive young niece Emanuella Torriani, a ballerina.

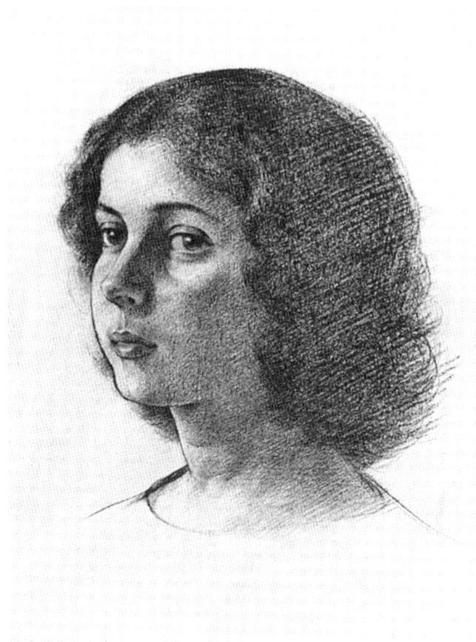

My drawing of Annigoni's niece, Emanuella Torriani

On 24 March the studio came to life again. Annigoni and company returned. He seemed pleased with my efforts in his study and invited me to go to Massaciuccoli again tomorrow. Great! A busy week ahead in the studio, plus my private commissions and more secretarial duties.

On 20 April Annigoni's life-size Madonna, painted for the church of the Claretian Fathers in Hayes, Middlesex, was detached from the support and rolled, ready to be dispatched by air to London. It was fascinating to watch the development of this painting of the Madonna of the Immaculate Heart of Mary (310 x 540 cm), which was started in 1961. The standing figure, robed in white with a voluminous blue and red shawl framing her head and body, has a strong Italianate face whose expression foretells the tragedy that is to befall the Holy Child cradled in the crook of her right arm, leaning against her breast. Her left arm and hand turn inward, pointing to her heart, which will suffer and finally break only 33 years later. The painting is full of symbolism and prophecy. Signifying the destruction of evil, one sandalled foot crushes a viper on the severed branch of a tree on which it rests, while from that same branch new life emerges as young green shoots springing out of the bark. In the bottom corner a white dove is about to alight on the earth, bringing peace to the world. The figure of the Madonna is encircled with flames of shimmering gold and silver leaf burnished onto the background, which add luminosity to the painting. In the low-lying far distance on one side, alluding to the reality of modern life and the industrial area around Hayes, a factory is under construction, surrounded by scaffolding and a crane – so subtly defined and unobtrusive that it in no way detracts from the dominant figure of the Madonna, who transcends time and place.

This picture started with a life model holding a weighted doll. Then a miniature clay model was made and clothed, from which the life-size painting evolved. The final addition was the dove alighting. To paint a dove in flight was difficult, even for a quick sketch. Florence is alive with pigeons,

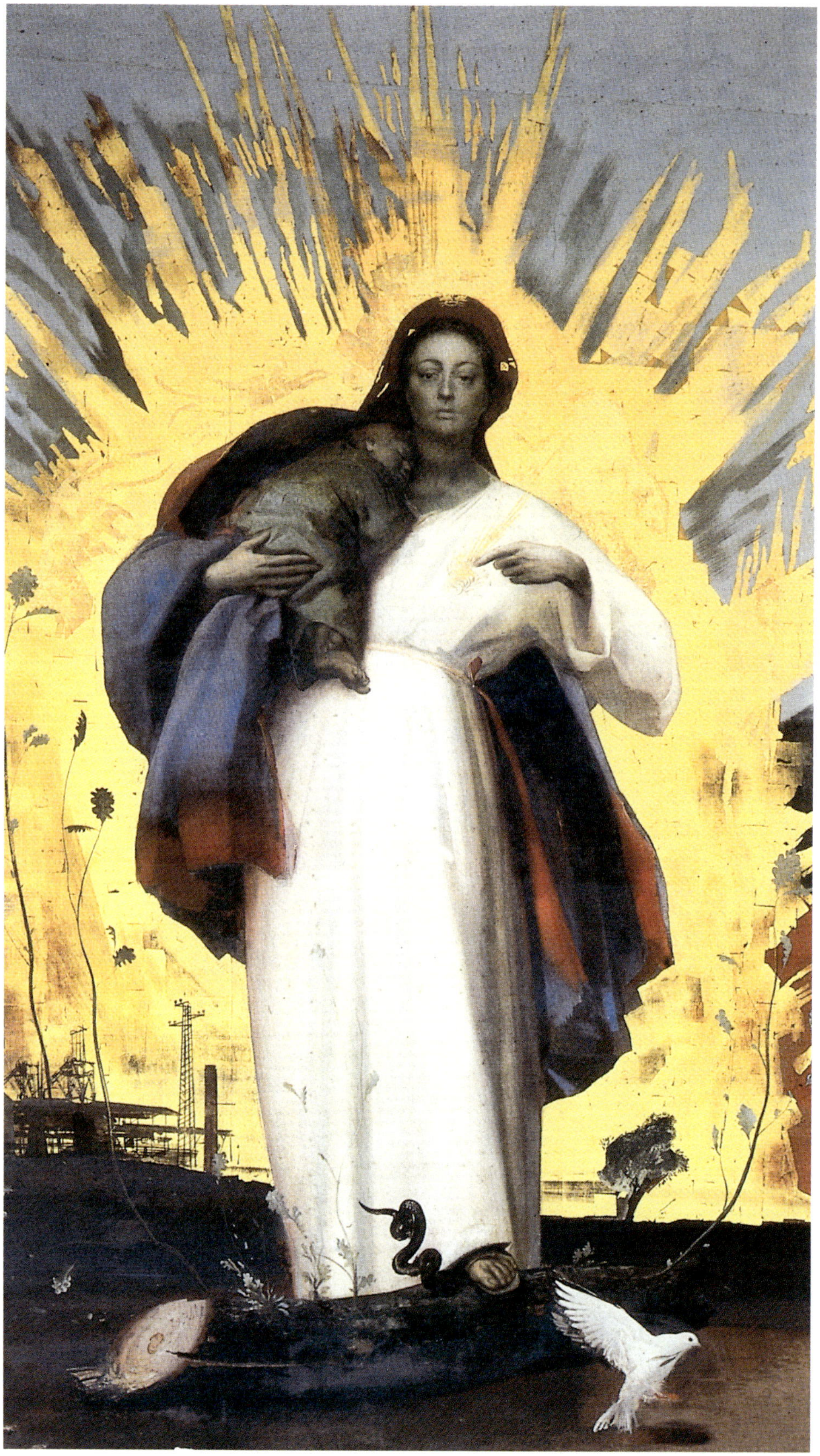

The Madonna of the Immaculate Heart of Mary (1961-62)

nesting and perching everywhere on roof tops. When the shutters are opened they appear from nowhere in a flurry of feathers and take off from every nook and cranny into the air. My task one morning was to continually open and close one of the studio windows, making as much noise as possible. Meanwhile Annigoni was ready with his sketch book to draw the pigeons as they landed – unfortunately, not always when, where or how he wanted. It took some time and patience for him to catch one in action. The pigeon was transformed into a dove and was the only other significant note of pure white in this striking painting

Talking of doves reminds me of a special Florentine custom on Easter Sunday. 22 April that year was a very hot day. A large crowd had gathered in the Piazza del Duomo to watch the traditional *scoppio del carro* (explosion of a wagon laden with fireworks). At the stroke of noon the wagon is set alight. This can be quite a hazardous operation when it works; however, for the second year running, this Easter Sunday it did not, much to everyone's disappointment. I have never understood the true significance of this custom and much preferred the, to me, more appropriate tradition of freeing dozens of caged doves into the sky – a portent of peace worldwide and a joyful and natural spectacle – accompanied by the ringing of bells all over the city proclaiming the risen Christ.

La colomba (the dove) is also represented as a traditional cake baked in the shape of the bird. The cake is synonymous with Easter, just as the famous panettone is synonymous with Christmas.

Annigoni Abroad

Annigoni was at that time painting many notable portrait commissions, particularly for the American *Time Magazine*. Of these, the most controversial was of John F. Kennedy. He was also the most difficult and tedious of sitters, stretching Annigoni's patience to the limit. He did not even give Annigoni private sittings; the artist had to join presidential press conferences, at the back of a crowded office filled with officials. Secretaries came and went and the horde of reporters and photographers waited outside in the corridors of the White House to pounce. Under such impossible conditions all Annigoni could hope to obtain were sketches in charcoal and sanguine drawn from the occasional glimpse of Kennedy momentarily static while he read, wrote or dictated to his secretary. Very occasionally he looked up. Despite these trying and exasperating circumstances, Annigoni managed to produce a portrait of what he saw as a man under great stress, his heavy-lidded eyes swollen with fatigue and his tie askew.

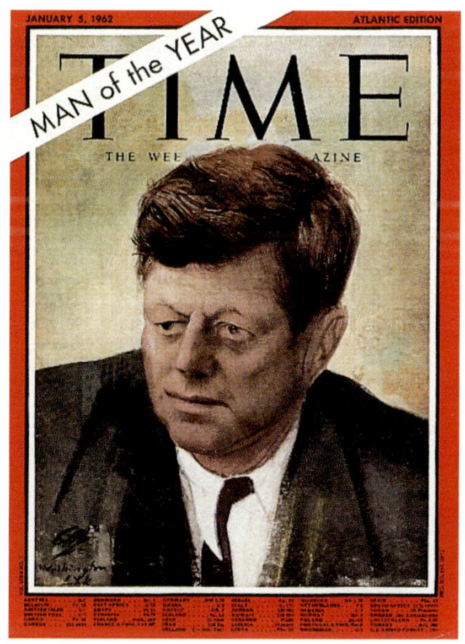

John F. Kennedy for *Time Magazine*

This rendering received very mixed comments in the barrage of letters to the editor of *Time Magazine* and to himself. These were equally divided between the enthusiastic and the appalled. One particular letter which arrived in Florence he passed on to me to answer. It was from the mother superior of an order of nuns somewhere in the United States, expressing outrage at the President being depicted as 'a weary and oppressed man', when he 'would never have been seen with his necktie out of place and his hair dishevelled'.

'Considering the burden of responsibility on his shoulders, it was a wonder that this tragically ill-fated man did not appear with six heads,' was Annigoni's comment.

I did my best tactfully to explain to the mother superior the exceptional circumstances under which Annigoni had had to work and the heavy burden of responsibility that the President had to bear, which obviously showed clearly in his expression. Despite the controversy that this second drawing had aroused, it was the one selected from three by Kennedy himself, but it was not printed until some time later.

Apparently, the editor was not at all displeased as there followed a further commission in June 1962 for a portrait of Pope John XXIII, yet another difficult sitter, either talking non-stop or falling asleep. Nevertheless, there was a rapport between him and Annigoni as well as a common language. The Pope approved of the profile portrait, which, in fact, had captured his strong and fulsome face perfectly, especially the extra large and fleshy ears for which in his youth as a seminarist he came to be nicknamed 'the elephant' by his contemporaries. The Pope recounted this story with amusement and gave his general approbation of the portrait. Annigoni found him a bad model but a truly saintly man, emanating a gentle serenity despite his physical suffering and the heavy load of his office.

Further *Time Magazine* covers were to follow: Chancellor Ludwig Erhard of Germany in 1963 and later that year the American-born Italian, Governor Volpe of Massachusetts, whom Annigoni liked immensely. He was a congenial and intelligent man whom he enjoyed painting, unlike the German Chancellor or the later American president, Lyndon Johnson (painted by Annigoni in 1964), who were difficult subjects. Prime Minister Harold Wilson was amiable and gave no problems, despite giving Annigoni only a one-hour sitting at Number 10. Shortly after this the Kennedy portrait appeared on the cover of *Time Magazine*, appropriately timed to follow the terrible assassination that shook the entire world. These few portraits proved to those who had categorized Annigoni as a painter of royalty and beautiful women that he was an equally accomplished painter of men of character.

More sittings with the Duke of Edinburgh (15.6.62)

An old friend of my family who was then on the board of directors of the Automobile Association had asked me if Annigoni would be prepared to paint another portrait of the Duke of Edinburgh, who was at that time their president, adding that they had only limited resources for the commission. This request was received with a wry smile by Annigoni, who realized what they were after. Moreover, he was not particularly enthusiastic about tackling the Duke again so soon after the commission from the Worshipful Company of Fishmongers. The AA board had ideas of a casual portrait, with the Duke leaning against his Lagonda sports car. Annigoni had other ideas. As the Duke had already agreed in advance to 10 sittings Annigoni decided to proceed with this idea of his own.

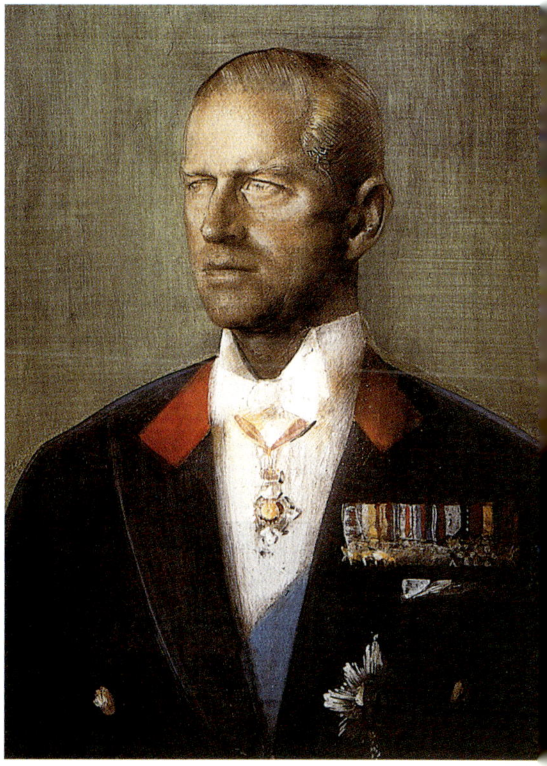

This time the sittings were not to take place at Buckingham Palace in the yellow drawing-room but at Windsor Castle. Here, between sittings, the Duke personally drove Annigoni around the Great Park, and a much more informal and relaxed atmosphere prevailed. The preliminary drawings in the usual mixed media so delighted the Duke that he asked him if he would paint the portrait for the family, as a private commission, depicting the Duke in what he referred to as 'the Windsor uniform', full dress-coat of blue with scarlet collar and cuffs, and brass buttons, medals and orders. With the drawings for reference, Annigoni returned to Florence and decided to paint the portrait as a fresco, an unusual decision, involving the heavy material of plaster on tile, and the complicated procedure of transposing the thin layer of painting onto canvas for easier transportation to England. He thought it would be different from all the other royal portraits, and probably unique. I found it fascinating to watch him at work.

Annigoni – the man and his family

Annigoni was a man of contrasting emotions. He possessed a wicked sense of humour and, when in the mood, would often indulge in crazy practical jokes. Once someone produced a miniature toy cannon from somewhere or other. This so intrigued him that nothing would suffice until he and Romano, like young boys with a new toy, had gone up onto the roof terrace with some gunpowder to see if it worked. Suddenly an enormous explosion came from above and all the pigeons in the neighbourhood took flight, while shutters were opened and anxious heads appeared.

He enjoyed and could tell a good joke, but he could equally easily explode in rage, as he did when protesting against the export of great works of art for

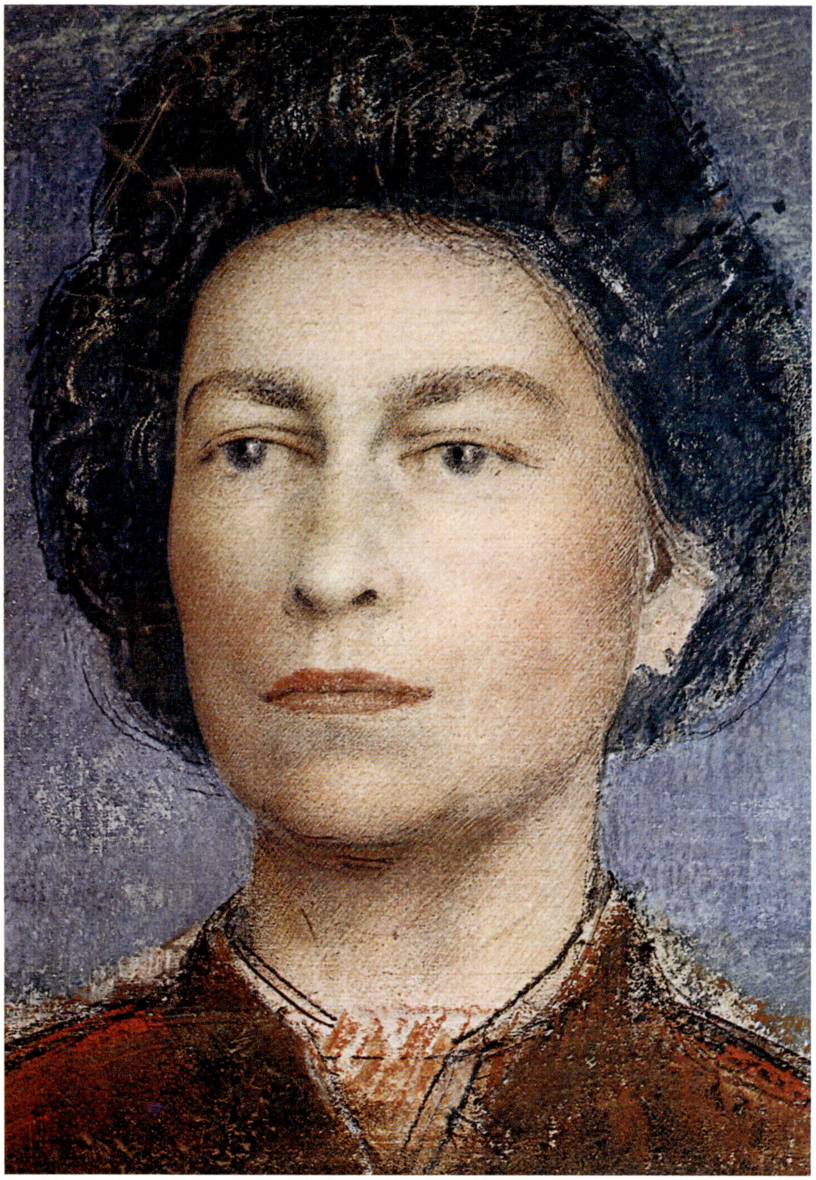

Study for the second portrait of HM The Queen in mixed media

exhibition in other countries, risking damage in transit and through atmospheric changes. He felt so strongly about this that he made a public demonstration by climbing up inside the tower of the Palazzo Vecchio, where he and some colleagues decided to lock themselves in, saying they would not come down until the authorities of the Fine Arts Department of the local government took notice of their protest. There they remained resolute, while friends sent up food and wine to sustain them overnight. These had to be hauled up in baskets with ropes. The protest certainly caught the imagination of the public and the attention of the press – even more so later in court when Annigoni called the mayor a 'buffoon' and was charged with contempt of court and forced to apologize. Ironically, on that same day – celebrating St Columbus (when America honours an Italian) – it happened to be Annigoni who was chosen!

There was a limit to Annigoni's tolerance, which would often snap when his patience was overstretched. Maybe that was a safety valve, for he seldom let down the self-imposed barrier that defended him from any unwanted approach. Being a fellow Gemini (with only a few days between our birthdays), I can well understand much of his complex character. He was deeply thoughtful, highly sensitive, often extremely lonely, single-minded, uncompromising, dedicated and also prophetic, as the painting 'Vita' demonstrates. This disturbing vision of life in the 1960s is even more relevant today.

In his second portrait of the Queen, commissioned for the National Portrait Gallery in London 15 years after the first, Annigoni painted a very different and controversial version of Her Majesty. Following the same procedure as for the Iranian portraits, he made a detailed study in pastel and, given a limited number of sittings at Buckingham Palace, returned to Florence to execute the almost full-length portrait.

This time he depicted the Queen standing against a very sombre, empty and storm-foreboding sky. He said he wanted to convey a sense of solitude and isolation. No concessions were made. The face wore a fixed and almost stern expression, uncompromising and unflattering. This time the Queen wore a dark ruby-red cape bearing the insignia of the Order of the British Empire. It was severe and in complete contrast to the earlier more romantic one. He talked about it frankly, and I remarked on the Queen's very set and impenetrable expression, to which he replied, 'Your Queen is a very lonely figure. When I first painted her she was a young woman on the threshold of a new and promising Elizabethan age (that portrait was often described as "chocolate boxy" because it was too realistic). I now see her as an isolated monarch facing a very uncertain future.'

Those prophetic words describe the situation that was to come about 30 years later.

One might have expected Annigoni to be gregarious and extrovert. On the contrary, he preferred the intimate company of his proven friends, to whom he remained loyal. I for one experienced this loyalty daily in the studio and by his frequent invitations to join his company for meals and on local painting excursions, yet inwardly, he was a man of solitude and often sadness, unable or unwilling to adjust to the changing world around him. Despite, or maybe because of, a broken marriage of over 20 years, he was devoted to his two children, his son Benedetto and daughter Maria Ricciarda.

He suffered three personal and profound bereavements. The first was the death of his father, during the terrible war years when Florence was bombarded and when no undertakers were functioning in the city, he was obliged to carry the body on a handcart to be buried. On 2 February 1968, his closest and oldest friend and companion, Riccardo Noferi, died instantly in a tragic motor accident in which Annigoni himself lost an ear. On 14 August

1969, following a long and fatal illness which affected Annigoni deeply, his estranged wife Anna also died. These deaths left deep emotional wounds and an irreparable sense of loss. Only his painting, into which he threw himself with even greater intensity, helped him to continue on his long and solitary road.

When my own father was slowly dying from cancer in that same fateful year of 1969, Annigoni found time to write me letters of sympathy and encouragement when I was at my lowest ebb. My mother died the following year. Nearly four years of my life were devoted to nursing my parents, without a break and with no time or energy left for painting, much less for returning to Florence. He understood my predicament and in writing gave me some hope during those terrible and seemingly hopeless years.

For Annigoni, some light returned to life when on one of many trans-Atlantic sea crossings he met a beautiful young Italian fashion model to whom he was immediately attracted. Her name was Rossella Segreto, and she became his close companion as their friendship and love deepened. After three years of meetings, travels and correspondence she eventually joined him in Florence. They had been together for seven years when they married on 29 January 1976.

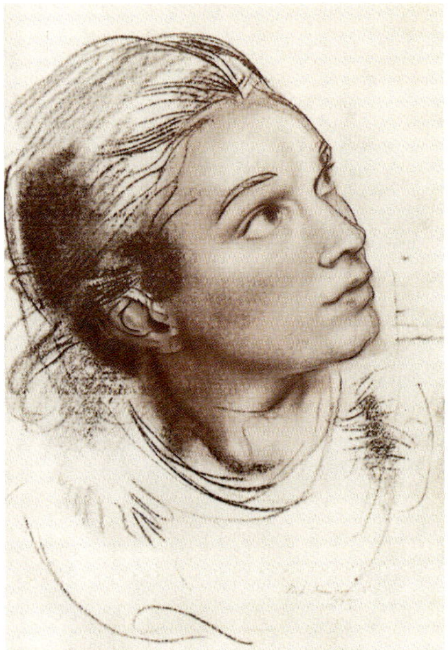

One of Annigoni's many studies of Rossella

Rossella was already his preferred and most painted model at that time, and had abandoned her career in fashion modelling to study for a degree in Biology at the University of Florence. She was also taking more and more interest in his fresco painting with which she was often able to assist him in later years. She modelled for many of the large religious frescos to which Annigoni devoted the last 11 years of his life. She was at his side throughout the painting of the huge fresco of the deposition and resurrection of Christ at the church of Ponte a Buggianese, a mammoth work, all of it done on scaffolding, from which on one occasion the ladder slipped and Annigoni fell heavily onto the stone floor. Being a man of some substance it was a miracle that he escaped any more serious injury than a torn ligament, but that alone (exacerbated by shock) caused him considerable pain and hampered his progress. He had fallen once on a previous occasion and was beginning to feel accident prone. Rossella was always at his side to support, comfort and care for him. In September of 1975, his great 'Last Supper' behind the altar of the same church was unveiled and consecrated by the Bishop of Pescia before a huge congregation of local inhabitants, friends and followers, and including former Prime Minister Fanfani. Outside a big crowd of well-wishers and press photographers waited. It was not surprising that Annigoni and Rossella chose this place for their quiet private marriage in a small civil ceremony conducted by the Mayor at the town hall a year later. Rossella brought Annigoni joy, love, companionship and a more ordered domestic life after the bohemian years of living alone in his studio and eating mostly in restaurants. They moved to an elegant apartment where there was peace, comfort, regular meals and a more tranquil private life to benefit his later years.

From London back to Florence

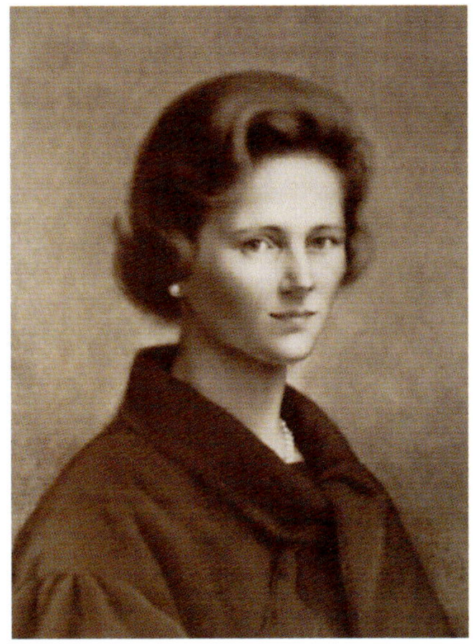

My portrait of Lady Serena Remnant

1963 was a very fractured year for me, both in work and travels. I had to return to England for a long period in order to nurse my mother, who was suffering from a serious and protracted illness, and care for my father. As soon as she had recovered and domestic life had been taken care of, I caught up with postponed commissions in London and looked for a studio there. After much searching I was fortunate to find a small studio-flat in Upper Cheyne Row, Chelsea – a very good address but extremely cramped accommodation. There was only one good living-room with a skylight, where I worked, ate and slept. The kitchen and bathroom were almost as minuscule as my 'Florentine cupboard' in Via Condotta, but with no view over the rooftops and no sense of community with my neighbours. But it was somewhere to start and near to the home of my first sitter, Lady Serena Remnant.

But oh, how I missed Florence, my friends and our gregarious way of life! In large cities one can be surrounded by crowds yet very lonely and isolated. I worked every day, with agreeable subjects to paint, but still felt claustrophobic in that room. I spent the few remaining hours of daylight visiting art galleries, where at least I felt at home. The 'swinging Kings Road' gave me no pleasure. I was homesick for Florence (although I looked forward to driving to my family home at weekends). I gradually made some social contacts through my sitters, which helped me to survive for the six months of my lease, but I was not sorry to leave.

Finally, in March 1964, I was back in Florence searching for another apartment, full of hope and enthusiasm again. I found an adequate pied à terre in the San Frediano quarter again, in Via dello Sprone. It was sunny, small, convenient and cosy, with no studio, alas, but then I did not need one as I was to resume my studies at Borgo degli Albizi 8. My spirits lifted as I began to live again in the old familiar atmosphere. Here was a sense of community and true joie de vivre that I had never felt in London. The unpredictability of daily life lent momentum and enthusiasm to my work.

The little annexe off the main studio was still unoccupied. One of the books in the deep shelves on the wall was an ancient hand-bound treatise on alchemy. It was printed on hand-made paper, ocre-aged and in barely legible Latin. When opened, the thick pages spread out fan-shaped making a fascinating pattern. Together with some old bottles of ink and powder the book created a perfect composition in itself, without arrangement. The different textures and subtle sepia tones were timeless, tranquil and meditative, appealing to me to be painted. I had prepared fresh colours and had already started the painting when one morning a colleague of the Maestro called to see him and then, coming to look over my shoulder, said, 'Ah! That is a fine subject. Do you know how that ink was made?' Apparently, it was from an age-old formula of an extract of acorns. This produced a particular shade of

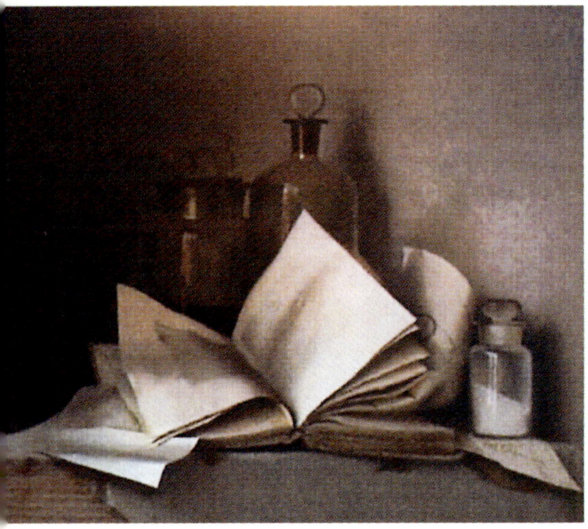

'The book of Alchemy' (oil tempera)

sepia which Leonardo and Michaelangelo used in their drawings, and which this man had studied, being an able exponent of pen and ink drawing himself. Shortly afterwards he brought me a small bottle of his own production which I treasured and used when trying to reproduce the text on the two barely exposed and foreshortened pages of the alchemy treatise in my painting.

This was certainly a very challenging subject and it took me many weeks to produce.

During this time the Sunday outings to Massaciuccoli continued but, with no shade for protection, on those still canal waters the increasingly hot weather made painting uncomfortable. Annigoni did not tolerate heat well, and I was prey to increasing mosquito attacks, so to escape both we often drifted through the canals towards the open sea. For me this was a chance for a refreshing swim. On one such day, heavy with lethargy-inducing heat, Annigoni had invited three old friends to join our outing: a charming couple, Avvocato Emilio Masari and his wife, and the Swiss painter Ponziano Togni. By mid-day painting was impossible, so we moored on the quay near to Viareggio and lunched al fresco at one of the many fish restaurants.

Towards sunset in perfect painting light, we drifted inland again to catch the golden hour on canvas. I found this extremely difficult, and the light faded fast. I was exhausted and hoped we would return to Florence, but the Maestro decided to go back to Viareggio for supper at La Bombetta to savour their speciality, *zuppa di pesce*. During the meal an imposing woman, dressed dramatically in a flowing cape, made a grand stage entrance and, seeing Annigoni, immediately approached our table. He recognized her and rose to greet this unexpected visitor while she enveloped him in an embrace, saying. *'Ciao Pietro! Che sorpresa!'* He, too, looked surprised and offered her a seat.

'Who on earth is she?' I whispered to Riccardo. No one seemed to know until Annigoni introduced her to everyone round the table as Jacquetta Hawkes, the famous English sculptor and explorer. I knew her by reputation only. Many years later, when she was the ageing widow of her second husband, the writer J.B. Priestly, she spent the last years of her life in the Cotswold town of Chipping Campden, near to my own home in Broadway, but I never met her again.

Painting continued quietly at the studio much as before, Annigoni at his easel and the various pupils fitting into the few spaces available. The visiting hour was as usual filled with comings and goings: framers, friends and visitors from all over the world. Of these I recall in particular a young couple, Fleur and Ludi Ferri, from Johannesburg. The wife, a talented painter, was already well established in her profession. The husband was Italian. There was an immediate rapport between us all, and a very convivial evening dining out with Annigoni followed. It was a spontaneous event which began a friendship between Fleur and me which has endured ever since. In 1982 I was commissioned to paint six portraits in and around Cape Town. I visited Fleur en route at her home and studio, in a magical garden setting of her own creation in the pleasant residential outskirts of Johannesburg. By then she had become the leading portrait painter in South Africa and was a talented artist in several genres.

At the end of 1964 I flew to Madeira for what developed into a working holiday as the guest of two very dear friends, Muriel and Antonio Ribeiro. Their beautiful old Portuguese home, the Quinta da Penha de França above Funchal, is set in a tropical walled garden full of jacaranda, palm trees and exotic flowers, and with a fine view to the old port below and beyond to the open Atlantic. Perched on this wall is a small gazebo which, a century ago, was originally used by young girls to watch unseen through the slatted shutters as the young men passed in the narrow lane below hoping to court them. This one time 'chaperone garden house' was now used as a store room for fishing and sailing tackle. My kind friends suggested that it could be cleared and converted into a temporary studio where I could work without disturbance. Here I controlled the very strong light (the gazebo faced due south) by opening and closing shutters. By now I was accustomed to working in confined spaces and was delighted. I started with Muriel as my first model. Her lovely face and fine bone structure were inspiring, and the portrait was so well received that commissions from some of the Ribeiros' friends quickly followed. I was hard at work again, in an idyllic setting, and extremely happy. Apparently, few of the resident artists painted portraits so I was fortunately able to capture a willing clientele. When not drawing people, I was equally happy painting the glorious flowers all around the garden.

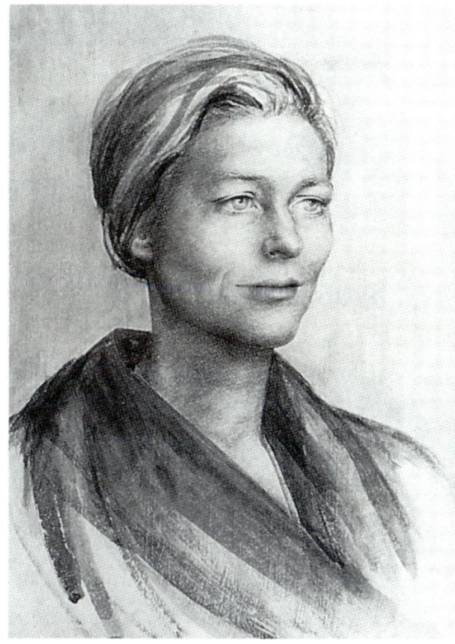

Muriel Ribeiro, pen and wash, 1965

Here I worked contentedly through the mild winter months, extending my range of subjects to some of the more characteristic peasant faces out in the country villages and the mountain areas inland – faces that reflected the hard life of the land and the sea. What a wonderful change and variety of characters I found! My sojourn was extended until March, but this blissfully happy life had to come to an end. I was long overdue in England to paint another rather tedious boardroom portrait of a company chairman in the customary formal suit, followed by the headmaster of a local school – the latter of which at least gave more freedom of style with the subject in his academic robe and stole.

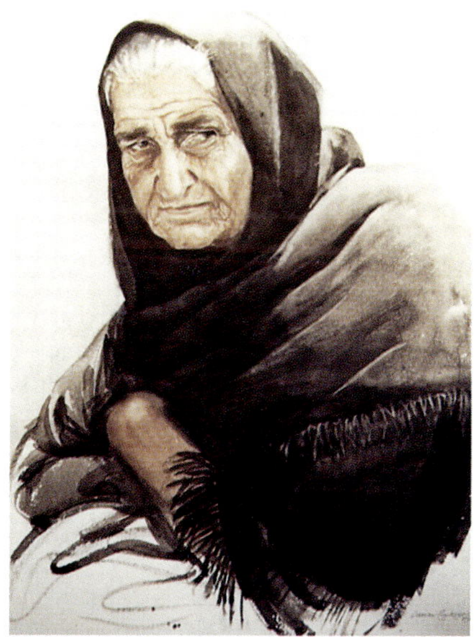

A Portuguese peasant, Madeira 1964, watercolour

This time-consuming work prevented my returning to Florence until the spring of 1965, when I had yet another change of address. By chance I heard of a very good apartment available in an old palazzo on the Costa San Giorgio. Only a few minutes walk from the busy Ponte Vecchio, this steep and narrow street winds its way up to the ancient walls of the city. Of all my five abodes in seven years this was the best. Indeed, it was all I could desire. Elegantly furnished with antiques and adorned with paintings, it belonged to the Conti Marzotto, who lived on the same floor. It was usually reserved for their visiting family but was temporarily vacant. I could hardly believe my luck. It had several rooms all looking out from the back of the palazzo

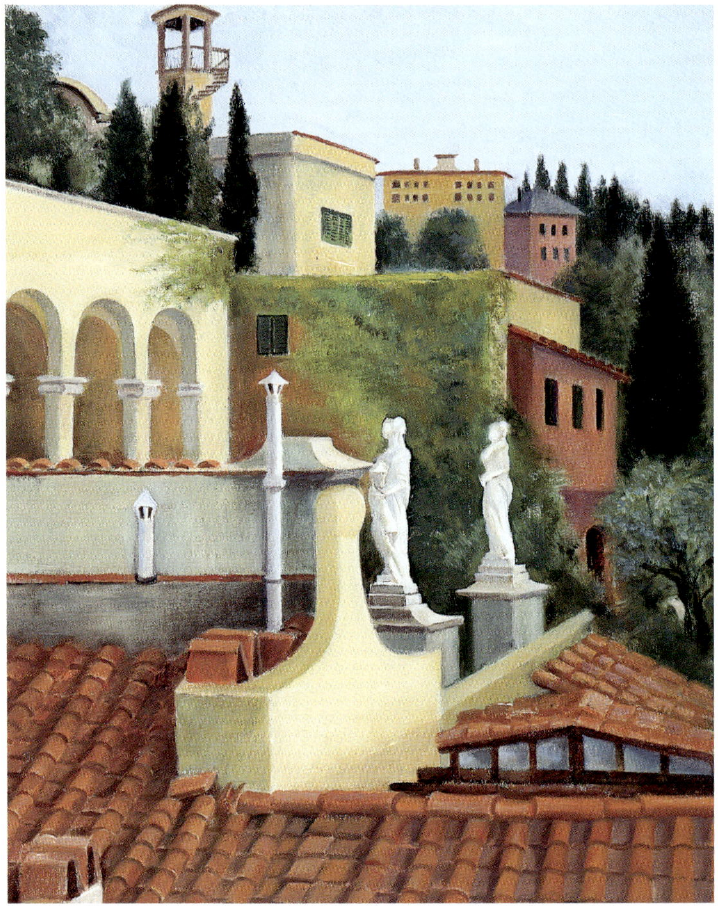

View from my window towards the Boboli gardens, 1965

towards the Boboli Gardens – an almost rural view. At last I had space and utter tranquillity, and, despite the increasing heat, it was cool inside the massive stone walls.

I had completed my best still-life so far and had gained Annigoni's approval – he told me that it was 'not bad', which was quite a compliment from this exacting master, even after six years of study. I had also drawn a portrait of Annigoni with one of his characteristic expressions. This was done without his knowledge, intended as a surprise, which I thought I had hidden among my other studies. But, to my embarrassment, one morning a visiting English journalist from the *Daily Express* saw it among some of my work and remarked to the Maestro that I had made him look like the Emperor Nero. I've no idea why, or what was Annigoni's reaction, but I knew the expression I had often noticed when he was scrutinizing the lake at the helm of his boat *Onda Seconda* on which we had painted so many times. When I later offered the portrait to him as the only token of gratitude I could think of for all that I owed him, he said it would go well in his bathroom, whether as a joke or because he was too embarrassed to decline to accept it I shall never know. It was left lying around the studio for a long time with other drawings, so I decided that if he did not want yet another portrait of himself, I would treasure it far more as a reminder – as if I needed one. I told him so, and the portrait has hung ever since in my studio and appeared in several exhibitions.

Among the many beautiful models who posed for Annigoni, one of the most striking was the beautiful Sharmini, originally from Ceylon. In her long flowing national dress she caused quite a stir walking down the Borgo Albizi, all the men turning to gaze at her. Annigoni made several monochrome portraits of her in pen and ink and wash, using Chinese ink and a fine pen to delineate her features and large free brush strokes of black wash for the hair that framed her face. The effect was striking. I have also used this medium frequently, especially for dark-haired Latin faces. However, it involves a lot of time and sittings which are not always freely available. In this case charcoal and/or sanguine is a good alternative.

Sara Coleman, Florence, 1964

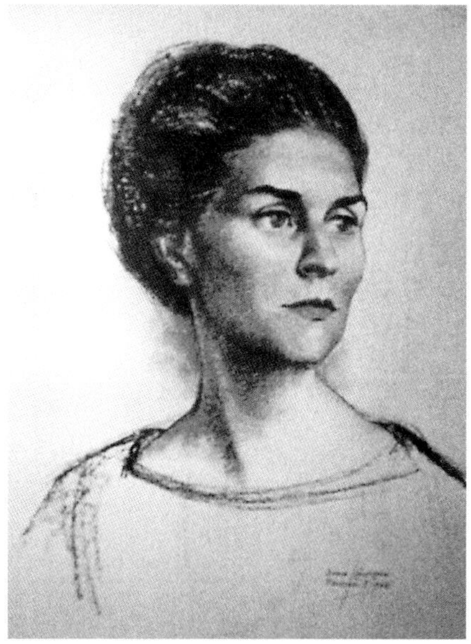

I gained a surprise commission to draw the daughter of one of Annigoni's previous sitters. Although an American citizen she had strong Italian features and a mass of dark hair. She was only available for a few sittings at my apartment.

Nerina Simi instilled her pupils that hard charcoal had to be chiselled to a fine point and never held as a pen so that the touch of the hand was light and free from pressure. She abhorred smudging and correcting was done by lifting the charcoal with a putty rubber, or better still with bread crumbs rolled into tiny pellets. We learnt to draw the hard and sure way.

A propitious encounter

26 July 1965 was a hot sultry day, especially at the studio. As I was leaving, Annigoni invited me to join him for dinner out in the country at Il Cigno, a favourite venue, particularly in the summer, on the bank of the River Arno. He wanted me to help entertain two important America businessmen. The day before – a Sunday – he, Benedetto and I had spent all day on Lake Massaciuccoli. It had been almost too hot to paint, with an oppressive Scirocco wind increasing the heavy atmosphere. It was a long and wilting day, with an inevitably late return to Florence. Consequently, the next day I was looking forward to an early night and asked Annigoni to excuse me. Evidently he was displeased, because when I returned home for lunch Riccardo telephoned me urging me to change my mind and accept, as his guests were very important. And so I did, albeit rather reluctantly. I was told to be ready to be collected by taxi at eight o'clock.

The taxi arrived, with Annigoni sitting by the driver. In the rear the two Americans, to whom I was briefly introduced, made room for me between them. Neither of them spoke Italian. The elder of the two, rather morose and unprepossessing, was evidently one of the directors of Wildenstein's Gallery in New York. His companion, in contrast, was a jovial, wise-cracking extrovert, an ex-show business entertainer turned World Sales Director of Coca Cola. They were two totally opposite characters. Both of them intrigued me, particularly the latter, Morton Downey, whom I was to entertain while Annigoni discussed serious business with the gallery director. We made an odd foursome, especially at this simple rustic trattoria where we sat outdoors to await the arrival of Signora Giuliana, the proprietress. Annigoni immediately ordered the usual wine, which Mr Downey declined, asking instead for Coca Cola. Giuliana, with barely concealed disapproval, replied that they did not even stock it, let alone serve it in *her* restaurant, which didn't go down very well with Mr Downey, who settled for mineral water. To avoid any embarrassment to Annigoni, I discreetly explained to Giuliana who these men were and that Mr Downey was a teetotaller whether she liked it or not! Fortunately, when a huge beef steak and fried potatoes arrived (and there was no request for ketchup) Mr Downey devoured it with such obvious enjoyment that her ruffled feathers were smoothed. Annigoni was mainly engrossed in conversation with the Wildenstein director, who occasionally requested my help with Italian translation, while I was being entertained with a colourful account of Mr Downey's theatrical career: his connections with famous film stars and the many bands and cabarets with which he had sung. I estimated him to be in his sixties, as he talked about singing with 'snake-hips' Johnson in cabaret in London during the war, when the nightclub was bombed and he was one of few to survive.

He asked me where I came from, and hearing my home town was Birmingham, he told me he had played at the Theatre Royal there. From then on we got along like a house on fire and he started questioning me: 'Have you ever been to the States?'

'Unfortunately, no.'

'Then it's high time you did. And you must come to New York.' And producing a visiting card with a heavily embossed name and Park Avenue address, he told me to get in touch with him. I accepted this politely but without much conviction of his sincerity or intentions.

Wining and dining al fresco under a vine-covered trellis and star-lit sky late into that balmy July night had mellowed the exuberant Mr Downey. The conversation turned to art and music. Suddenly he burst into song with such a fine tenor voice that all conversation ceased around the other tables. Giuliana came out from the kitchen to listen in amazement, and even forgave him asking for Nescafé at the end of dinner.

We returned to the city in a very convivial mood; even the sombre director was more affable. Mr Downey turned towards me and asked, 'How would you like to come over and paint my kids some time. They're great youngsters and very good-looking.'

'What are their ages?'

'Oh, they're both at university and very bright. You'll love them.'

I wondered, still apprehensive, about this very sudden proposal and pointed out that I was only one of Annigoni's more recent pupils.

'You must be pretty darned good to be in his studio, and I've seen some of your work there. It's fine by me.'

The others left me at my apartment well after midnight. Little did I imagine that that particular evening, which I had been reluctant to attend, was destined to be so important to my future career.

At the end of August, when most of the inhabitants desert the city for the annual *Ferragosto*, I was taken to the lovely island of Elba by a friend for an idyllic and relaxing holiday before returning to England in September. Late in the autumn a letter arrived from New York. It was from Morton Downey, recalling our meeting in July and his wish for me to paint his step-daughter and step-daughter-in-law, who lived respectively in Cambridge, Mass. and Washington D.C. He asked for my fees and how soon I could come and start work. Although inwardly excited at this great opportunity, I was still rather apprehensive. I immediately phoned Annigoni for advice about appropriate fees and also for some reassurance about Mr Downey before replying to him. I need not have worried. Annigoni told me not to undervalue my work, especially in America, and advised me to pay my own fare but to expect all living expenses to be paid. He assured me that Morton Downey was very well-known in New York, extremely wealthy and a shrewd businessman. Once again, *buona fortuna è in bocca al lupo!*

I wrote to Mr Downey with all the necessary details, saying that I could not undertake the commissions until the following year, probably starting in September and calculating that they would take two to three months. A phone call followed a few days later, accepting my fee and telling me to book a flight in good time.

'Could I possibly have some photos of your girls in the mean time to prepare me?' I asked.

'You won't need any,' he replied. 'They're both good-looking girls in their twenties. They're looking forward to the sittings, and you'll just love them! Fly to New York and stay at my apartment for a week so as to get acclimatized. OK? Let me know your dates. You'll probably need a visa, but *don't* apply for a work permit. Goodbye.'

He was brief and to the point and the ball was now in my court.

The rest of that year was taken up with portraits of two big business executives, which turned out better than I expected; the portrait of the headmaster of a local school and of one of the school governors, and the portrait of the then Archdeacon of Birmingham. I also painted many children's portraits, which took me to homes all over the country. Although demanding, these were a pleasant diversion from more formal portraits.

To America in the fall

1966 looked full of promise. The first three months were spent in Madeira. Intended as a winter break with my good friends Antonio and Muriel, this turned into a working holiday, with commissions waiting for me and ideal conditions in which to paint. The next three months were spent in England. In London during July and August the fortunate flow of commissions continued. I also exhibited with the Royal Birmingham Society of Artists and the Watercolour Society. I returned to Italy in September, far too briefly, as I had to prepare for my visit to the States.

I needed to take with me a lot of heavy painting equipment, including a portable easel, ready prepared wood panels for paintings in oil tempera, about 20 bottles of colours and a metal palette. On top of this, I needed clothing for three months of variable temperatures. How could I possibly take all this by air? I decided on a sea trip, not only because of the weight of my luggage, but also to help me adjust to the change with a few days of sea air and rest before work began.

I booked a passage on the liner *United States*, sailing from Southampton on 30 September via Cork, on a five-day crossing, but I never imagined there would be a force nine gale on the second day out.

Fortunately, my cabin was in first class, which was half empty, but I had to eat in second class for my special reduced fare. I was seated for dinner at a very assorted table of six passengers at the, (for me) very uncustomary time of 6.30 on the first evening. The only other woman, a middle-aged American, warned me that the crossing would be particularly bad in this ship. She preferred the *Queen Elizabeth*, which was far more civilized, and told me that we would probably not meet again as she would be taking all her meals in her cabin thereafter, and she advised me to do the same. Such foreboding reminded me of the *Titanic* and on the second night I lay awake while the huge liner pitched, tossed and rolled and my stomach accompanied it.

Although (so I had been told) this former battleship held the record for the fastest crossing of the Atlantic, its massive structure shuddered with a creaking and banging of doors and crashing of crockery while the turbulent waves exploded against my porthole and my belongings slid all over the cabin.

Next morning, as some light filtered through the storm, the thought of getting up, let alone facing any breakfast, made me feel nauseous. So I lay there letting my body 'go with the flow' until some time later there was a knock on the door and without waiting for an answer a black stewardess peeped in at me. 'Hi there! Howya doin'?' I groaned and thought it was obvious. Ignoring my apathy she suggested some food and a walk up on deck in some fresh air. 'Howdya like some coffee and bagels?' I managed to shake my head feebly while my stomach heaved and I appealed for some mineral water. She disappeared and returned with a huge glass of iced orange juice as well as mineral water, though she said an empty stomach was no way to face the day.

'Just put the tray on the floor please, and I'll get it later,' I pleaded. After she had put it down and left, it came to me instead, sliding perilously across the cabin and coming to a halt by my slippers. Somehow I managed to pull myself up from horizontal and grasp the glass of juice before it glided away. I staggered to my feet briefly, to grab my clothes and then collapsed on my bunk again. I had no idea of time and no desire to risk moving out of the cabin. I decided that I would rather go down with the ship if it came to that and vowed that I would never, never cross the Atlantic by sea again. Then, ashamed of such melodramatic thoughts, I struggled out into an empty gangway, grabbing a rail, and staggered up some stairs to the deck above. There were a few hardy passengers, bent double against the wind and drenched with spray, also staggering from rail to rail. I took some deep gulps of air and one look at the angry sea and deciding that discretion was the better part of valour, retreated to the safety of my cabin. I recalled how Annigoni, a well seasoned trans-Atlantic voyager and lover of rough seas, preferred to be up on deck studying the angry waves and cloudy skies of which he had made many sketches. He never mentioned whether he was ever sea-sick, but I doubt it.

And so we weathered the unceasing storm for the next three days, without dropping any knots, as the captain was determined to dock on time in New York. What little food I could manage to keep down was unenjoyable and mostly brought to my cabin by the buxom and over-jovial stewardess. On the last evening, when the gale had mercifully decreased to a steady swell, I ventured up to the lounge on the upper deck after the usual early dinner to sit and enjoy a coffee in some company.

A small band was playing and a few hardy couples had braved the dance floor when a fellow passenger approached and asked if I was alone and whether I would care to have a drink, adding that he'd seen me up on deck looking 'pretty rough' a day ago and hoped I was feeling better. The drinks came and we chatted about the purpose of our voyage and our different destinations on reaching the States. The band had started to play 'Strangers in the Night' and he invited me to dance. There was still a moderate swell and although I love dancing I did not want to land on the floor and jeopardize my mobility at this stage, so I suggested it might be somewhat risky.

'Not in my hands,' he assured me, leading me with a firm arm onto the dance floor.

It was more of a balancing act than a dance as he gripped and I clung while we slid from one side to the other, avoiding collisions with the few other dancers. Before long even he had to admit defeat as we swerved to the safety of our armchairs to find that our drinks had spilled over. Pity! He was rather nice and this could have been a more enjoyable ending to my miserable voyage. Whenever I hear Frank Sinatra singing that song it reminds me of that brief encounter.

I was up and packed early next morning, ready to watch the unforgettable approach to New York harbour past the dominating Statue of Liberty and the tie-up at Pier 86 with all the crowds, noise, bustle and confusion of landing. I checked all my luggage and equipment, which had been brought up from the hold, and got my passport ready for immigration control, which I had been warned would be a lengthy and tedious business. As I looked down at the docks and wondered when, where and by whom I would be met, I suddenly heard my name called: 'Would passenger Miss Dawn Cookson please report to the first-class lounge on A deck.' Everyone in the queue of second-class passengers looked around at me as I stepped out, rather like a schoolgirl called out of class for some misdemeanour.

A steward directed me, assuring me that my luggage would be taken care of. I was met by a small man in dark glasses looking like a mafioso, who asked for my passport and ushered me through queues of passengers waiting to land from another gangway. At the foot of this waited the welcome stocky figure of Morton Downey, now hardly recognizable in an oversized fur-collared, black overcoat, a black trilby hat and dark glasses. I was rushed through customs and immigration and Mr Downey and I were escorted by an official through a VIP channel and out to a waiting black-windowed stretch limo.

When my luggage eventually arrived it was piled so high on the trolley that the porter behind was almost invisible. Morton Downey laughed and remarked, 'Gee! How long do you intend to stay for? A year?'

Before I could reply, it was all transferred into the car's enormous trunk and I was ushered into the back seat with Morton Downey, while the 'bodyguard' took the wheel about six feet in front of us. We glided into a daze of traffic, noise and flashing lights, and I sank into the leather upholstery in a haze of disorientation.

Fortunately, Morton Downey was involved in a business conversation with the driver from the docks to up-town New York. I was in a state of limbo, my body still reacting to the turbulent motion of the sea, and now to the smoothly gliding limousine, which was almost as bad. I had hardly recovered from my sea-sickness before beginning to feel car sick. It was probably all nerves. We approached Fifth Avenue and the intersection with Park Avenue. The car pulled up outside No. 640, an imposing grey and white building with a striped awning over the sidewalk. A doorman in a grey frock-coat opened the car door for me. 'Wow! New York here I come!'

After ascending countless floors in the elevator to the Downey apartment, I did not expect the sight that met my eyes. The door was opened onto a long and elegant hall, at the end of which two della Robbia base reliefs faced me on either side of a fifteenth-century painting (they must be copies surely, I thought). Doors led off on either side to a large sitting-room and a dining-room, both furnished in exquisite taste, and most of all hung with fabulous and famous paintings, the living-room with six works by French Impressionists and the dining-room with six Utrillos. It also contained the longest table I have ever seen. There were French bureaux and escritoires, two Giacometti bronze figures, Italian intarsio marble tables and polished wood marquetry and objets d'art from all over the world – in fact, an overwhelming surfeit of riches.

I was introduced to the French housekeeper, who showed me to the elegant guest suite, three walls of which were covered with original paintings, and the fourth, with a large heavily draped window, looked onto Park Avenue. A luxurious adjoining bathroom and a walk-in closet, with more than ample space for me and all my luggage together, made a most welcome impression. The housekeeper, a dignified middle-aged woman, told me that Mr Downey would be in his office nextdoor and that I should phone him when I was ready. I remember flopping onto the king-size bed, gazing around at some eight or 10 paintings and wondering if I was dreaming. I must have dozed off, because I was suddenly awoken by telephones ringing and voices in conversation in the next room – as well as police sirens screaming outside, a sound that was to become all too familiar in the following days.

I came back to reality, did some unpacking and peeped into the corridor. The next room was Morton Downey's office, containing two enormous desks and several telephones which all seemed to be ringing at once. The bodyguard-cum-chauffeur was now the secretary, cradling one telephone receiver between his chin and one shoulder while holding another, into which he was speaking loudly while smoking at the same time. A huge television screen in one corner was showing a sitcom accompanied by screams of laughter. No wonder the 'secretary' looked harassed. Cupping his hand over one of the phones when he saw me, he indicated that Mr Downey was in the library waiting for me.

The library was a slightly smaller room, more homely and lived-in, with comfortable armchairs and a white grand piano, on which were displayed numerous autographed photographs of the Kennedy family and others of stars of stage and screen. Most of them had been signed with personal greetings 'to Mort'. One particularly striking photograph of a beautiful young woman stood out. Beside it was a vase of red roses. I gazed at it admiringly, unaware that my host had entered the room and was standing behind me.

'Don't you think she's lovely?' he asked.

'Oh yes. Is this one of your daughters?'

'No, she is my late second wife.'

I was embarrassed by my unwitting blunder.

'She was much younger than me and died not long after our marriage, so I inherited Catherine and her brother Christian. He is married to Nora and they live in Washington – you will paint her down there. Catherine and Christian's mother was previously married to Prince Höhenlohe – the brother of the notorious playboy who married Ira Fürstenberg. They divorced and later she married me. I had also been married before. I guess you aren't old enough to remember the film actresses Constance and Joan Bennett? Well, I married the third sister, but she also died, so I lost two wives.'

By this time I was getting lost with all these relationships, and he had hardly drawn breath. I must have looked bewildered.

'Don't worry, I know you'll do a great job and love both girls, so let's drink to it,' he said, opening a hidden door in the wall panelling to reveal a refrigerator stacked with every kind of spirit and even more cans of Coca Cola. 'What do you like with your Coke: gin, rum, bourbon or whiskey?'

'I really don't care much for Coke, so may I have just a small whiskey and soda, with no ice please.'

'You'll have to get to like it in this house – I mean the Coke and ice. That's all I drink anyway.'

This reminded me that he was the World Sales Director of the product. He told me that dinner would be at eight o'clock and that I should 'dress casual'. I retired to unpack, bath and change into something appropriate, but when he appeared in a short black Japanese silk kimono with bare legs and wearing slippers, I wondered if I should have chosen a bath robe!

However, our delicious dinner à deux, occupying less than a quarter of a table large enough for 20, was impeccably served and accompanied by excellent French wine. After it we sat in a cosier room for coffee and discussed plans for the portrait sittings at Cambridge and Washington. At the coming weekend my first sitter, Catherine, and her husband, Bill Cook, were arriving to meet me and to get acquainted before work started. Meanwhile, M.D. (as I preferred to call Morton Downey) told me what I should see, where I should go and which areas I should avoid in New York – the latter included the subway and Central Park. I could come and go as I pleased and have whatever food I wanted at any time. I had only to inform the housekeeper. M.D. would be out a lot of the time, but his secretary was always in the office if I needed help. The doorman would call be a cab, which I was advised to take everywhere around town. Didn't anyone walk, I wondered? Well, *I* needed exercise.

I decided that my priority was to visit the art galleries and museums. I started at the Frick, a treasure house of great works of art: fabulous paintings and sculpture as well as objets d'art and period furniture, all superbly displayed in a very imposing and dignified nineteenth-century mansion surrounded by skyscrapers. Then I explored the area on foot for the rest of my first day.

The next two days I spent visiting two old friends, John and Jan Wattles, in Upper Saddle River, New Jersey – a happy reunion after many years and a brief relaxing break, out in the country in peaceful surroundings. I returned to the noise and bustle of the Big Apple for dinner at an ultra chic restaurant on Fifth Avenue, La Grenouille, where I was to meet my first sitter, Catherine, and her husband Bill Cook.

I knew at once that I would enjoy painting her. She was an intelligent, cultured and extremely attractive girl who next day took me window-shopping on Fifth Avenue. What temptations to be resisted! New York certainly has a buzz, and I was lucky to be seeing it from the best side. The weather was wonderful, sunny and warm. The Cooks returned to Boston with some of my more necessary luggage. I was to follow by train a few days later.

Next day I 'did' the Metropolitan Museum of Art quite intensely all morning and the Guggenheim all afternoon. The latter is a fantastic building and a wonderful setting for modern paintings – some of them exciting but others appalling according to my taste and understanding of art – but by then I had reached saturation point. This was exacerbated by the spiralling levels of the gallery, which had a disorientating effect.

12 October was my last day of introduction to New York and coincided with the big public holiday that honours St Columbus. The street parades, processions, bands and majorettes twirling and tossing their batons blocked all the main streets. The sidewalks were packed with cheering waving crowds swaying to the beat of the drums. Quite a spectacle! New York, New York is certainly a wonderful town if you can take the pace.

Annigoni was also in town, staying at the city home of his old friend and patron Chauncey Stillman nearby on Fifth Avenue. He phoned and invited me to call that evening. I had already heard much about this intellectual and patron of the arts and could well understand why Annigoni felt at home in his apartment when I was shown into an interior furnished and decorated in the style of a Florentine palazzo. I was led through an elegant hall to a drawing-room in which was one of the most famous Italian masterpieces of the seventeenth-century, 'The Halberdier' by Pontormo, which dominated the room. To see such a superb original in a private apartment in New York was a surprise and a privilege. Mr Stillman was away at Wethersfield House, his country estate at Armenia in New York State where Annigoni had often stayed when painting his friend and his two daughters. There he had also started a series of frescoes to decorate a 'gloriette' (a highly decorated room). These were between marble pillars and covered the entire curved ceiling with romantic and allegorical compositions. Later the Pontormo was transferred to this room, where it formed the centrepiece of a classic setting containing Greek and Roman sculpture.

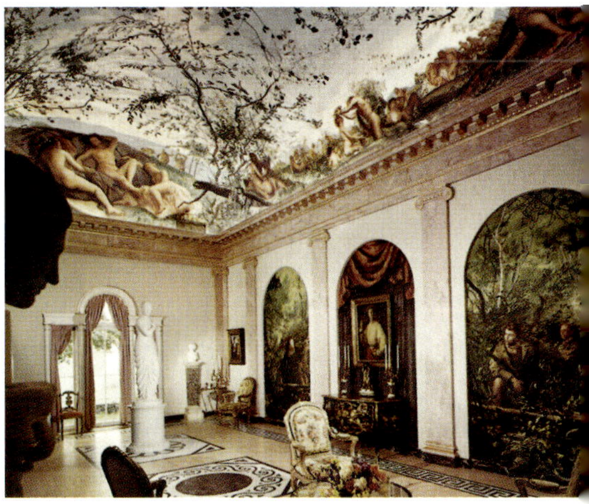

Annigoni frescoes at Wethersfield House, Armenia, New York State

Annigoni took me to dinner at his favourite Italian restaurant on Broadway – a familiar and relaxing atmosphere. We talked about his painting at Wethersfield and I asked his advice about certain aspects of the unknown environment in which I was about to paint the two young women in Boston and Washington. For me, so much depended on the outcome of the sittings, and I felt a sense of responsibility to him. We enjoyed an excellent meal – the only occasion I can remember being with Annigoni without other company – and drank some exceedingly good wine. Feeling in a good mood after this and in need of some fresh air and exercise, we mingled with the animated crowds in the streets of the Italian quarter, which was buzzing with life at that hour. Passing an amusement arcade Annigoni stopped and, to my amazement, said, 'Shall we go in?'

'What in *that* place? Are you serious?' I replied.

'Why always be serious? Let's go and have some fun.'

I happily responded to his frivolous mood. We played the slot machines and he did some target practice. We sat in the booth for automatic photos of each other pulling grotesque faces and for a few dollars had our names printed in headlines on a mock newspaper above some fictitious and ludicrous article. It was a lovely evening. I had never seen Annigoni so relaxed or felt more at ease myself. Maybe for him it was a reaction to the tension of work, added to the amount of wine we had drunk, and for me encouragement for the work I was about to start. That Italian evening in New York on St Columbus day was special.

Next day he was to return to Wethersfield, and I was to set off to Boston. Mr Downey could not understand why I preferred the train journey to a short flight. I just wanted a few hours of space and time to think. And so on 13 October I took a cab to Grand Central Station. My driver, a typical New York cabbie, looked up at me from his mirror and told me bluntly to 'sit back 'cos I stop fast', which advice I took as we raced downtown barely halting at traffic lights. In fact, when passing through a less than salubrious district he sped through the already changing lights while I clung to my seat with eyes closed and gasped.

'Look, lady,' he said, 'the guys in this area can stick a gun or a knife through the window while you stop at the intersections, and you either give 'em your dough or they get you and run. So I don't give 'em a chance. I even picked up a fare who stuck a gun in the back of my neck, told me to hand over the cash, and was out of the cab and running before we'd started.' He continued, 'Yer English, ain't yer? So that figures.'

Not wishing to prolong the dialogue, I sat back and shut up. Anyway he got me safely to Grand Central with a genial smile and a 'so long, have a good trip!', which I did, with time to recover.

Cambridge and Boston

I was met on arrival by Catherine and driven to the Sheraton Commander Hotel in Cambridge, where a very nice apartment had been rented for me. She then showed me around the centre of Cambridge, with its imposing university buildings and shopping area, which was in walking distance of the apartment. I liked the place and the atmosphere immediately. It was much smaller then than it is now, but it was always alive with youth. I hardly had time to unpack and decide where to set up my easel for the best light than I was whisked off to dinner at the young couple's nearby apartment. Bill was at Harvard and Catherine was at Radcliff, both studying for their finals.

Next morning I awoke to brilliant sunshine, which although welcome was not the light to paint in, as it would constantly change. Evidently, the booking had been made especially for the bright and cheerful room. When Catherine arrived for her first sitting I explained to her the necessity for a more constant light, ideally north-facing. Luckily, there was a suite available on the fifth floor facing due west. At least the sun would not shine in until late afternoon, so we both prepared for morning sittings. I moved up four floors with all my luggage and equipment, settled in again and tried to convert some space into a temporary studio.

I was anxious to get down to some serious painting as soon as possible. However, my hosts had other plans for the coming weekend. We were to drive up to their seashore cottage on Cape Cod especially for my benefit. I could hardly decline the invitation without causing offence, and I welcomed the opportunity to see some of that renowned and beautiful coastal region. So I packed a smaller bag and some drawing materials in readiness for our departure on the following afternoon, Friday 14 October. The 'cottage', so-called, on the exclusive private reserve at Hyannis, was a long, low-built timber house comprising 10 bedrooms and several bathrooms and a designer kitchen any woman would dream about. It commanded an uninterrupted view as far as the eye could see between sand dunes leading down to the silvery shore of the Atlantic Ocean. I wished that I had the time and the means to sit down and paint this breathtaking scene, but I was unprepared. All was utter peace and tranquillity, the only sounds being the lapping of waves on the beach and the cries of seabirds.

To reach this reserved coastal area, one had to pass through gates which were continually manned, with access given only to residents and their authorized visitors. This was the Kennedy clan's own private playground, where all members of that family had their summer homes within walking distance of each other, and their exclusive yachts moored in the harbour of Hyannis Port.

Although it was mid-October, the weather was unbelievably warm and sunny. Despite all the temptations for idleness, I insisted on starting a drawing of Catherine during the two mornings at the cottage. I gave in after lunch and went for a sail around the bay of the Cape in the Cooks' 40-foot yacht – an exhilarating experience, despite my reticence after the Atlantic crossing. What a life those young people had! Catherine was an excellent and innovative cook, and after the sea trip fresh lobster and succulent salads with excellent Californian wines ended a perfect day.

I rose very early on Sunday morning to take a long walk along the isolated beach, with only the twittering sandpipers for company, scurrying in and out of the water's edge foraging for food with their sharp beaks in the wet sand. I sat briefly on a rock to gaze at this unspoilt paradise, assimilating all its natural beauty and inwardly praying that I could accomplish my best work in these two portraits.

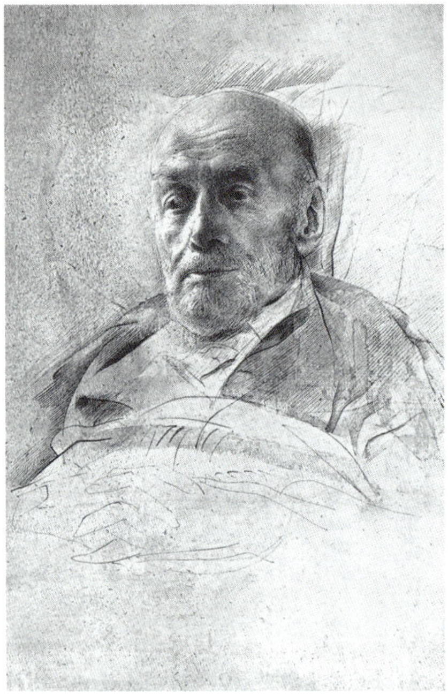

Annigoni's portrait of Berenson on his death bed

After breakfast I had another sitting with Catherine to complete a preliminary pastel study. In the late afternoon we three drove back to Cambridge, and I was left to settle in to my new apartment at No. 508.

The first week started well. I worked every morning from ten to one p.m., sometimes continuing with an afternoon sitting after a snack lunch in the apartment. Catherine had to study, so she posed reading a book resting on the window sill, the golden autumn light enhancing her long honey-blond hair and accentuating her features. The afternoons were filled with sightseeing, trips into Boston to meet some friends and several visits to the superb Museum of Fine Arts, which contains many of the world's great masterpieces. The Impressionist collection alone included 22 Monets, and that was only a part of the museum.

Another fascinating and more intimate and unique collection was amassed by the wealthy eccentric Isabella Steward Gardener, who had constructed a very credible copy of a Florentine Renaissance palace, albeit incongruously situated in the heart of twentieth-century Boston. She was an avid collector of fine paintings, largely bought on the advice of Bernard Berenson, the acknowledged connoisseur of fine arts, and also incidentally a friend and great admirer of Annigoni. Indeed, Annigoni drew a very sensitive pen and ink portrait of him on his death bed. The Gardener collection, fully endowed to the public in perpetuity by the philanthropic lady, contained hidden treasures as well as some oddities and a few dubious originals, all set around a large covered inner quadrangle filled with exotic flowering plants and trees. In fact, the idiosyncratic Mrs Gardener was known to have received guests for soirées in full evening dress seated high up on a branch of an acacia tree. In her will she stipulated exactly which species of flowers or plants were to be placed under specific paintings. The collection, also comprising objets d'art, furniture and sculpture, certainly reflected the very discerning and individual taste of that wealthy patron of arts and music. Concerts were still regularly performed in the glass-covered courtyard.

Portrait of Catherine Cook, 1966

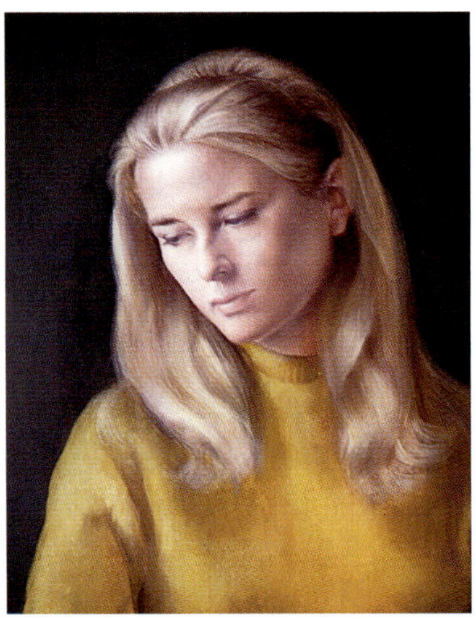

I was royally entertained by Catherine, Bill and other friends in Boston: at dinner parties at home and dining out at restaurants; at the theatre, where we saw a Congreve play; a superb concert by the Boston Symphony Orchestra, which performed my favourite Mahler; and not least at Cape Cod on three delightful weekends.

After 14 sittings with Catherine, I successfully completed the portrait in tempera, as well as two pastel drawings of her and one of Bill, which I gave to them. The other pastel I reserved as a gift for Morton Downey. By then it was early November, and remarkably mild and sunny until Sunday 6 November when it poured with rain all day long. The rain heralded some terrible news. When I attended early communion at the nearby Anglican church, the vicar told me that Florence had been flooded overnight. He knew the city well, and we were both shocked and distressed. My immediate reaction was to telephone Annigoni, but as I was unsure of his whereabouts I wrote to him care of Chauncey Stillman. The letter must have been sent on to Boston where he was painting Governor Volpe. He replied reassuring me that his family were safe and well, as were our mutual friends, but he was greatly disturbed and concerned about the suffering of the city in such a colossal disaster and was in constant touch with his son Benedetto for the latest news. The flooding hung like a cloud over both of us, so far away and unable to help. There was nothing we could do but wait for news from Annigoni's family and our friends and pray for the waters to subside.

My work had gone well and I had thoroughly enjoyed my stay in Cambridge with its many visits to nearby Boston and much kind hospitality – especially from Alex and Dick Norton, whom I'd met long before through a chance meeting of our parents in Florence, where so many friendships were formed and have remained. I returned to New York, where M.D. gave me a great welcome and was anxious to see my painting, about which he was enthusiastic. It was such a relief! He had already reserved a table at the famous 21 restaurant for a party to celebrate the occasion.

For a change I dressed up and felt ready to hit the town as we set off in the limo to be met by the maître d' as we entered. As he guided us through the closely packed tables everyone seemed to know M.D., including several film stars. At one table Frank Sinatra called out, 'Hi Mort!', and they greeted each other with friendly pats on padded shoulders. At another, the lovely Irish-American actress Maureen O'Hara blew him a kiss as we passed. I was introduced to her and then to his waiting guests with flattering remarks about the portrait, much to my embarrassment, and he invited his guests to come and see it next day at his apartment. The atmosphere was scintillating and the company cosmopolitan. Glamorous women sparkled with jewellery, well-tailored men in tow. I wished I had had a sketch book handy. Instead, an out-size napkin was placed on my lap and a magazine-sized menu into my hands while waiters bustled around us. My mind flashed back to Angiolino's – equally animated but poles apart from '21'. I remembered the simple Italian meal with Annigoni on St Columbus day. Such contrasts to savour and record in my diary.

The next day I managed to squeeze in a visit to see my colleague Julian Barrow, who was currently holding an exhibition of his work in a prestigious New York gallery. He has since had numerous others. It was nice to see him after our Florentine years and his latest paintings of New York and London, most of them sold. He had developed into a considerably accomplished painter.

After this I visited the Witney Museum of Modern Art, where there were startling exhibits on the top floor and some superb Sargents and Whistlers, which gave me more pleasure. I had to be back at the apartment early as the guests from the previous night's party, including Maureen O'Hara, were coming for drinks and to view my portrait. The other friends included a business colleague of M.D. who was the head of Pepsi Cola and also seriously rich. All were generous in their remarks about my work, but I knew better than to set much store by this. Contacts are important, but actions speak louder than words. I had done my best and pleased the Downey family.

Only one other person's opinion mattered to me and that was the Maestro's. I was going to meet him next day at the home of Chauncey Stillman, where I took my portrait for his criticism, together with a photograph of the subject, whom he had never met. It gained his approval and his *'Brava!'*, which meant everything to me. Then he took me out for a quiet dinner on Broadway. After a very long and full day, it was a lovely relaxing evening with which to complete my stay in New York. Annigoni was still preoccupied by the acute conditions prevailing in Florence and anxious to return home. I wished I also could return to my Italian home, but the next day I had to set off for Washington.

Washington and Georgetown

On 14 November I got up early, packed and set off for Pennsylvania Station to catch a train to Washington. I found myself in a carriage full of clerics attending a conference of bishops at the great cathedral at Mount St Alban. It was a very uninteresting journey of four hours, but at least it gave me time to catch up with myself.

I was met by my next sitter, Nora Höhenlohe, newly married to Catherine's brother Christopher. Both Nora and Christopher were studying law. She was quite the opposite of Catherine in looks and colouring and attractive in a different way. There was something about her that reminded me of the typical Italian Renaissance page who frequently appears in fifteenth-century paintings. Her dark shoulder-length hair and fringe framed a very sculptured pale face with penetrating brown eyes. She had a timeless quality, was highly intelligent and very easy to get on with.

The couple had rented an apartment for me at Carillon House on Washington Heights. This was within walking distance of the impressive cathedral, faithfully constructed in the Gothic style, the work of several generations of stonemasons and skilled artisans – mostly Italians, who three generations on, were becoming extinct. The building had taken nearly 60 years from the laying of the foundation stone in 1907 mainly due to the lack of qualified craftsmen. (Whereas, without the aid of modern engineering, and built entirely by human labour, the great cathedral in Florence took over 150 years to complete.) Inside, the massive building was a haven of calm to which I often escaped for peace and quiet meditation or to enjoy a traditional choral evensong to uplift my spirits.

The apartment block was another anonymous building of boxes largely occupied by the staff of the many embassies. The accommodation was adequate and the light good. I settled in, unpacked once more and set up my portable studio. I was ready to start the first sitting the next day. The weather was much colder but there were still clear blue skies and sunshine.

On Sunday 20 November I walked up the hill to the cathedral to attend the early communion service. It might have been in England with all its tradition, dignity and solemnity. The large choir and splendid organ music resounded throughout the architectural splendour of the interior, enhanced by the acoustics of the high fan-vaulted roof. It was a very moving experience.

After the morning sitting I spent the afternoon at the National Gallery, where I saw a small part of the wonderful Mellon collection. I lost count of the Rembrandts, Rubens and Franz Hals in the Flemish gallery and was very impressed by the audio recording that was automatically picked up (by the then wonders of technology) as one stood directly opposite a painting. This greatly added to the appreciation without one having to hire and carry a taped commentary. Each school and period of painting was superbly hung against a different background, compatible with the period, using subtle materials and harmonious colours. I planned to return there every Sunday during my month's stay to absorb as much culture and pleasure as possible, remembering Annigoni's adage that one could learn more from studying the actual paintings of old masters than from any teacher. *Magari!*

For this second portrait it was taking me longer to 'get into' my subject and there were several anxious days when I felt 'out of gear'. Adding to this disturbed state of mind, a letter from Else Steen in Florence made me even more depressed as it described the terrible aftermath of the flooding, with mud and oily sludge penetrating everywhere and causing even more damage than the flood waters. I wished I could be there to join in the recovery of thousands of precious and historical books and manuscripts. It was painstaking and time-consuming work separating the sheets of antique paper and then drying them with blotting paper. They were even covered with talcum powder in order to absorb some of the grease and grime, a technique also used upon the many priceless sculptures damaged. But here I was with a job to complete, and in a far from happy state of mind. While Florence in all its turmoil oppressed me, letters from home brought worrying news of my father's deteriorating health.

On 23 November I confronted the fifth and brief sitting and was then whisked off to join the rest of the family on Cape Cod for Thanksgiving Day and the weekend. Nora, Chris and I caught the shuttle to New York, where we joined Catherine and Bill, who had flown into La Guardia. From there we flew up to Hyannis on a specially chartered six-seater. This was a really fascinating flight following the coastline quite low over the sea in brilliant moonlight, with the illuminated skyscrapers of New York puncturing the black velvet sky and up towards Boston with strata of pearly haze above a tapestry of twinkling sequins reflected in the sea. I wished I had kept my camera handy, and even more that I could have captured that scene on canvas – almost impossible. It was a quite unforgettable sight.

24 November was my dear father's birthday. As the two couples opened up the family seashore retreat to celebrate Thanksgiving Day I wished I could be with my family. We celebrated with a huge lunch of roast turkey with chestnut stuffing and baked marshmallow pie – followed by some necessary exercise on the beach on a fine sunny day. I could happily have stayed on there and painted some scenery for a change. Instead, I was drawing a portrait of Bill as a gift to Catherine. On Sunday Catherine and Bill drove us back to Boston where Nora, Chris and I were left to catch the shuttle back to New York, with a tedious wait in an overcrowded airport for the next flight to Washington. Over 1000 miles of travelling for a long weekend on Cape Cod – a mere nothing to them, but I was quite exhausted.

The sittings continued but their outcome was not to my satisfaction, and anxiety and tension were building up. I remember someone saying that painting a portrait is rather like a horse race. You go along the flat and have to confront and overcome hurdles, and hopefully land safely for another stretch of flat before the next hurdle. Problems continually face the portrait painter, and everything depends on how you face them or, as my one-time teacher, the late Bernard Fleetwood Walker RA, put it succinctly, 'You know, sometimes God holds your hand, and sometimes it's the Devil.' I prayed hard to God in that penultimate week of daily sittings and many hours of work.

The bitter cold weather in Washington continued until 8 December, when it changed overnight. During the following day the temperature soared dramatically into the seventies; from frosty mornings and biting cold winds we were plunged into a mini heat-wave, for which I was totally unprepared.

Portrait of Nora Hohenloe

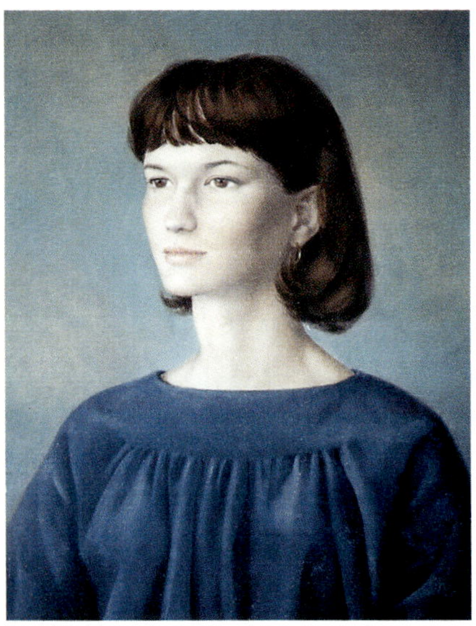

At the same time I managed to jump the last hurdle that had been impeding my progress despite 14 sittings with the patient and very co-operative Nora. Eureka! I had accomplished the second commission. I had also completed a pen and ink portrait of her husband in much less time. All the family came to view my work and expressed heartening approbation and pleasure, which brought me a great sense of relief.

On the following day, Sunday, I paid my fourth and final visit to the Mellon Gallery. I spent four hours there and I had still only covered three-quarters of the collection. After this, a tranquil evensong service at the cathedral had its usual therapeutic effect, bringing a sense of calm, peace and thanksgiving.

My young hosts and their families and friends had shown me such hospitality and kindness, inviting me to dine at their homes and at a variety of restaurants. They had taken me sightseeing and shopping in nearby Georgetown, with its elegant houses around which Washington high society mingled with ambassadors and there was a continual round of social activity. I found it all fascinating but was reaching the point of saturation and mental fatigue. I wanted the pace of this social world to slow down and let me get off and go home.

The intemperate heat wave disappeared as fast as it came and by 13 December it was snowing heavily and I was rushing around hastily doing some last-minute Christmas shopping. Then I did my packing before flying to New York on the one-hour shuttle next day. I was met by the stretch limo at La Guardia and driven back once more to the now familiar 640 Park Avenue on 18 December.

M.D. was delighted with my portrait of Nora. My commissions from him were completed, as well as four pastel studies, a pen and wash drawing and two sanguine drawings which I gave to the families and friends who had entertained me so warmly. These remained behind in different homes while I returned to mine empty-handed but well rewarded, and enriched by all my travels and experiences.

Christmas was approaching and crowds were out shopping and window-gazing amidst the wonderful illuminations, transforming the city with the sparkle of anticipation of the coming festivities. Only five days remained until my departure for England and home. Before that M.D. had arranged yet another party for me, with his family and close friends, as a farewell and pre-Christmas celebration. This time the venue was Luchows, renowned for its fine German cuisine and as the gourmets' restaurant since 1882. Oh dear, another gargantuan meal! But it was also a memorable evening.

While I was in Washington, Maureen O'Hara had contacted M.D. to ask if I would fly out to California to paint her daughter. This he strongly urged me to do while I was in the States, but I had had a premonition that all was not well at home, and very reluctantly had to decline what might have been a golden opportunity and another turning point in my career. I had made many contacts thanks to him and said I would return as soon as possible, but now I had more urgent priorities. He had been extraordinarily kind and generous throughout my 10-week stay. My return flight was booked and arrangements were made for all my heavy luggage to accompany me. I dreaded to think of the overweight charges, but M.D.'s super-efficient secretary took me to Kennedy airport and escorted me through immigration with no problems or charges. I was given VIP treatment and was taken right onto the TWA jet like a film star. I revelled in it. Life would be very different after this.

When I greeted my father, who was waiting for me at Heathrow, I could see that he was very ill, although he did his best to disguise it. Nevertheless, I was home for Christmas with my own family. What a wonderful year it had been!

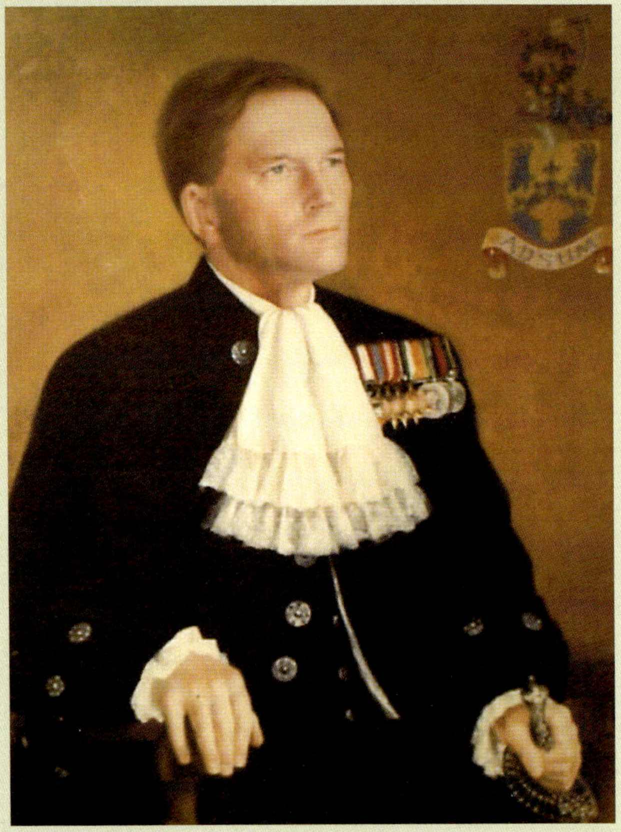

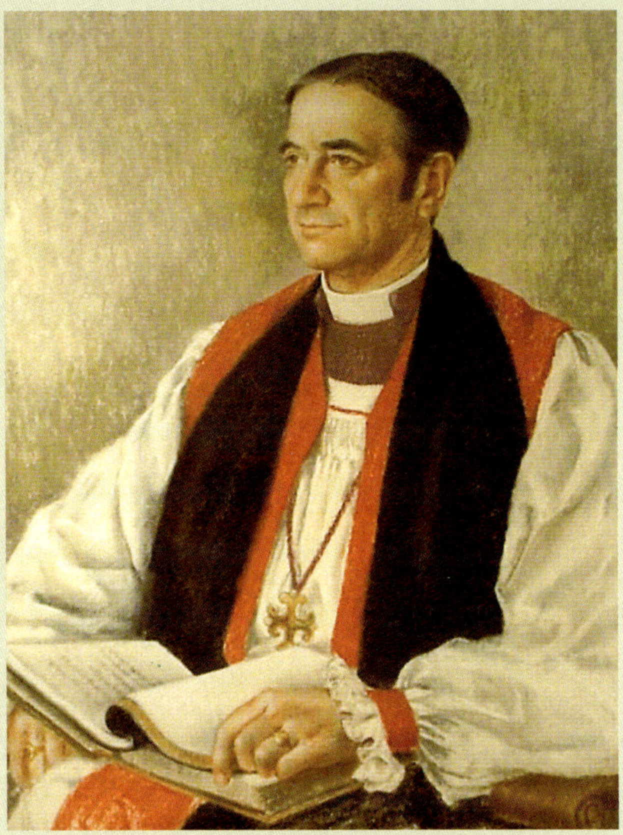

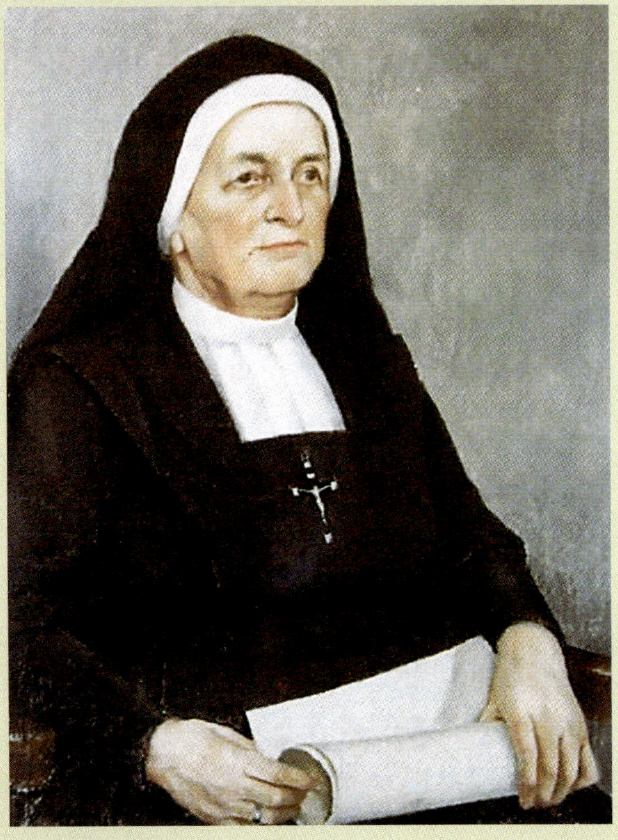

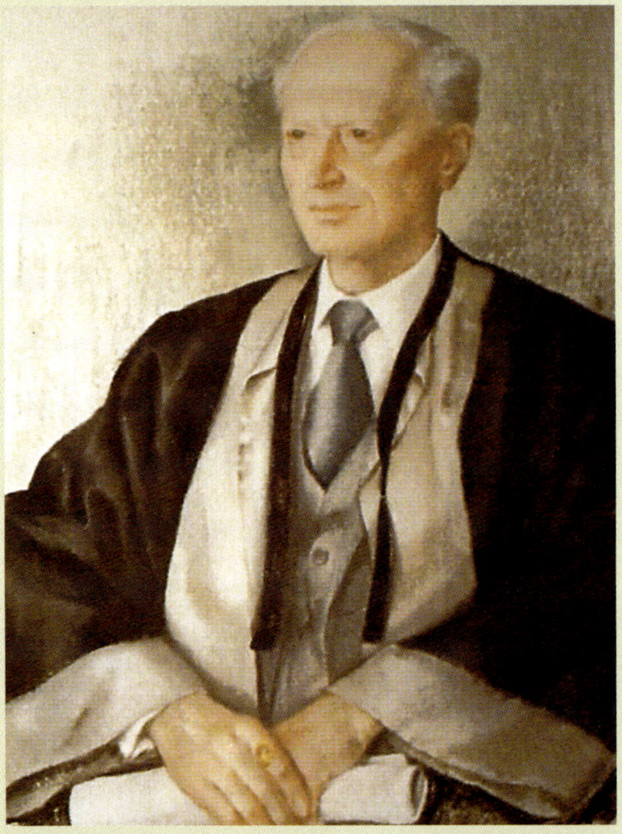

RETURN HOME

Troubled Times

I returned to England on the crest of a wave, but it seemed inevitable that this could not be ridden for long. More portrait commissions were awaiting me, but it took some time to adjust to the very different pace of life after those exhilarating months in the United States and so much travelling. I was glad to work from my home-based studio for a while, where I painted some local clerics: the Archdeacon of Birmingham, S Harvie Clarke, and an extraordinary 84-year-old Irish nun, the Mother General of St Paul's Convent in Selly Oak, Birmingham. I also painted two governors and the headmaster of the Blue Coat School in Harborne, where I lived. Later that year I went to Surrey to paint Henry Dumas, then High Sheriff of the county. All these subjects wore the robes and costume of their different offices, which gave more colour and interest to the painting and provided different materials to tackle – so much more appealing than the board room suit from the painter's point of view (although I had to undertake many of the latter in subsequent years).

My fears for my father's state of health were confirmed when he was diagnosed with cancer and thyroid problems, while my mother simultaneously developed heart disease. These conditions naturally affected my life. Plans to return to Florence that year had to be postponed and my commissions had to be fitted in around the domestic and nursing duties which were to take up most of my time for the foreseeable future.

During a brief remission my parents were able to travel to Madeira during the winter months and I returned there with them to paint some more fascinating Portuguese faces – already on a waiting-list from the previous year on this my third and very fruitful visit. I still missed Florence and felt a great longing and need to recharge my run-down batteries and revitalize my flagging spirits.

On the morning of 2 February while painting in my studio I heard on the radio the terrible news of the car accident on the outskirts of Florence involving Annigoni, Riccardo and another friend. I was so shocked that I phoned the

Opposite clockwise from top left: Henry Dumas, High Sheriff of Surrey; Dr Stuart Blanch, the late Most Reverend Archbishop of York; Dr Bernt Hjejle, President of the Law Society, Copenhagen; The Reverend Mother General of St Paul's Convent, Selly Oak, Birmingham

Birmingham Post for details and was told that Annigoni, in the passenger seat, had escaped but that his left ear had been completely severed by the smashed wing mirror. Riccardo in the back seat was killed instantly by the impact and the driver was unhurt. This news appalled me and I tried desperately to telephone Adriana, Riccardo's wife, and Else Steen, but both lines were unavailable, so I wired them. I was too upset to do anything but wait for more detailed news and hope that the Maestro was out of danger. I finally got through to Else next morning, when Riccardo's funeral was to take place. Poor, dear and devoted Adriana! Annigoni had held on to his severed ear as he was rushed to hospital, fortunately nearby. A surgeon replaced the ear using 45 stitches and no anaesthetic and Annigoni was retained in hospital in a state of shock. So he was spared the attendance at the funeral of his dearest friend. He tried to discharge himself from hospital that day but was forced back to bed for several days of observation before being allowed home. During that time they discovered that he had high blood pressure, but worse was to follow. It was soon apparent that the ear graft was not taking, despite a further 30 stitches – which must have been an extremely painful ordeal. Three weeks later, Annigoni had to accept the fact that he would lose the ear and be left with an unsightly wound. However, the far deeper wound of the loss of his friend of 40 years made an even greater impact on his life.

A month later I managed to return to Florence and was greeted in the studio by a very subdued Maestro. Never one to show his inner-most feelings, with typical irony he was wearing a plastic ear over the wound. Aware of my surprise at this very realistic and convincing substitute, he suddenly pulled it off, as one would an eye patch, and held it towards me in mock amusement, pretending not to have heard my comments. I had written all that I could express of my sympathy at his great loss and my own affection for Riccardo and concern for Adriana, and felt that further discussion of the tragedy would only add to the grief that he felt but did not show.

He then told me the sad news of the death of old Koshland in Lisbon only a few days before his ninety-first birthday – another faithful friend and admirer of many years. Annigoni had helped and supported the old man who spent his last 10 years in total blindness. Despite his endless and boring chatter, he was very knowledgeable and there was mutual respect between him and Annigoni. Annigoni never forgot him.

Work continued as usual in the studio, but I too missed Riccardo's almost daily ebullient visits. Even the outings on the lake were not the same. Annigoni and Riccardo had been closer than blood brothers. He was now like David without Jonathan.

Palmiro Meacci stepped into the breach as a much-needed secretary and agent to handle the increasing business affairs, studio management and commissions. And Rossella stepped in to console and distract Annigoni. 1969 would bring further grief for him, as it also did for me. I soon had to return home to nurse my parents, who needed care between long spells of hospital treatment. Painting was impossible and all my strength and energy was directed to them. Annigoni wrote letters of concern and encouragement as the situation worsened. Florence seemed another world. Illness and all its demands enveloped me. But one has unknown reserves when needed, and I was given the strength to cope in these long and arduous days of worry and depression.

My father died shortly after my birthday on 13 June 1969, which also fell ominously on a Friday. I felt a terrible sense of despair and desolation. Life would go on, and I had to support my ill and grieving mother. I needed to get down to work – the only real cure for getting back to life and normality. Fortunately, later during the summer I was able to catch up on the many portrait commissions that were pending throughout a wide area of the Midlands. These concentrated my mind and focused my attention on creativity rather than grieving and depression.

My oldest Italian friends, in Bolzano, near the Austrian border, cabled inviting me to visit them. I arranged for my mother to be cared for during my absence and flew to Venice on 13 September. From there I travelled by train to Bassano del Grappa in the *dolce Veneto*, which I had often visited. It was wonderful to be in Italy again even if I could not fit a visit to Florence into only 10 days. I needed a rest and found it, as always, in this peaceful area of the Veneto. My friends' beautiful villa was just outside the ancient town, renowned for its famous wooden bridge and also its fiery grappa, made from the residue of grape seeds after the wine pressing – a potent but pure spirit. The house stood amidst olive trees and vines, and looked down onto the River Brenta – *pace e riposo in paradiso, grazie a Dio!* (peace and rest in paradise, thank God!). The peace and rest was short-lived. Further serious illness soon befell my darling mother. The worry and full-time nursing precluded any painting for a year. She died at Christmas after a long and agonizing struggle. The bottom fell out of my world.

My diary was blank. I had no time or inclination to write and nothing but foreboding and sadness to write about. I also had practical necessities to cope with: lawyers, accountants, a house to be sold and a move to the Cotswolds to the already half-converted house to which my parents had planned to retire. I had little enthusiasm and even less energy, but the mammoth house move had to be undertaken. I wanted to run away, return to Italy, but I had to face reality and be responsible for the plans already in action.

Some days after my mother's funeral, I was sitting alone in our family pew in the local church of St Peter in Harborne staring up at the blank wall to the right of the chancel. I was in deep despair following the loss of my beloved parents who were the best of all my friends. Suddenly, out of the gloom that enveloped me, I knew exactly what I had to do. The idea became a vision: a mural painting of St Peter.

Since my Florentine days I had had an unfulfilled desire to paint a

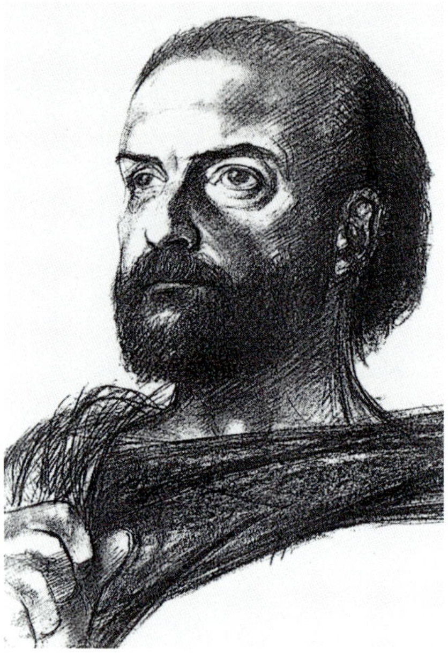

First charcoal sketch of Martim da Camera

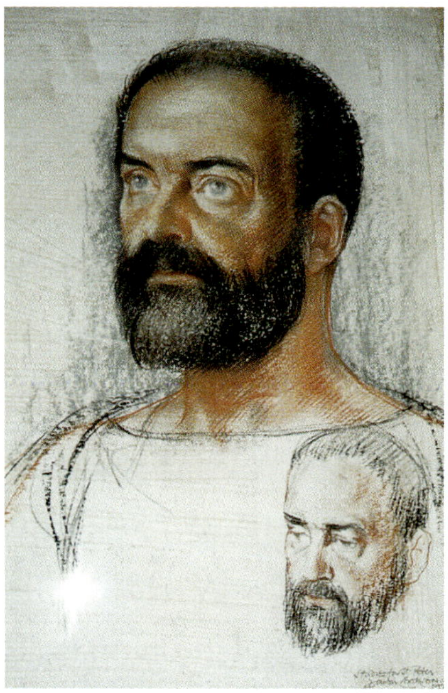

Second pastel study of Martim da Camera for head of St Peter

religious subject for a church. Here was the opportunity and stimulus to do so, as a memorial to my parents and a gift to our church. However, this would have to wait until I had moved to Broadway and established myself in the much more spacious studio that was being made out of an old coach-house there. Before that I needed another break to restore my body and spirit after all the trauma and the upheaval of the move.

In May 1971 I was able to return again to Madeira for some sun and sea, and it was there that my concept of St Peter began to take shape. The man I envisaged was not the customary representation of the aged saint towards the end of his life, with a long grey beard and worn down by the weight of the keys of the Kingdom with which Christ had entrusted him. I wanted to paint the younger Peter, the fisherman, vigorous and in his prime – the strong figure that must have made an impression upon Christ at the Sea of Galilee when Peter was told to follow him, becoming a fisher of men and finally the founder of the Christian church.

I knew that this must be a strong and solid figure of a man but with more than merely the looks and build of a typical fisherman. There also had to be intelligence, strength of character and courage – even if all these qualities were to fail him when faced with his master's crucifixion. I could see the face clearly in my mind, but I needed a live model to work from. I wandered around the harbour of Funchal with my sketch book and camera, searching among the many fishermen and boat hands working around the busy port. No face I saw seemed appropriate and I thought I would have to rely on my imagination – until I remembered an old Portuguese friend, a man of the country and mountains rather than the sea but essentially the sort of head I had in mind. His was an unusual face with a short beard and penetrating blue eyes. I persuaded him to come to my little gazebo studio, where I drew his head in charcoal and then in pastel. At least I had made a start. I knew that I must return to Florence to do all the necessary studies, with male models in an atmosphere where I knew I would be stimulated and inspired and, equally important, under the stern criticism of Annigoni.

So for the first three months of 1972 I was back again in the familiar studio after an absence of three years. Annibale was the first to pose for me, for studies of his hands which were strong and worn, with gnarled veins after many years of manual work. He stood patiently for hours, between answering the phone and opening the door! My colleague Romano Stefanelli kindly spared me some time and posed for the robust body; having been a boxer in his earlier youth he had just the right torso. I made a number of anatomical studies of the figure in charcoal before the final half-scale drawing passed the Maestro's approval. I then had this photographed and enlarged on a transparency which could then be projected high up onto the wall of the studio. This was to see how the proportions would be affected when viewed from below, foreshortening the figure. Added height had to be allowed for. I drew around the projected image on paper fixed to the wall in order to save time working up a drawing to scale. Meanwhile, Annibale posed again, this time barefoot on the cold, stone-tiled floor, poor old man. However, his feet were too old and thin to be those of a fisherman accustomed to walking barefoot or in sandals. I would have to find more suitable feet elsewhere for these studies.

I was fortunately able to utilize the whole of the mezzanine floor of Annigoni's studio, but the final painting on a wood panel of 9 x 6 feet would have to be undertaken back in my newly converted and more spacious studio in Broadway, involving more problems and a complicated procedure.

During those winter months I had settled back with my old familiar friends. Relatives of Riccardo's wife Adriana had commissioned me to paint portraits of their two children outside Florence at Figline in the Valdarno. It was a chance to earn some lire, but it was hard work keeping two very spoilt young sitters still. Being able to play 'I Spy' in three languages was my only resource to hold their attention, but it was exhausting. Since then I must have painted literally hundreds of children of all ages and nationalities and it doesn't get any easier. I noted that Annigoni painted few and I can understand why.

By mid-February I was working on the life-size cartoon on an enormous sheet of paper in Romano's studio, which he was kindly allowing me to use for a couple of evenings. Somehow or other, this would have to be rolled and transported back to England in a tube, together with all my usual clutter of luggage.

I returned home in March and set about trying to obtain a suitable panel of seasoned poplar wood, which proved to be a greater problem than I expected. I searched all the local timber yards and boat-builders without success. Then the Broadway based firm of Gordon Russell, renowned for quality furniture, came to my rescue. Poplar was unobtainable, let alone a panel of those proportions, but blockboard of several laminates was guaranteed not to warp or be affected by damp, and this was supplied to me. A foot had to be cut off the ideal height and width in order for it to pass through my studio door. Even so, it took two men several hours to manoeuvre the panel in and then fix it firmly to one of the walls. By this time several months had elapsed since my return from Florence so full of enthusiasm and longing to get started on my most ambitious subject.

I was having a one woman exhibition later that autumn in Broadway and had to produce a lot of paintings for this. However, the base for the St Peter was ready, prepared with a covering of fine linen canvas which had been adhered to the surface by hot press also thanks to the Russell factory. All I had to do was to prepare the surface with a strong gesso base – a mixture of slaked lime and animal size as prepared by the apprentices of the old masters for centuries, and still in the Annigoni studio, where pupils were trained in traditional groundwork. I had learnt the procedure by watching my colleagues and then by practising myself. The panel then had to dry out and season

St Peter in progress

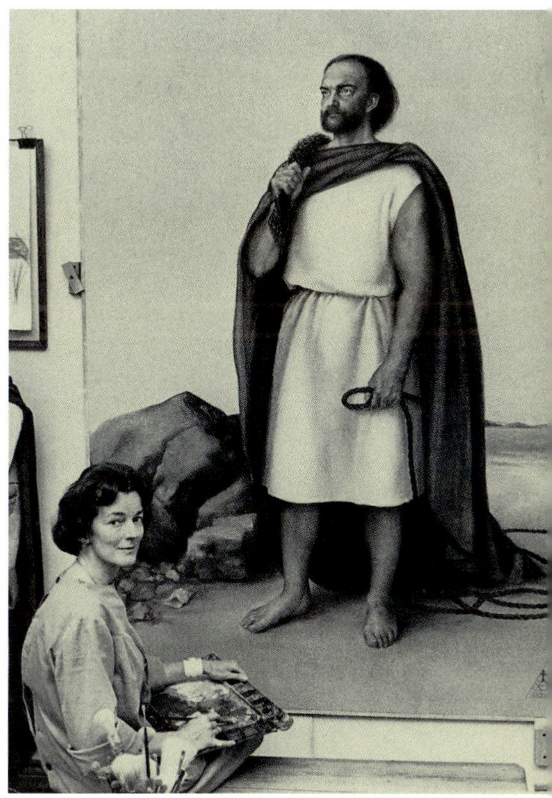

through the autumn, while I was busy preparing for my first solo exhibition. This was fortunately a great success and a boost to my morale.

In the mean time, I had procured two more male models for the limbs of St Peter. One was my gardener, an ex-regimental sergeant major with fine muscular arms, and the other an old friend with just the right broad feet, on which he stood patiently in a tray of sand for many hours while I drew them. My figure of St Peter was finally composed of five different models: a Portuguese, two Italians and two Englishmen. The resulting anatomical combination gave me the basic structure, leaving my imagination to conjure up the rest. The vast empty white canvas looked challengingly down at me. The final life-size drawing was unrolled and transferred onto the panel by the ancient process of pouncing. All I had to do now was prepare enough fresh tempera colours for the work involved. I worked steadily on the painting day in, week out from the beginning of 1973, alone with the inevitable problems and hurdles, up and down a step-ladder or standing on a dais or crouching on the floor. At times I was despondent and depressed, at others exhilarated and inspired. I had taken up the challenge and there was no question of retreat. By then I had a deadline. The fear of failure had to be overcome by the determination to succeed and please all the many people concerned. The painting, which became a work of faith, hope and love, was completed at the end of May. I called in an expert restorer to apply the varnish with a spray gun. It is a professional task to obtain the even covering that brings matt colours to life and also seals and protects the painting from absorbing too much dirt or damp.

The mural was dedicated by the Bishop of Birmingham in a packed St Peter's church on 24 June 1973. My mission was accomplished at long last. This was the most satisfying and rewarding work I had ever done, to the memory of my parents, an offering to our church and in recognition of all I owed to Annigoni.

EPILOGUE

I am sure that anyone reading this reflection of my years with Annigoni will appreciate that it is inevitably a very subjective record. I lived in close proximity to Annigoni, a man with a strong personality, over a number of years. However, this does not mean that I have always sympathized with or understood everything he painted or did. I admired his overall integrity, his undoubted ability to express his feelings in his art without being influenced by others, and his courage to follow a solitary road with total conviction throughout his life. This brought him fame and success during his lifetime.

Obviously, such a controversial figure aroused much criticism. In the foreword of the first and most comprehensive biography of Annigoni, by

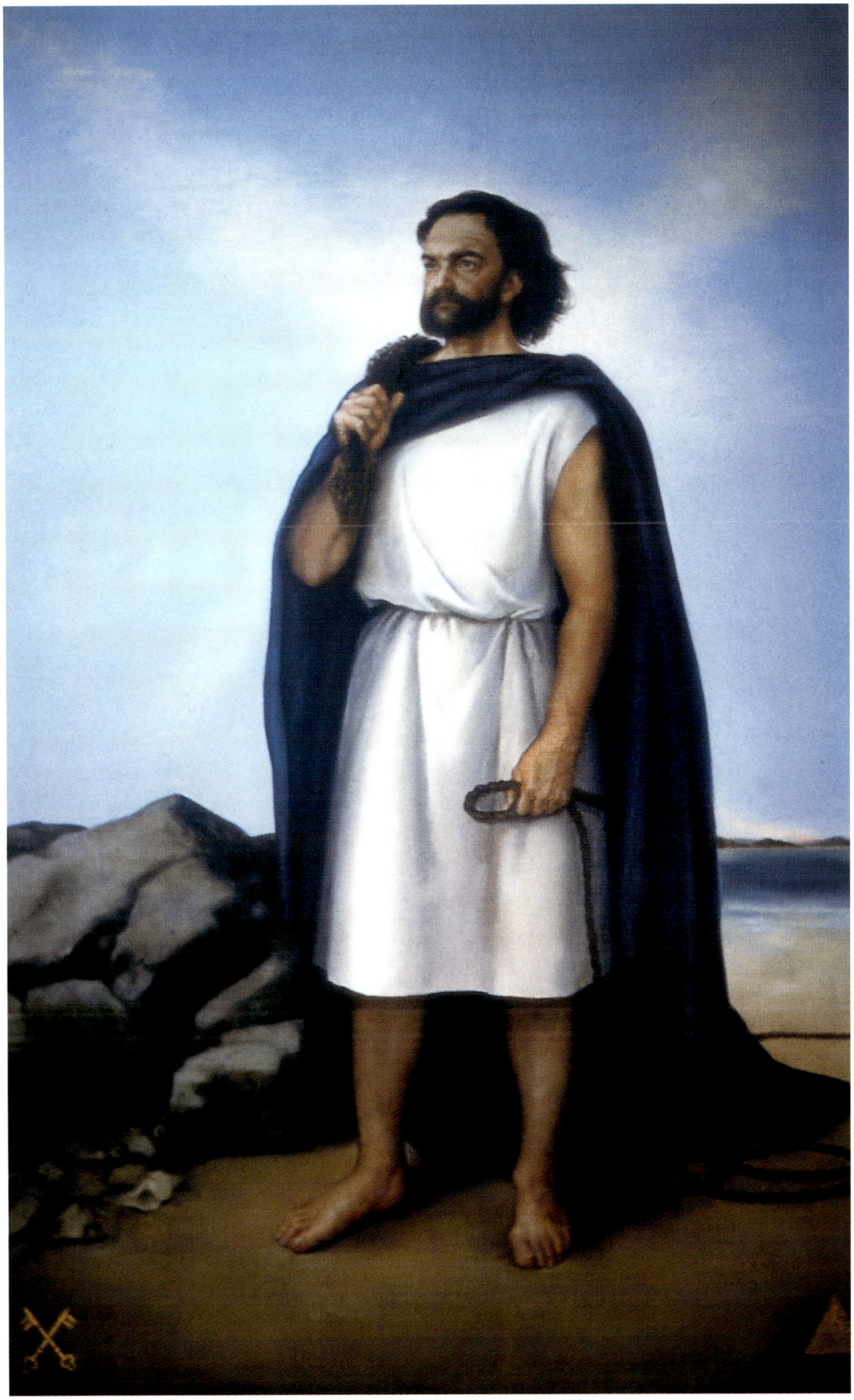

Nicolò Rasmo, several interesting opinions are quoted from his critics, leading Italian writers and painters of his time; those who praised his paintings and those who dismissed them altogether. I would like to quote here a few lines from the Italian painter Giorgio de Chirico, a contemporary, who wrote:

> 'In Florence there is also the painter Pietro Annigoni, an artist of great talent and immense seriousness. He, in contrast to many of his fellows, is a great worker and possesses a technique of which the majority of the painters today, not only Italians but also foreigners, have not the faintest idea. Pietro Annigoni works seriously and goes straight along his road without heeding the chatter, snobbery, intellectualism and foolishness of our unhappy period, and also without taking any notice of the spite which such work arouses. He is an able draughtsman and an etcher of the first rank.'

This comment was included in de Chirico's own biography, written in 1945, long before Annigoni's fame spread worldwide.

Annigoni's Renaissance-style studio was, as far as I know, unique. It was out of character with our century as in fact in many ways was the man himself. He frequently expressed his strong reactions to contemporary art and antagonism to its often facile abstraction. Such art cannot be constructively criticized in any coherent way, and its critics tend to leave the public bewildered and confused. No wonder Annigoni turned to the masters of the Renaissance for his inspiration.

He often used to remark, 'After all, bread has been baked since time immemorial as the most basic food of which we never tire; it is good and nourishing and has been tried and tested.' In a similar way the art of past centuries is still alive today in the galleries and museums of the world, to which millions flock for intellectual, spiritual and emotional sustenance and stimulation.

Many of the works of our present age certainly reflect the disturbing and distressing times in which we live, times in which there is more rebellion than harmony, more arrogance than humility, more outrage than ability, more confusion than explanation and, most of all, an almost hostile denigration of skill and artistry. This subject can be argued at length, but only time will reveal to future generations the validity of what may remain of the art of today, which in many cases requires no skill, study, training or even tools to produce.

One might ask what place Annigoni's art and teaching has in the twentieth century. It is not for me to justify his art, although I am convinced of its importance; it speaks for itself. As for his teaching, he instilled the importance of good draughtsmanship through observation, concentration and discipline. In the most difficult study of the human form he taught the mind to feel and assimilate the subtlety of light, shade and atmosphere, and the hand to execute it. The advantage of such a system was that it gave pupils the ground work, knowledge and ability necessary to express their artistic instincts. This valuable teaching is now hard to find in art schools, colleges and institutions, which lack such skilled and dedicated tutors. Many consider that too much academic teaching inhibits free expression, but after all, a musician must be able to read scores and must practise scales daily before he can play an instrument or compose. A writer must have considerable knowledge of language, grammar, spelling and vocabulary in order to write a book. A dancer must train assiduously in the movements of the body to be able to control and co-ordinate them to music. An architect cannot plan a building without a knowledge of perspective, engineering and drainage, and the ability to design and draw accurately. All of these professions require hard and long training. And so does art even when the artist has genius.

Annigoni's pupils were expert in their craft: in drawing and painting, and some also in etching, lithography, fresco painting, gilding and modelling. This enabled them to undertake important commissions, execute large frescoes and paint all manner of subjects in various media. Most have since progressed as professionals in their own right, exhibiting and working far and wide. The nucleus of the older Italian pupils remains in Florence, but others live and work in the UK and USA. Nearly all of us have worked and exhibited in many other countries. We were expected to be worthy of the high standards of the studio, as a reflection on the Maestro.

There is a great need for such a system of apprenticeship that aims at the pursuit of excellence, but such a system requires a strong and able painter who can inspire his pupils through his own painting, and a dedicated and vocational teacher with considerable knowledge and talent, and most of all time to teach. It is almost impossible to do both.

I have pointed out the great advantages we derived from Annigoni's studio. Through his generosity we were able to progress with self-assurance, developing our own individual styles rather than consciously or unconsciously merely copying his (although such imitation is sometimes noticeable). I have spent some fruitful years teaching and passing on what I have learnt, and I have found it absorbing and rewarding, the demands of time and energy and the relatively small financial return aside. In the end one has to earn a living and decide which road to take. I have never regretted taking the road I took when fate intervened and gave me the golden opportunity to study in that exceptional studio. Nor have I regretted all that has led from this study.

Ever since my own particular halcyon decade, now long past, I have been aware of a subtle thread that has woven its way through my working life linking me to that memorable studio and reminding me what drew me to, through and beyond it. Other pupils came before and after me, many of whom have since achieved fame or fortune. All of us were privileged to have passed under the guidance and influence of one of the great painters of the past 70 years, to whom I pay tribute with gratitude.

APPENDIX

Formula for oil-tempera medium

For those who may find the procedure of personal interest:–

To make the emulsion:

Eggs, in the proportion of one whole egg to two yolks, 4 parts

Mastic varnish	1 part	
		Equalling half the quantity of eggs
Stand oil	1 part	

To make an average mix of approximately 18–20 colours (this varies according to size of painting) 18–20 eggs are needed, as they often vary in size.

Colours (in ground powders)		**Dry Quantity**	**Emulsion**
1	Titanium white	100 grams	110 grams
2	Cadmium yellow light	100	140
3	Cadmium yellow dark	100	200
4	Raw umber natural	100	200
5	Burnt umber	100	120/25
6	Burnt siena	100	120/25
7	Yellow ochre pale	100	120/25
8	Yellow ochre dark	100	120/25
9	Red pozzuolo	100	120/25
10	Crimson lake	100	180
11	Cadmium red (dark and light)	100	140
12	Cadmium orange	100	140
13	Cobalt blue	100	250
14	Ultramarine blue	100	180
15	Emerald green (viridian)	100	200
16	Morellone	100	
17	Black (ivory)	100	250
18	Prussian blue – if necessary (very strong colour; only small quantity)	100	180/200

The eggs must be carefully separated and poured into a glass cylinder in multiples of 3 at a time, dividing quantity exactly in half to add the appropriate amount of emulsion. Then this mixture transferred to a suitable metal container to whisk thoroughly for half an hour in order to amalgamate the mixture which becomes a creamy white colour and smooth consistency. An electric mixer saves time and energy. Meantime the powder colours are carefully measured according to the various amounts required, starting with the lightest colours, and each one mixed on a marble slab with dry white wine, using a spatula or palette knife, and then measured carefully against the appropriate quantity of emulsion in a thoroughly cleaned container and mixed well together. The resulting liquid poured into clean plastic bottles and well capped and sealed. When mixing the powder colours, add very little wine at a time to form a paste which should not be too liquid; when the colours are added to the emulsion they become more liquid and therefore shakeable.

Obviously a larger amount of white is needed, next the earth colours, yellow, blues and green and lesser quantities of reds and black. So select different sized plastic bottles accordingly.

This process demands precision, care, time and patience. The slab, palette and mixer container must be washed thoroughly between each mixing. When the desired selection of colours are mixed, bottled and sealed these should be placed in a suitably large ceramic or plastic bowl containing damp sand and kept moist in a cool place – away from heat or cold. This way they will keep for up to 4–6 months, after which colours deteriorate and begin to smell strongly!

Before using each time, every bottle must be well shaken. A special metal palette with small pans attached around the edges to hold the liquid colours is necessary, taking care to only pour out sufficient quantities for each day's work. These can be covered with strips of dampened cloth to avoid them drying out overnight. So that they can be used or added to for several days. However, do not return any excess paint back into bottles. There is inevitably some wastage, as with oil colours and this has to be discarded. Therefore only put out small quantities at a time.

When using and mixing the desired colours, water is used and added by brush on the palette – not into the colour pans. The colours can be used as thickly as with oils for an 'impasto' base, and thinly as with watercolours for glazes and fine drawing.

The possibilities of this medium are endless but not for a beginner or a speedy painter 'alla prima'!

ACKNOWLEDGMENTS

Although this account of my experiences is based on my diaries and numerous letters written throughout those years, I have also referred to works by others published during the intervening years. These include:

Pietro Annigoni: An Artist's Life. As told to Robert Wraight. London.
Annigoni: Introduction. Nicolo Rasmo. Florence, 1991.
Annigoni Diario (1946-69). Published privately. Florence.
Don't Look Round: the autobiography of Violet Trefusis, with an introduction by Peter Quennell. London.
Life of a Painter: the autobiography of Antonio Ciccone.

Thanks to all my friends and colleagues mentioned in this book and to those who have supported me and encouraged my writing.

In particular, I should like to thank Felicità Pask-Hughes who, in urging me to study in Perugia, led me to Florence; and most recently Dr Puck Wertwyn without whose initial assistance this book would never have been produced. Thanks also to Anna Hatch, and last but not least to Benedetto Annigoni for his continual help and encouragement and for allowing photographs and other materials from his archive to be reproduced.

The author and publishers of this book would like to thank all those who have given permission for portraits, drawings and photographs to be reproduced, and apologise for any inadvertent breach of acknowledgment.